THE ROUGH GUIDE to

Macs & OS X

2nd Edition

by

Peter Buckley and Duncan Clark

 PAUL WEBB

Credits

The Rough Guide to Macs & OS X

Text, Layout & Design:
Peter Buckley & Duncan Clark
Proofreading: Susannah Wight
Production: Rebecca Short

Rough Guides Reference

Editors: Peter Buckley, Tracy Hopkins,
Sean Mahoney, Matthew Milton,
Joe Staines, Ruth Tidball
Director: Andrew Lockett

Acknowledgements

All pictures of Macs and iPods courtesy of Apple Computer

Publishing Information

This second edition published January 2008 by
Rough Guides Ltd, 80 Strand, London WC2R 0RL
345 Hudson St, 4th Floor, New York 10014, USA
Email: mail@roughguides.com

Distributed by the Penguin Group:
Penguin Books Ltd, 80 Strand, London WC2R 0RL
Penguin Putnam, Inc., 375 Hudson Street, NY 10014, USA
Penguin Group (Australia), 250 Camberwell Road, Camberwell, Victoria 3124, Australia
Penguin Books Canada Ltd, 10 Alcorn Avenue, Toronto, Ontario, Canada M4V 1E4
Penguin Group (New Zealand), Cnr Rosedale and Airborne Roads, Albany, Auckland, New Zealand

Printed in Italy by LegoPrint S.p.A

Typeset in Minion and Myriad to an original design by Peter Buckley & Duncan Clark

The publishers and authors have done their best to ensure the accuracy and currency of all information in The Rough Guide to Macs & OS X; however, they can accept no responsibility for any loss or inconvenience sustained by any reader as a result of its information or advice.

A catalogue record for this book is available from the British Library

ISBN 13: 978-1-84353-873-8
ISBN 10: 1-84353-873-3

1 3 5 7 9 8 6 4 2

Contents

contents

PICTURES

VIDEO

SECURITY & MAINTENANCE

MACOLOGY

INDEX

About this book

Macs aren't perfect. But with their elegant design and ergonomic OS X operating system, they come much closer to a futuristic digital Utopia than the ugly, virus-infested Windows alternative. Indeed, on the whole, modern Macs are a joy to use. We wouldn't have written and designed this book using them if we didn't think so. In fact, we wouldn't have written this book at all.

If you're reading this, however, you probably don't need much convincing. Chances are you're either a Mac user already, or you're sick of PCs and are thinking of defecting. Either way, *The Rough Guide to Macs & OS X* has something for you. It covers everything from buying and upgrading Macs, via making music, editing pictures and creating DVDs, to online security and customizing your system with extra software.

We've avoided the patronizing walk-throughs common to much computer publishing ("This is a mouse – try clicking the button!"), so as to pack in more of the stuff that you'll actually find useful and interesting. As well as background information and scores of tips and tricks, we've included plenty of links to websites and downloadable goodies, plus the occasional bit of wider context – such as the weird world of Apple obsession covered in Chapter 38.

about this book

This book focuses on OS X version 10.5 – aka "Leopard" – and covers all its major new features, such as Spaces and Time Machine. If you purchased your Mac before autumn 2007, and you haven't upgraded, then you'll have an older version. In that case, a few of the things we describe will be missing, or different, on your Mac, but the vast majority of what you read will still apply.

Finally, a couple of things to note. Prices are stated in US$ and UK£ (real prices, not conversions), though in the case of software downloads you'll often see only one currency listed. That's because you'll pay in this currency regardless of where you are in the world, either by credit card or via a safe online payment service such as PayPal (www.paypal.com). And if you find yourself confounded by some strange hieroglyphics – the likes of ⌘⌥⌫ – these are simply instructions for keyboard shortcuts. To find out how to interpret them, see p.50.

Frequently asked questions

Macs & PCs

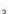

1

What's a Mac?

A Mac is one of a series of personal computers produced by a company called Apple. Macs – which take their name from the McIntosh, an apple variety grown in northern USA – have been around for more than two decades, though today's slick-looking models don't look or work much like the machine released to much fanfare back in January 1984.

Macs come in various shapes and sizes: laptops and desktops aimed at both the consumer and professional markets. Despite their varied portability and firepower, however, all Macs work in the same way, since they all run the software operating system OS X (more on this overleaf).

What's a PC?

PC stands for personal computer, so in that broad sense a Mac is a kind of PC. But in everyday use, the term "PC" means something far more specific than just any old personal computer. It refers to a particular type of machine capable of running Microsoft's Windows operating system (not to be confused with Microsoft's Office programs, such as Word and Excel, which are available for both Macs and PCs).

In this more standard sense, PC is short for "IBM PC compatible", reflecting the fact that modern-day PCs are based on a model released by IBM back in 1981. Today, however, PCs – unlike Macs – are made by countless different companies; you can even purchase the various components and build your own. For more on PCs, see *The Rough Guide to PCs & Windows*.

How many Mac users are there?

Apple is an amazingly visible and influential company – especially in this era of iPod adulation. But Macs account for only a very small percentage of the world's personal computers. Figures vary, but most current estimates give Macs a 2–3 percent market share globally, and 4–5 percent in the US and Europe. Some studies claim to show that Macs score better when you measure the "installed base" of computers – those actually in use – but there are also figures that suggest the opposite.

Which is better, a Mac or a PC?

Macs and PCs both have their die-hard devotees, so be careful posing this question or you might find yourself on the receiving end of an impassioned rant. In truth, both camps make some fair points.

Operating systems

Every modern computer features an operating system, or OS: the underlying software that acts as a bridge between the hardware (the physical bits), the application software (programs such as word processors or image editors) and the user (you). On current Macs, the operating system is OS X. On PCs, it's usually Windows, though it may also be Linux or various others. For more on OS X, see p.7.

The main argument in favour of PCs is that you get better value in terms of sheer bang per buck. That is, if you take a Mac and a PC with the same price tag, the Mac will be slightly slower at accomplishing most tasks. Why the price difference? It's partly because Apple use high-quality components and throw in lots of good software, but competition between PC manufacturers also has a lot to do with it. Apple's design budget must also be factored in: everything from the computers to the boxes they come in are produced with almost obsessive attention to detail. You might also make the case that, since whole industries (such as publishing) are effectively locked in to Mac use by industry-wide convention, Apple's pricing of high-spec computers strikes a balance between winning new consumer users on the one hand and maximizing the revenue from commercial sales on the other.

Intel, Wintel, MacIntel...

Traditionally, the defining feature of a "PC", as opposed to a Mac, was that its central processor, or CPU, was a member of the x86 family. This type of processor was first produced by Intel, who still dominate the market. Since most PCs combine these Intel-style processors with the Windows operating system, they're commonly referred to as "Wintel" machines.

Apple, by contrast, for years favoured PowerPC processors (such as the G3, G4 and G5) manufactured by IBM. However, in 2006 Apple switched to PC-style x86 processors – more specifically the Intel Core Duo chip. Supposedly, the reason was that IBM failed to keep up with its own development "roadmap", but many commentators have suggested other reasons (such as Apple wanting to score bargain iPod chips from Intel).

Intel-based Macs, sometimes dubbed "MacIntels" or "Mactels", are faster than their PowerPC-based predecessors and offer various other advantages. For example, they can run Windows in addition to OS X (see p.12).

So why choose a Mac?

Despite their slightly higher price tags, Macs have a whole lot going for them. For a start, since the core hardware and software components are designed by the same company, the whole package "just works" to a much greater extent than with PCs. In the course of a Mac's lifetime, you're far less likely to run into hardware conflicts, inexplicable malfunctions and the like.

Even if you do have problems, you may find a Mac easier to troubleshoot. Millions of people will have exactly the same Mac model as you (unlike with PCs, where each producer combines a slightly different selection of components). This means that, when you run into trouble, someone else has probably come across precisely the same annoyance – and posted a solution on the Web.

Another advantage of Macs – and one that's becoming more important every year – is that they're far less susceptible to online woes such as viruses and spyware (see p.284). This has less to do with the way Macs are designed, and more to do with the fact that malicious programmers tend to focus their misdeeds on Windows. To date, there's never been a serious virus outbreak on Macs. For as long as this continues, Mac users don't have to worry about virus-scanner subscriptions and other such pains.

Then there are aesthetics to consider. Apple was the first company to make computers that are actually pleasant to look at, and it remains almost impossible to find a PC with even the slightest visual appeal. And when it comes to computers, beauty isn't always skin deep. Macs score highly on build quality, as well as other not-so-obvious things such as laptop battery life.

As for software, PC users may have more available overall, but a huge percentage of it is ugly, unreliable and, potentially, full of spyware. Nearly every major application is available for OS X, as well as tens of thousands of other programs, plug-ins, widgets and utilities, many of them downloadable via the Apple site.

But probably the single most persuasive reason for buying a Mac is the operating system, OS X…

OS X

What's OS X?

As already explained, every personal computer has an operating system, or OS. This is the software responsible for controlling the physical hardware of the machine. It also provides the "platform" on which other programs run, and features a set of tools to help you browse, copy and delete files, and choose which application to open them into. Modern operating systems typically come bundled with a wide range of extra programs, from Web browsers (see p.153) to simple word processors.

The operating system found on Macs is called, logically enough, Mac OS (at least that's been the name since 1996; before then it was just called "System"). The current generation of Mac OS is the tenth, hence the term OS X – pronounced "ten" not "ex". The first edition of OS X was released in 2001, replacing OS 9.

Why X not 10?

There are a couple of reasons why Apple chose "OS X" over "OS 10". First, while many previous updates to the Mac system had been relatively minor (OS 8 doesn't look or feel very different from OS 9, for example), OS X was a total redesign. The "X" helped Apple make the difference as apparent as possible.

OS X on a PC?

Mac OS has always been available for use on Macs and Macs alone. But now that Macs are based on Intel processors (see p.5), it's technically possible to run OS X on a PC. Various techie types have already made it happen. Apple, however, have no professed intention of heading down that path, so although a number of PC manufacturers – including Dell – have suggested they might be interested in offering "Mac PCs", this looks unlikely in the immediate future. In the longer term, it seems perfectly plausible that Apple will find the opportunity to eat into Microsoft's monopoly too tempting to resist. But until then, OS X PCs will remain the domain of geeks interested primarily in the technical challenge of making it work. Far preferable is running Windows on a Mac – see p.12.

What's UNIX?

UNIX is a powerful multi-user operating system known for being stable and secure. First developed in the late 1960s by staff at AT&T, it's now available in many different versions – some free, others commercial. Initially used primarily in academic and scientific contexts, UNIX later became popular for Internet-related tasks, but wasn't used on personal computers until the advent of Linux (a free, open-source UNIX-based system) in the early 1990s. UNIX finally entered the consumer market mainstream when Apple chose to use BSD – the UNIX version developed at Berkeley University – as the basis of Mac OS X. Technically, OS X is not actually "a UNIX system", as it isn't certified to meet the Single UNIX Specification, but that's pretty much detail. Anyone who knows UNIX can roughly find their way around OS X's technical back-end – via the Terminal utility – and Macs can even run UNIX applications, though only once the applications have been "recompiled".

The second reason is that OS X is based on another operating system called UNIX, and there's a long tradition of UNIX-based systems having names ending in X – Linux, Minix and Xenix being just a few examples.

Which is better, OS X or Windows?

Modern versions of both Mac OS and Windows are incomparably better than their predecessors. Both systems are relatively stable, and both feature a host of useful features. As to which is better, it's largely down to personal preference, though many people who are experienced with both systems (including the authors of this book) find OS X *much* nicer to work with.

Comparing the two systems available at the time of writing, OS 10.5 ("Leopard") feels much more intuitive, flexible, elegant and powerful than Windows Vista. This is partly down to some excellent "surface" features, such as the Dock, but it's also because of how and when it was developed. At its base is the security, stability and power of the venerable UNIX system, but the interface (the "look and feel") was designed pretty much from scratch only a few years ago, and has been energetically improved every year since.

By comparison, Windows, with its global monopoly clearly established, has been substantially improved only once every few years, with each new version feeling like an unhappy compromise between real invention and a fear of changing too much.

"OS X 10.5.1 Leopard". Eh?

Every year or so Apple release a new edition of the Mac operating system, complete with new features and other improvements. These new versions are not radically different enough to be branded "OS 11" or "OS XI". Instead, they're considered new versions of OS X and are numbered accordingly: v10.1, v10.2, and so on. The latest edition is given away with new Macs, and is also available to buy as an upgrade for existing Macs (see p.37).

Beside these major new versions, Apple also releases interim upgrades to each version to fix problems, improve security and perhaps add a feature or two. These interim upgrades add another decimal point to the number. If you installed OS X v10.4, your Mac's Software Update tool (see p.46) may flash up offering you v10.4.2. A few months down the line, you'll get v10.4.3, and so on.

As well as a number, new versions of OS X receive a name, all of which so far have been big cats – Jaguar, Panther, Tiger and Leopard. Such names are presumably intended primarily to aid marketing: "Tiger Unleashed!" certainly has more of a ring to it than "10.4 Unleashed!". It also gives Mac users a shorthand that's more friendly and memorable than a number with one decimal place.

The choice of giant felines stems from the fact that OS X version 10.0 and 10.1 were codenamed Cheetah and Puma in Apple HQ during their development. Such codenaming is quite normal in the world of software: Windows XP was codenamed "Whistler", for example, and Vista was known as "Longhorn".

Can I install OS X Leopard on my Mac?

Possibly, but it may not be worth it if you have quite an old machine – especially where you are currently running OS 9. Turn to p.37 for more information on upgrading your operating system.

OS Wars

For an in-depth and balanced comparison of OS X and Windows, visit:

Mac vs Windows
macvswindows.com

The site examines and rates nearly every element of the two operating systems. The overall scores at the time of writing are: 643 for OS X and 557 for XP home, with updated data for OS X Leopard and Windows Vista expected soon.

Mac vs **Windows**

2 Thinking of switching?

Will I find a Mac difficult to get used to?

If you're used to Windows, switching to a Mac is inevitably a touch confusing for a while, though most converts find the transition to be relatively painless – not least because Mac OS X is a very user-friendly and intuitive system. Furthermore, unless you're quite technically savvy anyway (in which case you won't struggle at all), most of your computer skills are related to specific applications, rather than the system itself. These applications don't vary much: using, say, Microsoft Word on a Mac really isn't very different from using Microsoft Word on a PC.

If you're terrible with computers, and it took you years to master your PC, then the changeover will undoubtedly be a tad more confusing. But work your way through this book and you'll probably end up far more clued-up and skilled on your Mac than you ever were on your PC.

Will my PC documents, data, emails and applications work on a Mac?

Not long ago, Macs and PCs spoke very different languages, but these days compatibility is not much of an issue for the average home user. That said, don't assume that everything on your PC can be effortlessly migrated to your new Mac.

It's easy to physically copy all your documents, photos, emails, contacts and so on onto the Mac. The question is whether you'll actually be able to open them. Many common file types won't pose any problems – photos, PDFs, simple text files and so on. But other types of file require you to install the appropriate application. For example, if you want to open and edit Microsoft Word and Excel documents, you'll need Word and Excel installed on the Mac.

Unfortunately, you can't install PC versions of programs on a Mac (at least not without the hassle of using Boot Camp – see box overleaf). So you'd have to acquire the Mac version of the application in question. That's easy enough for common tools such as Word and Excel, but impossible for some more obscure programs that are not available for Macs.

In some cases, files can be opened on a Mac but only after a certain amount of fiddling around. For example, you might want to move all your old emails from Outlook Express (on the PC) to Apple Mail (the Mac equivalent). This can be done but only via a faffy process involving IMAP mail (see p.76). For more on actually copying your emails, files and more from a PC to a Mac, see p.71.

Are Macs OK for Microsoft Word?

First, let's get a few things absolutely clear, since this is a common point of confusion. Word – and the Office "suite" that it is a part

Running Windows – or Windows hardware or software – programs on a Mac

If you want to run Windows programs on a Mac, or connect to Windows-only hardware or networks, there are two main options…

Boot Camp

If you have a Mac with an Intel processor – which you can check by selecting About This Mac in the menu – it's possible to install a fully functional version of Windows on your Mac. Each time you switch on, you can choose either Windows or Mac OS.

Thanks to Boot Camp – a piece of software that's built in to OS X Leopard or available as a download for OS X Tiger – installing Windows on your Mac shouldn't be difficult. Boot Camp walks you through the process of "partitioning" your hard drive (allocating a fixed amount of space to each of the two systems) and getting everything up and running. It's a non-destructive process, so you shouldn't lose any data, but it's a good idea to back up everything before you start the installation.

Boot Camp works with Windows Vista or recent versions of Windows XP (ie those with Service Pack 2). See apple.com/bootcamp for more information.

PC emulators

If you want to run a Windows program right inside the OS X environment, as opposed to switching between the two systems, then you could install a PC emulator package on your Mac. Running a program this way can be a bit slow (the Mac has to crunch a lot of data in the background) but it's usable enough for most tasks.

There are various emulators on the market – see macwindows.com for details – but the most popular is Microsoft's Virtual PC, which even puts a Windows Start menu in the OS X Dock. Find out more at mactopia.com.

of – is separate from Windows, despite the fact that both are made by Microsoft, and despite the fact that some new PCs are sold with Word pre-installed.

Word is available for both Macs and PCs, and though the Mac version looks a tiny bit different from the PC version, they're essentially the same. A Mac with Word installed *can* open, edit and resave a Word doc created on a PC – and vice versa.

Currently, new Macs ship with a trial version of the whole Office suite (including Word), which works for a couple of weeks. After that, you can pay online to turn the trial version into a full version. Alternatively, acquire Word or Office from elsewhere.

What about my music files?

Music files in the MP3 format, as well as any AAC files created or purchased using the PC version of iTunes, will work fine on a Mac. The other popular format – WMA (Windows Media Audio) – may be more problematic. WMA files you created yourself by importing from CD should be OK. But if you purchased music from a non-iTunes download service you may find they are protected by Digital Rights Management code and won't play on a Mac. There is usually a way around this (see p.209), but it's not ideal.

Will my printer and peripherals work?

Practically all recent printers are compatible with Macs. Indeed, in most cases you can just plug in a printer and it will work straight off; OS X comes preloaded with around one gigabyte's worth of printer drivers, so you shouldn't need to mess around with the CD that came with the printer. Note, though, that Macs don't have a parallel socket – the long sockets with teeth and screws used to attach older printers – so you'll need a printer with a USB connection.

Other PC peripherals that should work fine with a new Mac include monitors, external hard drives and keydrives (also known as thumb drives and USB flash drives). Most scanners and digital cameras are also compatible, though it's worth checking with the manufacturer (or doing a bit of research via Google) to make sure, especially if the device is more than a few years old.

However, there are also many peripherals that won't work on Macs – at least not without advanced technical tweaking way beyond the skills of most people. These include webcams and Wi-Fi adapters, many MP3 players and gaming devices, and some older scanners, cameras and printers.

For a full list of devices that OS X can handle without any driver installation, see:

OS X Upgrade apple.com/macosx/upgrade

My friends use PCs. Does that matter?

Switching to a Mac won't affect your ability to email, share pictures and instant message with your PC-using friends and family. One thing to note, however: video conferencing with a webcam between PCs and Macs will currently only work via Skype or AOL Instant Messenger.

What about my work?

If you're wondering whether a Mac would be suitable for work as well as home use, think about which applications you use at your place of employment. If it's mainly Word, Excel, PowerPoint and other standard office programs, you shouldn't have many problems, assuming you install Microsoft Office on the Mac. Occasionally there might be annoyances – a document written in a PC typeface, for example, might look slightly different on a Mac – but you won't often run into more serious problems.

For any other applications, however – from corporate systems to graphics packages – it might be more difficult, or simply impossible, to do the work on a Mac. So be sure to enquire with whoever runs the computer system at your workplace before splashing out.

What's with the one-button mouse?

One thing that has long infuriated PC users when they try out a Mac is that the mouse (or laptop trackpad) has traditionally only had one button. Today, however, Macs actually come with a two-button mouse – and they also work with standard PC mice. As for older Macs, clicking while holding down the **Control** button does exactly the same as right-clicking. Macbook users can also right-click by tapping with two fingers simultaneously.

Can a Mac and a PC share files, Internet and printers in a home network?

Absolutely – and unless your PC is ancient, it shouldn't be difficult to set up. For more information on networking and sharing files and Internet, turn to p.61. For printer sharing, see p.147.

Buying & upgrading

Where to buy, when to buy

3

The obvious place to buy a new Mac is from the Apple Store – either by phone or on the Web. The main advantage of this option is that you get to customize the computer with a different hard drive size, extra RAM and other such options (see p.38).

Apple Store UK apple.com/ukstore • 0800-039-1010
Apple Store US apple.com/store • 1-800-MY-APPLE

Other dealers typically won't let you customize the Mac – at least not to the same extent – but their prices might be fractionally lower than Apple's. Also, different sellers may throw in different extras, so it's worth shopping around. The easiest way to do this is using a price-comparison agent such as, in the US:

Froogle froogle.com
Shopper.com shopper.com
Shopping.com shopping.com

…and in the UK:

Kelkoo kelkoo.co.uk
PriceRunner pricerunner.com
Shopping.com uk.shopping.com

Tip: At the time of going to press, the Apple Store will lower their price on Macs and other Apple products by up to 10 percent to match lower prices found elsewhere. Note this doesn't apply to educational buying, and the compared prices don't include delivery, sales tax (in the US) and other extras. For more details, call the regular Apple Store number.

In the US, you can keep track of ▶
the various offers, discounts and
rebates available on all types
of Macs at the buyers' guides at
macreviewzone.com
and dealmac.com.

Buying abroad

Many prospective UK Mac owners stumble across the US Apple Store website and notice a significant difference in price – especially when the pound is strong against the dollar. The obvious question is: should I wait and get a friend to bring me back a Mac from the US? Many people have done just this and made savings, though if you're considering it, you should bear in mind the following: though you're unlikely to get fined, it's technically illegal unless you declare it at customs; the prices you see on the US Apple Store don't include sales tax, which adds up to 7.25 percent; a US Apple warranty will work in the UK for laptops but not desktops; and you'll need to get a UK plug to attach to the US adaptor.

One problem with buying over the Internet or phone – including from Apple themselves – is that you can usually expect around a week's wait for delivery. Some online retailers tend to be quicker, including the best known of all:

Amazon US amazon.com
Amazon UK amazon.co.uk

But if you want the Mac the same day, your only choice is to visit a "real" store. In the US – and in London, Birmingham and Manchester in the UK – that might mean heading straight to one of Apple's own retail stores. For a list, see:

Apple Retail Stores apple.com/retail

Or to locate other approved Mac dealers, follow the "Where to buy" links from:

Apple Hardware US apple.com/hardware
Apple Hardware UK apple.com/uk/hardware

Pre-owned Macs

Refurbished Macs

Apple, and a few other retailers, offer refurbished Macs and other special deals. These are either end-of-line models or up-to-date ones which have been returned for some reason. They come "as new" – checked, repackaged and with a full standard warranty – but are reduced in price by 10–45 percent.

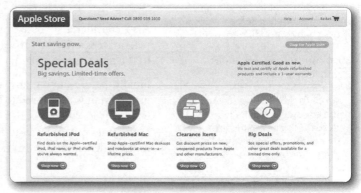

Until recently, you could only access the UK refurbished selection on Wednesdays from 10am. But as Mac sales have gone up, the range has become bigger and more consistent. To see what's on offer, follow the refurbished link at the bottom-right of the Apple Store homepage.

Used Macs

Buying a used Mac is much like buying any other piece of used electronic equipment: you might find a bargain but you might land yourself an overpriced bookend. That said, the standard Apple warranty is, in practice at least, transferable, so if you buy one that is less than a year old (and with the documentation to prove it) you should be able to get it repaired for free if anything goes wrong early on. Obviously, that will rely on the type of damage being covered by the warranty. It will also rely – except in the case of laptops, which are covered internationally – on the Mac having been purchased in the country where you want to get it repaired.

Macs on eBay

Though it's better to see any used item before you buy it, the online auction site eBay does cover your back to a degree. You can ask the seller as many questions as you want via email before you commit to a bid – something you may not feel able to do when responding to a classified ad. And by selling on eBay, the vendor enters into a legally binding contract that they will supply a product in exactly the condition they have described. So even if you're one of the tiny minority who get scammed, you may be able to recover your cash. The only problem is that there's such demand for Macs on eBay that you're unlikely to save much cash compared to buying new.

eBay UK computers.ebay.co.uk
eBay US computers.ebay.com

If you do buy a used Mac, make sure you see it in action before parting with any cash (except if you're shopping on eBay – see box), but remember that this won't tell you everything. Like all computers, Macs can develop hidden hardware problems that lead them to cut out unexpectedly. Or a particular component – the FireWire port, say – might be broken. In the case of laptops, also think about battery life, which diminishes over time. If any laptop battery has had heavy use, it may soon need replacing – which will add substantially to the cost; see p.297.

Also consider that older models won't necessarily support more recent accessories or software, and will run slowly if you upgrade to the most recent version of OS X.

Finally, before buying any used Mac, investigate to see whether a new version is rumoured to be coming out in a few weeks' time (see below). If so, you might be better off waiting, because when the new Mac comes out, older used models are suddenly less expensive and more widely available on the second-hand market.

To buy or to wait?

When shopping for any piece of computer equipment, there's always the tricky question of whether to buy the current model, which may have been around for a few months, or hang on for the next version, which may be both better and less expensive. In the case of Macs, the dilemma is even worse than normal, because Apple are famously secretive about their plans to release new or upgraded versions of their hardware.

Unless you have a friend who works in Apple HQ – and an opportunity to get him or her drunk – you're unlikely to hear anything specific from the horse's mouth about new Mac models until the day they appear. So, unless a new one came out recently, there's always the possibility that your new purchase will be out of date within a few weeks. About the best you can do is check out some sites where rumours of new models are discussed. But don't believe everything you read...

Apple Insider appleinsider.com
Mac Rumors macrumors.com

Which model, which specs

Once you've decided to purchase a Mac, then comes the hard bit: picking which model to plump for and choosing a set of specifications suited to your needs and budget. The following few pages may help. We've avoided giving detailed information on the specs of each Mac model, since it would probably be out of date before this book even rolled off the press. Instead, we've focused on the general issues and options that you need to consider before you buy.

The first decision is whether to go for a laptop (notebook) or a desktop. If you need to work on the move, then the decision is already made, but many people also buy laptops for home use, as they're so easy to move between rooms and hide away when not in use. Indeed, since 2005 laptop sales have been higher than desktop sales in many countries. Perhaps the most attractive thing about a laptop is that, thanks to wireless Internet, you can browse the Web, email and chat anywhere in the house or garden.

On the other hand, a desktop Mac offers a much bigger screen and bigger hard drive for the same money – or, in the case of a Mac Mini, the opportunity to save money by using an existing non-Apple monitor.

Mac names

For a long time, Macs aimed at the professional market were labelled "Power", while consumer and education models were usually prefixed with an "i" or "e". More recently, however, Apple have changed the names of their products to include the word Mac (eg MacBook and Mac Pro).

Mac laptops

Since 1999, Apple have produced two laptop families: one aimed primarily at the consumer and education market (the plastic-cased MacBook and its iBook predecessors) and the other aimed mainly at professionals (the aluminium MacBook Pro and its PowerBook predecesors).

MacBook vs MacBook Pro

If you decide to buy a Mac laptop, you'll first need to choose between a MacBook and a MacBook Pro. There are various differences between the two, but they're far less fundamental than the difference in price might suggest. Indeed, when Apple brought out the MacBook range, they significantly shrunk the gap between their consumer and pro laptops. At the time of writing, the main differences are as follows:

▶ **Horsepower** At any one time, the central processors offered in the MacBook Pros are faster than those in MacBooks. But the differential isn't usually huge.

▶ **Hard drives** The MacBook Pros come with bigger hard drives by default,

*The MacBook Pro 15"
(pictured left) and 17"
(pictured right) are great for
working with video, images
and page layouts.*

but if you buy a MacBook from Apple you can upgrade the drive size if you really want the extra space. Moreover, the MacBook hard drive enclosure is accessible, so upgrading to a larger drive in the future shouldn't be difficult.

▶ **Graphics** The MacBook Pro features a much faster graphics processor than the MacBook does, but in most cases you'll only notice the difference if you play processor-intensive 3D games.

▶ **Size** The MacBook Pros offer bigger screen sizes and thinner bodies. The flip side is that they're also slightly heavier.

▶ **External screens** Both models can drive external monitors, though the MacBook Pro can handle larger screens with higher resolutions.

▶ **Ports and slots** Some MacBook Pros offer a faster FireWire port (non-essential for most home users), and feature a PCMCIA ("PC Card") slot for devices such as 3G data cards (see p.64). They also have one USB port on each side (as opposed to two on the left-hand side as found on the MacBook) – useful when connecting an external mouse, for example.

▶ **Impact resistance** MacBooks are not completely indestructible, but they're much closer to being so than most computers thanks to their

Tip: At the time of writing, the MacBook is available in two white versions and one, more expensive, black version. Note that the extra cost of the black version is only partly justified by its bigger hard drive. If you buy online from Apple, you could choose the next model down, in white, upgrade the hard drive size to match that of the black model and the overall cost will be 10–20 percent lower.

polycarbonate plastic shell – made from "the same high-grade material used in bulletproof glass", according to Apple. This durabillty is one of the reasons MacBooks are popular with the education market.

▶ **Battery life** Fully charged, a MacBook battery will run for slightly longer than that of a MacBook Pro. At the time of writing, the difference is 30–60 mins (a maximum of six hours for a MacBook and five for a MacBook Pro). For more on maximizing your laptop's battery life, see p.297.

Our conclusion? Unless you plan to do serious video or sound editing, you'll get far better value for money with the MacBook. (Indeed, much of this book has been edited and typeset on a MacBook!) If you have leftover cash, spend it on extra hard drive space or RAM (see p.295).

Desktops: Mac mini, iMac & Mac Pro

Mac desktop computers currently fall into three families: Mac mini, iMac and Mac Pro. As with laptops, some of the differences – such as hard drive size – can be cancelled out by customizing the machine when buying via the Apple Store, but others, such as internal firepower, cannot. Here's a quick briefing on the main pros and cons of each of the three types of desktop Macs available at the time of going to press.

Mac mini

Released to much acclaim in January 2005, the Mac mini is designed primarily for PC users wanting an inexpensive way to switch to a Mac. The mini comes without monitor, keyboard or mouse, the idea being that you use the ones you already have for

The Mac mini doesn't leave much room for upgrades, but third-party extras make it possible to keep expanding. This MicroNet miniMate, for example, sits snugly under a mini, providing 400GB of disk space, four USB ports and three FireWire ports.

Tip: As we explain on p.296, it's possible to use one Mac as an external hard drive to another Mac. This is particularly useful for Mac mini owners. For example, you could take your Mac mini from home and open its files on a desktop Mac at work.

The iMac is like a large laptop on a stand. For another iMac pic, see p.3.
▼

your PC. Simply replace the PC's body with the diminutive Mac (6.5" x 6.5" x 2") and switch on.

Any monitor – DVI or VGA – should work fine with a Mac mini, though the keyboard and mouse need to be the type that connect with USB rather than PS/2 (the old-school round-ended connectors). If you do have a PS/2 keyboard and/or mouse, you can pick up an adaptor for around $15/£10, or buy new ones. For the keyboard, at least, it's worth considering an Apple model ($49/£29 at the time of writing), partly so you don't have a Windows key in place of a command (⌘) key, and partly because an Apple keyboard comes with two USB ports handily positioned on the back.

But the mini isn't only for PC users thinking of switching. It's also the single least-expensive way to get a Mac – even if you have to buy a monitor to go with it. It's portable, too, so can easily be taken, say, from home to work. (That said, you have to factor in a pretty bulky power adapter.)

As for processing speed, the mini isn't exactly a powerhouse, so it's not ideal for video editing or gaming. But it's more than capable of holding its own for the vast majority of tasks – especially if you get extra RAM when you buy.

iMac

If you fancy something with a bit more kick or a built-in screen, then consider an iMac. The first iMac, released in 1998, was one of the most radical computer products ever released. The machine may have lacked power and upgradability, but its slick design and out-of-the-box user-friendliness was a real breakthrough. The "i" is said to have originally stood for Internet, since this was the first personal computer to be ready to connect out of the box.

In 2002, Apple completely revised the iMac to add a flat screen, and a further overhaul, which saw all the components integrated into the casing of the screen, followed in 2005. Another major revision, with a switch to a metal enclosure, arrived in 2007.

There's nothing an iMac can do that a top-end Mac mini can't. However, iMacs do come with higher specifications and crisp, wide-screen, high-resolution displays, which makes them ideal for multimedia work such as video, music and picture editing. They also function very well as DVD players and can be easily moved between rooms.

Other recent Mac models

If you're in the market for a second-hand Mac, here are some other models you might come across:

▶ **iBook** The predecessor to the MacBook. It's a similar basic design, but a bit chunkier. Not the fastest Mac on earth, but the more recent G4 models are still serviceable for basic Internet and word-processing tasks.

▶ **PowerBook** The predecessor to the MacBook Pro. Pretty well identical from the outside, but a bit slower on the inside. Again, the more recent G4 models are perfectly good for most tasks that don't require serious firepower.

▶ **eMac** Originally released as a bigger-screen, education-oriented version of the original iMac, the eMac was for years the best-value Apple computer available. As with the laptops above, the later models, with G4 processors (pictured), are fine for basic tasks such as Internet, iTunes, Word and digital photos.

For (much, much) more on old Mac models, see:

Low-End Mac lowendmac.com

The Mac Pro.

Mac Pro

In pre-Intel days, Apple's top-end computer was known as the Power Mac and generally referred to by its processor ("G5" or "G4"). Today, however, it's simply called the Mac Pro.

The main advantage of a Mac Pro is its sheer speed, which it achieves courtesy of two high-speed 64-bit CPUs, super-fast bus connections and a massive RAM capacity (up to 16 gigabytes at the time of going to press). Unlike other Macs, it features a "tower"-style case, which leaves room for multiple hard drives as well as PCI and AGP slots to host (among other things) professional-level video cards capable of powering up to two enormous screens. And there are scores of ports to boot – from Bluetooth antenna to optical audio – including some handily stationed on the front of the case.

Do you really need this kind of power and expandability? If you plan to do professional-level graphics, video or sound editing, or supercomputer-style number crunching, then perhaps you do – in which case the Mac Pro is a matchless computer. If not, it's both overpriced (note that no monitor, camera, speakers or microphone are included in the advertised prices) and oversized (it's 15 times heavier and 36 times bulkier than a Mac Mini).

Which specs?

Once you've chosen which type of Mac to buy, you need to pick a specific model. And, if you buy the computer via the Apple website, you'll be offered various customization options at the time of purchase. Here are some of the factors you will need to grapple with when making your decision:

▶ **Processor** The processor, or CPU, is the brain of a computer: the bit that actually does the computing. This is a key factor in determining a Mac's potential speed, but don't think that it's the only one – getting a slightly slower-processor model and spending the extra money on plenty of RAM (see p.39) will often result in better overall performance.

▶ **Screen size** A bigger, wider screen is always nice to have. It comes into its own for watching DVDs and working with professional-level applications in which the "palettes" of options take up quite a lot of screen real-estate before you even open a file. Note, however, that the dimensions of a screen in pixels are just as important as its actual physical size.

▶ **Combo Drive** or **SuperDrive** All Macs come with either a Combo Drive (which will playback CDs and DVDs and burn recordable CDs) or a SuperDrive (which will do the same but also burn DVDs). Burning DVDs is useful for distributing your home videos to friends and family, and also for backing up data. But if backing up is your main aim, you could consider spending the extra money on an external hard drive instead.

▶ **Hard drive capacity** The hard drive is a computer's storage cupboard where all your documents, music, applications and other files live. There are different types of hard drive but, when customizing a Mac, the only thing you can choose is the drive's capacity, measured in gigabytes (GB). See below for more on choosing how large a hard drive you need. The first thing to know is that a decent chunk of the space will be used up even before you've saved your first file. One reason for this is that all hard drives offer around 7 percent less space than advertised (because manufacturers

Megs & gigs

The basic unit of computer data is the "bit", which represents either a zero or a one in the RAM or hard drive. Roughly speaking, eight bits make one "byte" – the space required to describe a single character of text.

▶ **1 KB** (kilobyte) = 1000 bytes

▶ **1 MB** (megabyte) = 1000 kilobytes

▶ **1 GB** (gigabyte) = 1000 megabytes.

Mathematically minded readers may be interested to know that all these figures are actually approximations of the number two raised to different powers. A gigabyte, for example, is two bytes to the power of thirty, which equals 1,073,741,824 bytes.

use gigabyte to mean a billion bytes, when in reality it should be around 2^{30} = 1.07 billion bytes). Another reason is that OS X and the applications that come with a Mac take up many gigabytes themselves. So an "80GB" hard drive, for example, offers something closer to 50GB of empty space. In that space, you'll be saving all your files, including the following:

Music	Video	Photos	Documents	Software
Allow around 1GB per 200 songs in iTunes. Or, for making your own music at CD quality, 1GB equals around 90 minutes.	Unedited footage imported from a DV camera takes up around 1GB per 5 minutes of footage.	Depending on the camera and setting, you'd fit around 1000 pictures in 1GB.	Text documents such as Excel and Word docs with no pictures are relatively tiny. Almost not worth factoring in.	Allow around 1GB for each major software suite (eg Microsoft Office or Adobe CS). Smaller applications take up much less room.

▶ **Memory** or **RAM** When you open an application or document, the relevant files are pulled from the hard drive into the RAM (Random Access Memory) so that the processor can quickly access them. So the more RAM the system has, the more files and programs it can handle at the same time. RAM makes an enormous difference to performance – even more than the processor in terms of the price-to-power ratio – so be sure to choose a model that allows room in your budget to add some extra. However, unless you're buying a Mac mini, consider adding the RAM yourself, as Apple rarely offer the best price (see p.39).

▶ **Keyboard and mouse** All Macs apart from minis and laptops come with the standard Apple keyboard and mouse. A wireless set means less desktop clutter and greater portability, but on the other hand doesn't feature the handy USB ports that reside on the back of the wired keyboard. Moreover,

Wireless connections

These days, all new Macs come with two forms of wireless connectivity built in:

▶ **Wi-Fi**, often referred to as 802.11x or just "wireless", is the technology used for creating wireless networks to share Internet, files and printers in homes, offices or cafés. Apple used to refer to Wi-Fi as "AirPort" or "AirPort Extreme", but now they reserve these monikers for their wireless base stations, which has helped clear up a lot of unnecessary confusion. Wi-Fi has a range of up to a couple of hundred feet, depending on the number and type of walls in the way. Note, though, that you'll also need a wireless router (see p.67) to connect to the Internet wirelessly. If you have, or are buying, an older Mac without Wi-Fi, you may be able to buy a card or USB plug-in to add this feature (see p.65).

▶ **Bluetooth** This short-range wireless technology is used for connecting to nearby Bluetooth-enabled keyboards, mice and printers. It also lets your Mac talk to your mobile phone, either to sync contacts and calendars (see p.146) or to connect to the Internet (see p.65). It's possible to add Bluetooth to older Macs at any time using an inexpensive third-party USB Bluetooth module – which you can also move between computers.

unlike infrared mice and keyboards, the Bluetooth models offered by Apple have a habit of consuming batteries pretty fast – especially the mice.

▶ **AppleCare** All Macs come with Apple's standard one-year hardware warranty (international on laptops; country of purchase on desktops) and 90 days of phone support (for Apple applications, OS X and hardware issues). The AppleCare scheme bumps up both streams of support to three years. So is it worth it? If you're terrible with computers and likely to make extensive use of the phone support, then perhaps. Otherwise, it's probably not good value: there's lots of technical support available for free online (see p.306), and though it's gutting to have any piece of equipment go wrong soon after the warranty period, Macs are known for being comparatively reliable.

Finally, you'll be offered lots of accessories, many of which are discussed elsewhere in this book. For example, an AirPort or AirPort Express Base Station (see p.67) or a .Mac account…

.Mac

Apple's .Mac service ("dot Mac") is a suite of tools and services that you can sign up for at a cost of $99/£69 per year. This buys you a large slice of online storage space – 10 gigabytes at the time of writing – along with tools for using it in various ways, such as:

An example of a .Mac Web Gallery created in a couple of clicks in iPhotos and hosted on .Mac.

▶ **Photo and video sharing** Using iPhoto and iMovie, respectively, you can publish your photos and home movies to the Web in seconds.

▶ **Web hosting** iWeb (see p.182) can be used to publish websites, blogs and photo galleries straight into your .Mac web space.

▶ **File transfer** The .Mac iDisk allows you to store and transfer any type of file via your .Mac web space.

▶ **Email** An email account accessible online and via a mail program. You'll get an address in the form yourname@mac.com. For more, see p.164.

▶ **Backup** An application for automatically backing up key files to your iDisk or external media such as hard drives, CDs and DVDs.

▶ **Sync** With a .Mac account, it's possible to synchronize your contacts, calendars and bookmarks across more than one Mac.

▶ **Remote Access** With .Mac's "Back to My Mac" feature, assuming your Mac is turned on and connected to the Internet, you can browse its files remotely from any other machine that is set up with your .Mac account (see box opposite) and also has the "Back to my Mac" feature enabled under **System Preferences > .Mac > Back to My Mac**.

One of the most useful aspects of .Mac is your online homepage, where you can log into and access all your published sites and galleries, as well as email, calendars, contacts and Safari bookmarks. The page also gives you access to loads of useful tips and tutorials.

None of this is essential and there are free alternatives to many of the services – such as email and Web space. Equally, it's perfectly possible to do backups without any special tools. Still, .Mac remains attractive due to its sheer ease of use and seamless integration with the tools on your Mac.

Apple will nag you to sign up for a free 60-day trial at every opportunity, but if you want to find out more or can't wait to be asked, either open **System Preferences > .Mac** or visit:

.Mac mac.com

.Mac preferences

Once you have set up a .Mac account you can register specific Macs to use the account via their **System Preferences > .Mac** panel. To synchronize contacts, calendars and so on across multiple Macs, each machine needs to be registered and have its preferences set under the **Sync** tab (pictured below). You can check the status of all synced Macs, or de-register one at any time, by clicking **System Preferences > .Mac > Sync > Advanced**.

The .Mac Preferences panel also allows you to enable the Back to My Mac feature. Unlike with .Mac syncing, however, this feature only works if both Macs are running OS X Leopard.

5 Upgrading

If your Mac hardware or operating system is past its best, or you want to expand your set-up to store more files or add extra firepower, you'll be in the market for an upgrade. This section takes a look at what kind of upgrades are possible, and which ones are actually worth the time and money.

Upgrading to Leopard

Though Leopard is easily the best version of the Mac operating system yet, it's not necessarily sensible or possible to install it on older Macs. First, you'll need to work out whether your Mac is up to Apple's specified minimum requirements: G3/G4/G5 processor; FireWire port; 512MB of RAM (physical, not virtual); 3GB of available hard drive space; and a drive that can read DVDs, as the operating system ships on DVD rather than CD.

Even if your machine matches these requirements, however, consider its speed: Leopard will more than likely be frustratingly slow on anything less than a G4. And if you want to run many applications simultaneously, 1GB of RAM is a more realistic minimum.

Buying and installing

The easiest way to get your hands on a copy of Leopard is to visit the Apple website and order a copy. However, OS X is not available

OS X versions

There's been a new release of OS X roughly once per year since 2001, when v10.0 Cheetah appeared. Each new version added a few significant new tools as well as hundreds of minor improvements:

▶ **v10.1 Puma (2001)** added DVD playback (p.255) support.

▶ **v10.2 Jaguar (2002)** added Address Book (p.144), iChat (p.175) and Universal Access (p.51).

▶ **v10.3 Panther (2003)** added faxing tools (p.150), Exposé (p.103) and greater Windows compatibility.

▶ **v10.4 Tiger (2005)** added Spotlight (p.96), Dashboard (p.108), Safari (p.153) and Automator (p.122).

▶ **v10.5 Leopard (2007)** added Time Machine (p.287), Spaces (p.104), Quick Look (p.86) and Stacks (p.81).

For the full story, visit: wikipedia.org/wiki/Mac_OS_X. Or, If you are determined to track down an earlier version of OS X, look on eBay, where they can be picked up relatively cheaply.

to download, so if don't want to wait for a boxed copy to arrive on your doorstep, you'll have to visit a retail store (see p.20). At the time of writing, a single-user copy will cost you $129/£85, while a five-user Family Pack costs $199/£129.

Installing the software from DVD is easy, but can take a while. Just in case things go wrong, it is advisable to make a complete backup of your entire system (see p.287) before you start. This is easily done with an external hard drive and a copy of SuperDuper:

SuperDuper shirt-pocket.com/SuperDuper

Classic mode

The OS X "Classic" mode allows users to run any old-style OS 9 Mac applications within OS X. Note, though, that this only works on pre-Intel Macs running older versions of OS X (up to and including v10.4 Tiger) and does *not* feature as part of Leopard – so take this into account if you are thinking of upgrading.

Upgrading Mac hardware

Macs, like all computers, can be upgraded in two ways: by getting under the hood and adding or replacing internal components, or by hooking up external peripherals. Sometimes you can achieve the same effect by either means.

The number of internal operations that you can perform on your Mac without voiding the warranty varies widely between different models. For tasks that Apple considers manageable for punters, you should be able to get easy-to-follow PDF instructions on the Apple site. Visit apple.com/support and follow the link for your model. Alternatively go straight to Apple's online DIY centre:

Apple DIY apple.com/support/diy
Apple DIY UK apple.com/uk/support/diy

You may also find the following site useful as a source of info as well as for buying parts (UK only):

MacUpgrades macupgrades.co.uk

If you decide the upgrade you want is beyond your capabilities, any authorized Apple dealer should be happy to take over. But, depending on the job and your particular set up, you may find that it's cheaper to opt for an external add-on. The following is a quick look at the most common upgrade jobs.

Tip: To check exactly what hardware currently comprises your Mac, click > **About This Mac** and then click the **More Info...** button.

Opening a Mac mini

Unlike other Macs, the mini doesn't theoretically have any DIY upgrade potential – not even the addition of RAM. However, many users have opened their Mac mini using two thin putty knives to prise off the case. Apple has given mixed messages about whether or not this will invalidate your warranty. If you don't damage anything, the answer is probably no; if you do, the answer may be yes. For more advice, see the Mac mini sites listed on p.303.

RAM

Adding extra RAM to any personal computer can make an enormous difference to performance. Applications will start and run more quickly, and when you're dealing with large files or performing many tasks at once, the improvements will be particularly marked. One of the best places to buy trustworthy RAM is the Crucial Memory website, which features a handy tool for picking exactly the right chips for your system.

Crucial US crucial.com
Crucial UK crucial.com/uk

When choosing how much RAM to buy, bear in mind that, annoyingly, your Mac won't necessarily have an empty RAM slot – so you may have to remove, say, an existing 128MB or 256MB chip to make way for the new chip that you've purchased.

Hard drive

If you run out of hard drive space, try clearing out old files. If that doesn't have any effect, the best solution in most cases is to buy an external hard drive to connect to your Mac via a FireWire or USB2 cable. Not only is this solution foolproof and comparatively inexpensive, but an external hard drive is also a very useful thing to have around – for backing up and transferring files between machines.

If you are set on adding an internal drive, it isn't difficult in any tower-style Power Mac or Mac Pro. But for other models you'll need to replace your existing drive, which means reinstalling your system from scratch (or a tricky process to get the data from one drive to the other). Furthermore, for many Mac models, replacing an internal hard drive often requires substantial disassembly of the machine – not an ideal job for an amateur.

RAM is usually sold in modules of 512MB, 1GB or 2GB. Desktop computers use DIMM chips, while laptops use SODIMMs.

Tip: When handling internal computer components – such as RAM chips – be aware that a small static electric shock from your hand could be enough to fry your newly acquired piece of kit. To avoid this, touch something unpainted and grounded (eg a tap or plumbing pipe) before touching any components and avoid placing parts on carpets.

Processor upgrades

With most Macs, there's no easy way to upgrade the processor. But it is possible in some models, such as old G3, G4 and G5 towers, Mac cubes and Mac Pros. For more information, browse CPU upgrades under the Hardware Reviews section of: macreviewzone.com.

SuperDrive

Unless you have a Power Mac or an iMac G5, you can't easily add a SuperDrive (DVD burner) to your machine. It can be done, but unless you're happy to invest substantial time or money, you might be better off considering an external DVD burner, such as those made by:

Lacie lacie.com

AirPort (wireless) card

If you purchased your Mac new in the last couple of years it should already have wireless capability. Many older Macs, however, can't use wireless until you install an AirPort card. Installing the card is simple enough, but finding one can be tricky, as Apple no longer sell them. A good place to start is eBay.

First, however, trawl the support section of the Apple website to work out whether your Mac requires an old-school AirPort card or a newer AirPort Extreme card. Then locate the AirPort slot (it's behind the CD tray on an eMac, and under the keyboard on a iBook or PowerBook), drop in the card and attach the tiny antenna cable. Switch on and you're ready to connect to a wireless network.

For more details on upgrading your Mac, try the model-specific websites listed on p.304. And for advice on importing data from an old Mac or PC, see p.74.

Setting up

Welcome to OS X

If you're new to OS X, you'll need to get used to an interface that is slightly different from the one you're familiar with from Windows or "classic" Mac systems. If you're completely new to Macs, you'll also need to get acquainted with an Apple-style mouse and keyboard. This chapter takes you through from switching on for the first time, via the basics of the OS X environment, to speeding up with Mac keyboard shortcuts.

Your first time...

When you fire up your Mac for the first time, you'll be prompted to enter various bits of information. It's largely self-explanatory, though a couple of things are worth noting:

▶ **Details** If you don't have Internet and email details or other info to hand you can ignore these stages and set it all up later (see p.60 and p.166).

▶ **Registering** If you don't want to register with Apple, or you have trouble entering your country information, press the **Q** and ⌘ keys simultaneously to quit the process.

When you first switch on your Mac, you'll be offered the services of the Migration Assistant tool, which allows you to hook up to an existing Mac and have everything transferred automatically. But the old machine needs to have OS X v10.1 or later, and you'll need a standard 6-pin to 6-pin FireWire cable. If you don't have one to hand, you can run the Migration Assistant later. For more on migrating data from old Macs and PCs, see p.74.

What's where in OS X

1. menu Aka the "Apple menu", this is always there, whichever application you are using; it holds log out and shut down options, System Preferences, and more. To customize the menu, see p.119.

> **Tip:** To find out about your Mac's hardware, click **About This Mac** in the menu for the basic specs, and then hit **More Info…** for the full techie version.

2. The desktop Similar to the desktop of a Windows PC, this is a place for storing docs currently in use and so on. The desktop can also be located as a folder within your "home" folder. To customize the desktop, see p.115.

3. Finder window Double-click any folder to reveal its contents in one of these. For much more on Finder windows, see p.90.

4. The Dock Home of quick links to applications, folders, Stacks, minimized windows and the Trash, the Dock is also used for switching between open applications. To read more about the Dock, turn to p.79.

Running along the top of the OS X screen is the menu bar, which holds application menu headers and, depending on how you set it up, status indicators, a clock, the current user's name (see p.53) and a Spotlight (see p.96) button.

5. Macintosh HD The default name for your Mac's hard drive. If you imagine that everything in your Mac lives within a family tree of folders, this is the folder at the top.

6. System Preferences The home of scores of options and settings – a bit like the Windows Control Panel. Accessed via the menu and the "cog" icon on the Dock.

> **Tip:** If an item is greyed out in System Preferences, you don't have privileges to access it (see p.59).

7. Info panel To see details about any file or folder, select it, hit ⌘I and one of these panels will appear. As well as giving info, these are used for changing icons (see p.120) and the application used to open a file (see p.87).

> **Tip:** If you're really confused, you could try the feature-stripped version of OS X: **Simple Finder** (see p.55).

Other basic concepts

Finder

Finder is the application at the centre of the Mac user experience, allowing you to find, copy and delete files, organize them into folders, launch applications, switch between tasks, connect to servers… and much more.

Finder doesn't *seem* like an application, since it's inseparable from OS X as a whole. Yet Finder is an application nonetheless, complete with all the prerequisite parts, such as menus, Preferences and an icon (the long-standing Mac smiley face, which is permanently welded to the Dock). Unlike most applications, it doesn't feature a "quit" option, but if Finder ever misbehaves or freezes up, you can relaunch it (see p.294).

Whenever Finder or another application needs your input or approval, it will display a so-called dialog box (just like in Windows). If a button is highlighted in blue, it can be activated by hitting the Enter key instead of clicking. You can also often activate a button by holding down the ⌘ key while hitting the first letter of the word displayed on the button.
▼

Home

Your "home" folder is the place where all your documents and other files (including the items on your desktop and various files related to your use of applications) are stored. If there is more than one account set up on a Mac, each user has their own home folder. The various home folders live within **Macintosh HD > Users**.

Applications

Applications, or programs, are pieces of software for anything from writing a letter to composing a piece of music. An application can live anywhere on your system, but usually they reside in the **Applications** folder. For more on applications, see p.100.

Trash

When you delete a file, it isn't really deleted: it's sent to the Trash, where it stays until the Trash is emptied. To do this, choose **Empty Trash** from the **Finder** menu, or click and hold the Trash icon on the Dock. Alternatively, use this shortcut: ⌘⇧⌫

Tip: Even when you empty the Trash, the file may remain on your drive, from where it could potentially be recovered (see p.298). If you really want to delete the Trash's contents for good, select **Secure Empty Trash** from the **Finder** menu.

◀ *The Trash icon changes to let you know at a glance whether it contains "owt" or "nowt".*

Drives and discs

When you connect an external hard drive (or other "volume" such as a key drive or virtual disk file) to your Mac it'll appear on the desktop and in the sidebar of any Finder window, usually with a white disk drive icon, ready for you to open it up and add, copy or remove files.

CDs and DVDs also appear on the desktop and in sidebars when inserted. If blank, they are labelled CD-R, DVD-RW, etc, and you can drag files onto them. When you're ready to write the disc, select it on a Finder sidebar and press **Burn**.

When you've finished using an external drive or a CD or DVD, you need to eject it – don't just unplug a drive or you might damage it. To eject a drive, either press the eject icon next to its name in the sidebar of any Finder window, or drag the drive or disc to the Trash, which will morph into an eject icon the moment you start dragging.

Tip: If you would like to watch some animated silliness while you trash files and folders, download the splendid FunTrash freeware application from: web.mac.com/cafeville/ Cafeville/FunTrash.html

Software Update

Apple ongoingly updates OS X and its various applications to make them more stable and secure or to add extra features. Whenever you're connected to the Internet, you can click **Software Update** in the menu to check for the latest updates and have OS X install them for you. Even if you don't, OS X will, by default, automatically check for updates every few weeks.

When you check for updates, you can choose which items to install and which to ignore. Unless you have a specific reason not to (such as a grindingly slow Internet connection), install everything. And, at the very least, accept anything related to security. With regard to online threats of all kinds, keeping your operating system up to date is more important than installing third-party virus software.

Mac Help

Mac OS X comes with a reasonably comprehensive Help tool, so if you get stuck or want to know how to do something, select **Mac Help** in Finder's **Help** menu – or use the shortcut ⌘⇧?

Shut down, sleep, log out

To switch off your Mac, select **Shut Down** from the menu. Alternatively, just leave it on, and within a few minutes it will go into a low-energy "Sleep" mode, ready to be quickly awoken next time you need it. If you have a Mac laptop, simply shutting the lid has the same effect – and you can safely carry a Mac laptop around in Sleep mode.

If more than one user account is set up on the Mac, you could also **Log Out** from the menu to return to the screen where the next user can log in.

Tip: Software Update has its own panel in **System Preferences**. Here you can stop OS X checking for updates automatically, and make various other changes.

Tip: OS X offers good power-management features, which you'll find under the **Energy Saver** panel of **System Preferences**. Here you can schedule your computer to switch on and off at the same time each day, set how long it should wait before entering Sleep mode and, if you have a laptop, alter the settings for battery use.

Mouse & keyboard

The Mighty Mouse

Traditionally, Macs have been associated with simple, single-button mice – something that has put off many potential Apple converts. In recent years, however, iMacs and Mac Pros have shipped with a Mighty Mouse that, despite its simple appearance, offers four ways to click – left-side, right-side, depressing the scroll button or squeezing left and right with thumb and middle finger.

These four buttons can be used in various different ways. For example, the squeeze function can be set to activate Exposé or Dashboard. To customize the way your Mighty Mouse works, open the **Keyboard & Mouse** panel within **System Preferences**.

Right-clicking without a Mighty Mouse

If your Mac only has a one-button mouse or trackpad you can still "right-click" by holding down the Ctrl key while clicking. Alternatively, plug in any two-button USB mouse.

MacBook owners can also right-click by tapping the trackpad with two fingers. To turn this feature on, choose **System Preferences > Keyboard & Mouse > Trackpad > Tap trackpad using two fingers for secondary click**.

> **Tip:** If you let your mouse hover over an item, button or command, a small label pops up to tell you a little bit more about what you're about to click.

> **Tip:** If you have a Bluetooth mouse and keyboard, the relevant System Preferences panel can also be reached from the Bluetooth icon on the menu bar.

49

Tip: If you're coming to Macs from a PC background, you'll find that the ⌘ (Command) key is the equivalent to the Control key in Windows. So while **Ctrl-X** is "cut" on a PC, **⌘X** does the same on a Mac.

Tip: Many keyboard shortcuts are listed to the right of commands in application menus. They're usually represented using the same symbol system used in this book.

Tip: The various keys in a keyboard combination don't need to be hit simultaneously. The instruction ⌘C, for instance, means "hit **C** while holding down ⌘" – just as you'd create a capital letter by hitting a letter key while holding down **Shift** (⇧).

Tip: If you connect a PC keyboard to a Mac, the **Windows** key becomes the ⌘ key.

Keyboard shortcuts

Throughout this book you'll come across hotkeys or shortcuts: special combinations of keys that allow you to quickly perform a function in a particular application or across your system without using your mouse to trawl through menus and icons. It's worth taking the time to get used to shortcuts – they greatly increase your computing efficiency (as well as reducing your chances of developing repetitive strain injury).

Most shortcuts revolve around a handful of keys found in the bottom corners of the main section of the keyboard. If Macs are less confusing than PCs in general, these keys are an exception, since each can be referred to with various names and symbols:

> **Command** = ⌘ = ⌥ = **Apple**
> **Option** = ⌥ = **Alt**
> **Control** = **Ctrl** = ^
> ⇧ = **Shift**

In this book, we've stuck to the symbols when describing keyboard shortcuts (eg ⌘V or ⌘⌥S) but you might come across the above names when reading elsewhere. One other key symbol we use is:

> ⌫ = **Backspace** (not delete!)

Many applications feature their own panel for setting shortcuts (in Word, for example, look in the **Tools** menu under **Customize**). OS X system shortcuts can be set in **System Preferences** within the **Keyboard & Mouse** panel. Here you can also apply shortcuts to particular menu commands to work in all applications.

Universal Access

If you have any difficulty seeing, hearing or using the mouse and keyboard, you may find that OS X's impressively comprehensive set of accessibility features make your Mac easier to use. You'll find them within the **Universal Access** panel of **System Preferences**, which you can open from the menu. The most important accessibility features include:

▶ **VoiceOver** Provides spoken feedback to help you navigate between items, windows and applications with the keyboard.

▶ **Zoom** Once activated, the shortcuts ⌘⌥= and ⌘⌥- zoom in and out on any area of the screen, following the mouse pointer around. Things don't become clearer (higher-resolution) as you zoom in; they just get bigger.

▶ **Display** Lets you switch your screen to **Grayscale** (like a black-and-white movie) or **White on Black** (like a film negative). To toggle between the modes, hit ⌘⌥^8.

▶ **Enhance Contrast** Increases the starkness of the difference between dark and light. The shortcuts ⌘⌥^. and ⌘⌥^, have the same effect.

▶ **Flash** A visual alternative to the alert sound.

▶ **Sticky Keys** Allows you to enter key combinations in sequence rather than simultaneously.

▶ **Mouse Keys** Turn on this feature to control the mouse pointer using the numeric keypad section of your keyboard. On a Mac laptop, you'll need to hold down the **fn** key to access the numeric keypad.

▶ **Cursor Size** Makes the mouse pointer larger.

In addition, you might wish to activate the OS X Speech Recognition features (see p.200).

7

User accounts

If more than one person uses – or will use – your Mac, consider setting up separate user accounts. This way, each person has their own personal set-up, complete with their own folders, iTunes Library, desktop background, custom settings and so on. It's almost as if each user has their own computer – except, of course, only one person can use the Mac at any one time.

When you first got your Mac out of the box and set it up, you will have been prompted to enter a name, "short name" and password (and also to pick a twee little image from a selection including a butterfly, snowflake and billiard ball). Whether you realized it or not, you were setting yourself up with an account – and, more specifically, an account with "administrative" powers.

Tip: The way that Accounts work in Macs – with home folders, access privileges and so on – is entirely inherited from UNIX (see p.8). Multi-user capabilities were one of the key aims during UNIX's early development back in the 1960s.

Tip: It is possible to remove administrator privileges from the user who originally set up the Mac – but only if another user has been given admin status, since there must be at least one administrator at any one time.

Every Mac has at least one administrator – a person who has power to make system-wide changes, install updates and applications, and generally be fully in control of the computer. When you add other users, you can choose whether to make them administrators (if you trust them not to do anything stupid) or standard users (great for technophobes and kids).

Managing accounts

All the settings for user accounts can be accessed via the **Accounts** pane of System Preferences. Here, you can add and remove accounts – if you're an administrator – using the standard "+" and "–" buttons. You can also make changes to…

Name, short name and password

When you enter the name for a new account, a matching "short name" will be generated, but you can override this and pick anything you like. The short name is, in short, the name that will appear on your home folder (see p.46), and though you can change your name at any time, you can't easily change your short name.

If you do really want to change your short name for an account that already exists, the easiest option is to create a new account with the correct name, copy all your files across and then delete the previous account; for instructions, visit www.apple.com/support and search for

Tip: Only those with administrative powers can make changes to all user accounts, and even then they will have to enter their password to do so.

Tip: By default, your account password will also be the password for your "Keychain", which exists to save you remembering lots of other passwords. See p.280 for more on Keychains.

Forgot your account password?

If you forget your password, ask any user with administrator privileges to log in, open **Accounts** from **System Preferences** and let you reset your password. If there are no other administrators set up, try this:

▶ **Turn off** your computer, and insert the Mac OS X CD that came with your Mac or copy of Leopard.

▶ **Press C** while you turn on the Mac and keep it held down until the Apple logo appears.

▶ **Choose Reset Password** from the Installer menu and choose your username – *not* "System Administrator". Then follow the prompts.

This shouldn't affect your Keychain or any other passwords.

106824. There are some other workarounds, but they're for technically advanced users only.

Next you have to choose whether or not to pick a password. You don't have to use one if you don't want to. Not having a password makes it quicker to log in, but it means anyone with physical or network access to the Mac will be able to instantly access your files.

Picture

If the default pics don't appeal – for some strange reason you don't have yourself down as a dog or a baseball – hit **Edit** and load something else. Either press **Choose** to browse for a pic on your Mac; drag an image directly into the Edit window from a folder, from a webpage or from iPhoto; or click **Take a video snapshot** to take a picture with your webcam. Then use the slider to zoom in and drag the pic around to select the area you want to use.

Parental Controls

The Parental Controls built into Leopard allow administrators to restrict or monitor the computer usage of children or others with non-administrator accounts. To set this up, click **System Preferences**, choose **Parental Controls** and select the user whose account you want to manage.

Under the various tabs you can specify, among other things, that the user can only access certain applications, view certain websites, email certain friends, and use the computer at certain times. You can even hide swear words from their dictionary.

The logs tab lets you see what your beloved offspring have been looking at (or trying to look at) online, and what they've been discussing with friends in iChat.

For really young (or indeed really old) users, try checking the box for **Simple Finder**, a foolproof version of OS X with big icons, simplified menus and so on.

If an account has any parental controls activated, it is labelled as "managed" in the Accounts pane of System Preferences.

Login Items

This panel lists the programs or files that will launch automatically every time you log in or switch on. To add and remove Login Items, use the standard "+" and "–" buttons. If you like, use the check boxes to tell OS X to hide applications once they've been launched. This simply saves you from facing a screen full of windows each time you log in.

Remote set-up

If you have more than one Mac, you can manage the Parental Controls on one from the other. To enable this, open **System Preferences > Accounts**. Choose the account you want to manage, click the cog icon near the bottom-left of the window and choose **Allow Remote Setup**. Once that's done, administrators on any Mac on the network can find and edit the account under **System Preferences > Parental Controls > Other Compters**.

Tip: If there are techie-looking items in your Login items, leave them be – they probably relate to a specific application feature that runs in the background.

Logging in & out

OS X offers various options for how your Mac handles the accounts – what happens when you switch on the machine, for example, and how to switch between accounts once someone is logged in. Open **Accounts** from **System Preference** and click **Login Options**.

If you are the only user on a machine and you're not worried about people seeing your data in the event of the computer being stolen or otherwise accessed (see p.277), set OS X to automatically log in to your account. Otherwise, choose **Display login window** and select whether you'd like the Mac to request both the **Name and password** of whoever is logging on, or present a **List of users**, in which case you just click your name and enter your password. The latter is convenient, though fractionally less secure.

Fast User Switching

Also within the Login Options pane you can enable Fast User Switching – and you probably should. This useful function allows one user to log on without out the current user first logging off. Any documents, applications or webpages that the current user has open stay active "in the background": hidden from view and password-

> **Tip:** Fast User Switching provides a convenient way for everyone to, in effect, use the machine at the same time – but this can take its toll on system resources. If there are ten accounts running in the background, each with many open applications and documents, your Mac may run much more slowly.

> **Tip:** Users can access the **Accounts Preferences** panel from the Fast User Switching menu on the menu bar, though if they are not authorized to make changes, they will find all the options greyed-out.

protected (assuming the account does have a password). When you switch back, it will be as if you never logged out.

When Fast User Switching is activated, the current user's name (or a generic icon) appears in the menu bar, next to the clock. Click here to reveal a menu that lets you switch between users – complete with a cool cubic pirouette. It can take a few seconds to log in a user this way, but switching between users who are already logged in is almost instant.

Private & shared folders

Each user set up on the system has a home folder, pre-loaded with sub-folders labelled **Documents**, **Music**, **Pictures**, **Movies**, etc. You can use, ignore or add to these folders as you see fit – though it's better not to delete or rename them, especially the **Library** (see box overleaf).

The various home folders reside in the Users folder within the top level of the hard drive, which is probably labelled **Macintosh HD**. When you're logged in, your home folder bears a little house icon, but other users' homes look like standard folders, and the items in

Libraries

On a Mac, **Library** folders hold all manner of system- and application-related files, from preferences and fonts to widgets. You may have noticed that there's one Library here:

Macintosh HD > Library

… and another here:

Macintosh HD > Users > Your Name > Library

This arrangement allows functions or features to be installed either for one or all user accounts. When you choose a typeface in a word processor, for example, the fonts on offer consist of all the ones in the general Library and all the ones in your personal Library – but not those in the Libraries of other users. The same goes for widgets, screen savers and many other items.

Tip: If you regularly access either the **Shared** user folder, or a particular **Drop Box**, drag its icon onto your Sidebar (see p.91) or Dock (see p.79) for quick access.

them won't be accessible. Note, though, that anyone on the Mac with a bit of technical know-how can still access your files – unless you follow the instructions in this book's Privacy & Passwords chapter (see p.277).

Sharing files between accounts

If you *do* want to pass files between users, you have a few options. The easiest is to drop the files into one of the following folders, both of which can be accessed by any user on the machine:

▶ **Macintosh HD > Users > Shared**
▶ **Macintosh HD > Users > Your Name > Public**

Alternatively, if you want to give a file to another user without putting it somewhere public, put it in the other user's Drop Box – a special folder that anyone can put things into but whose contents can only be seen by the user. You'll find their Drop Box here:

▶ **Macintosh HD > Users > The User's Name > Public > Drop Box**

A final option is to use OS X's permissions setting (see box opposite). However, this is only worth considering if you need to set up a more complex sharing arrangement.

Sharing music & photos between accounts

If you choose **Share My Library** in iTunes **Preferences** or **Share My Photos** in iPhoto **Preferences**, other users of the Mac will be able to play or view (but not change or delete) your songs and photos. This is very useful, though if you want more than one user to really

Ownership & permissions

OS X, like other UNIX-based systems, provides a "permissions" file-management system that allows complete control over which users can access which files.

By default, the user who creates a file is considered the **Owner** and only they have access to it. But users with administrative powers can change these settings by selecting a file or folder, pressing ⌘I and looking under the **Ownership & Permissions** pane. Here, you can specify access – read, write, both, or none – for specific users (under "groups") or for all users (under "others").

Permissions settings can be very useful, but unless you're technically confident and have a specific reason to make use of them, this is one area of OS X that's definitely best left alone.

"share" a single iTunes Library, with both parties able to add tracks, create playlists, etc, the only option is to employ a techie work-around using permissions. It's beyond the scope of this book to go into the details, but if you're determined, search online for more information.

More sharing between accounts

You can share your screen savers (see p.117), widgets (see p.110) and fonts (see p.136) with other users by dragging them from their folders in your personal **Library** to the corresponding folders in the top-level **Library**.

8

Connecting to the Internet

All Macs come ready to connect to the Internet, but to get online at home you'll also need an account with an Internet Service Provider (ISP). This chapter takes a quick look at connecting to your existing connection or choosing a new one. It also covers getting online when you're out and about with your Mac laptop. For much more detailed information about everything Internet-related, pick up a copy of *The Rough Guide to the Internet*.

Connecting at home

If you already have an Internet account at home, then it should work fine with your new Mac. If you don't already have an ISP account, then it's time to sign up (see box on p.62).

Connecting via wireless

All recent Macs have built-in wireless, allowing you to connect to any wireless network. Click the fan-shaped icon in the menu bar to reveal networks in range, and click one to connect, entering a password if required.

If your Mac doesn't display the fan icon, then it may be an older machine without built-in wireless. Depending on what model you have, you may be able to track down and install a suitable AirPort or AirPort Extreme card to add this feature. For more information, see p.40.

If you don't yet have wireless set up at home, then you'll need to buy yourself a Wi-Fi router (see p.67), either to connect to your broadband modem or to function both as a router and a modem.

Connecting via Ethernet or USB

If you have a broadband account already set up and your modem or router has an Ethernet socket on it (like a fatter version of a phone jack), then no configuration should be needed – just plug an Ethernet cable from the modem or router to the Mac and you'll be online. The same should work at friends' houses and in some offices (in other cases, you'll need to get a system administrator to approve and configure your Mac before it works on the network).

In the UK, many ADSL modems connect by USB and lack an Ethernet socket. If you have one of these, you'll need to install the modem's software on the Mac. Dig out the CD and instructions that came with the modem; if you can't find them, try getting online by any other means and downloading the relevant software from the website of the modem manufacturer. If the modem doesn't appear to be compatible with OS X, phone your ISP for advice.

Tip: Don't connect a USB modem to your Mac before you install the software that came with the modem. This is a common cause of problems. If you can't get your USB modem to work, try disconnecting it, uninstalling the software, restarting the Mac, installing the software and only then reattaching the modem.

Sharing an Internet connection

Even if you don't have broadband or a router, it's perfectly possible to share your Internet connection between two computers (either Macs or PCs), allowing both machines to be online at the same time. To find out how, see p.66.

Sign up for broadband

Macs are designed for broadband Internet. You can get by with old-fashioned dial-up access if necessary, but if you can get broadband, you should. Though slightly more expensive than dial-up, broadband offers three crucial advantages:

▶ **Speed** Broadband provides a faster ("higher-bandwidth") connection. That means webpages load faster, file downloads happen quicker, and video and music can be streamed more easily. It also makes broadband more suitable for setting up a home network and sharing the connection between more than one computer.

▶ **A freed-up phoneline** Unlike dial-up, broadband lets you make and receive calls while online – even when it works through the phoneline. (One exception to this rule is satellite broadband, which sometimes requires an outgoing dial-up connection.)

▶ **Always-on access** With dial-up, each time you connect to the Net you'll need to spend around 30 seconds actually "dialling-up". But broadband is usually "always on", so when your Mac is switched on, you're online.

There are various different types of broadband connection, the most common being cable and ADSL. Cable broadband arrives via the same wire that provides cable television and is usually served up by the same companies. ADSL, by contrast, uses your phone line and is usually provided by phone companies or standalone ISPs.

Neither ADSL nor cable offer any great advantage over the other. The main things to look out for are the speed – generally measured in Mbps (millions of bits per second) – and the download allowance (which determines how much you can use the account before incurring any extra fees).

If you can't get ADSL or cable in your area, you could consider satellite broadband, but it's not as desirable, partly because of its higher cost and higher latency (time lags between you clicking and anything actually happening).

Once you've settled on a connection type, you're ready to select an Internet Service Provider. The best approach is to ask around, read Internet magazine reviews and see which companies others recommend. If someone swears by an ISP, and they seem to know what they're talking about, give it a go. That's just about the best research you can do. However, there's lots of information available on the Web – so if you can already get online, you could try consulting one of these sites:

ADSL Guide adslguide.org.uk (UK)
ISP Check ispcheck.com (US)
ISP Review ispreview.co.uk (UK)
The List thelist.com (US)

Once you've picked an ISP and contacted them via the phone or Internet, they should provide you everything you need. If it's a dial-up account, that's probably just a few details, which you can key into your Mac as described opposite. If it's broadband, you may have to wait for the ISP to send you a router or modem, and then you'll have to set it up. If you get stuck, try searching for the name of your modem or router at:

Apple Discussions discussions.apple.com

Connecting via dial-up

If your Mac has a dial-up modem built in, then setting up a dial-up ISP account simply involves connecting to a phone line and plugging in the relevant details – phone number, user name, password and so on. However, most Macs manufactured in or after 2006 *don't* have a dial-up modem; if your computer falls into that category, you'll need to buy a USB modem attachment (pictured, right).

If you don't know your login details, but they're set up on your old PC, boot the PC, look for **Network Connections** or **Dial-up networking**, find the relevant ISP account, right-click it and choose **Properties**. This will give you the phone number, username and any other details except the password; if you don't know the password, phone the ISP.

Once you have all the required details, you'll need to plug them into the Mac. Open Internet Connect from **Applications** (or via the phone icon near the clock) and click on the **Internal Modem** button. Key in the details and press connect.

The Apple USB modem is available from the Apple Store for around $49/£30.

Internet Connect

If that worked, you should now be able to connect and disconnect via the phone icon in the menu bar – or by using Internet Connect. If it didn't work, you'll find more options in the **Network** panel of **System Preferences**. Choose **Internal Modem** in the **Show** menu and explore the settings.

Tip: Some dial-up accounts require you to input more data than just the phone number, username and password. You might also need the details for a proxy server, DNS servers and more. You should be able to recover this info either from your old computer or ISP.

To locate hotspots, try the JiWire hotspot directory widget, free from *jiwire.com/macosxtiger.htm*

Network finders

The AirPort menu bar entry does a pretty good job of showing you which wireless networks are within range, but if you'd like to be able to check for wireless networks without even opening your bag, investigate Kensington's handheld WiFi Finder: kensington.com.

Connecting on the move

If you're out and about with a Mac laptop, there are various ways to get online...

▶ **Wireless** Public wireless "hotspots" are now a common feature in cafés, hotels, airports and elsewhere. Just click the fan icon to see if any are in range. Some hotspots are free, but often you'll have to pay – either directly or via an online sign-up process. In the available networks list, those that require a password to log in will display a padlock icon, so try those without first when browsing the airwaves to see what's available.

▶ **Via a mobile phone** For maximum mobility, try connecting your Mac laptop via a cell phone. The basic requirements are a data-compatible phone – ideally one with a fast connection such as 3G, EDGE or GPRS – and a way to connect it to the computer. The best solution is to use Bluetooth wireless technology, which is built into most modern phones and all recent Macs. (If you have an older Mac without Bluetooth, you can add it with an inexpensive USB adapter.)

To get the connection going, click on **Bluetooth** in **System Preferences**, and then hit **Set up new device…** and follow the prompts. If the set-up seems to work, but you can't get online, contact your phone provider to make sure your tariff allows data calls.

▶ **Via a card phone** If you have a MacBook Pro or PowerBook, you could opt for a high-speed PCMCIA card phone – such as the Vodafone 3G Card (pictured). That way you can get a fast Internet connection anywhere you can get phone reception. Such cards are usually not expensive to buy, but you'll be hit with monthly, hourly or per-meg usages fees. Ask in any phone shop for more details.

▶ **Via another computer** If you're at a friend's house and you want to share their Internet connection but they don't have a router, run an Ethernet cable between the two machines and quickly set up Connection Sharing (see p.66).

▶ **Phone sockets** If you have a dial-up modem and ISP account (many broadband ISPs provide a dial-up "backup" number), you may be able to get online wherever you can find a phone socket. You can use Internet Connect as usual, adding any relevant national or international dialling codes. But before shelling out on dialling long distance, check with your ISP to see if they have a local number in your current location.

Tip: If you're connecting via a mobile phone, why not download your numbers into Address Book while you're at it (see p.146).

iPhone & iPod touch

Though you can't use either an iPod touch or iPhone to connect your Mac laptop to the Internet, both offer a more-than-acceptable browsing experience via Wi-Fi hotspots and, in the case of the iPhone, your phone provider's EDGE network. For the full story, track down this title's two sister volumes, *The Rough Guide to the iPhone* and *The Rough Guide to iPods, iTunes & Music Online*.

More than one computer

Connecting two or more computers together enables them to share files, printers and an Internet connection. And these days it's very easy to do – even with a mixture of Macs and PCs. Don't be put off by the jargon: a "network" or "LAN" is simply two or more connected computers. As this chapter explains, the computers can be connected either directly, or via a central hub called a router. And the computer and router can communicate either via cables or wirelessly.

The first thing to do when setting up a home network is to work out whether you need any extra hardware. That depends on whether you want a typical router-based network or a money-saving computer-to-computer network…

Router-based networks

Traditionally, a network requires a router – a physical device that acts as the junction between the various computers. In a typical set-up, the router is attached to the Internet via a broadband modem

Tip: If you're trying to network a PC and a Mac but the PC doesn't have an Ethernet socket or Wi-Fi, you'll need to add one of these things to the PC with either an Ethernet or wireless adapter. These are relatively inexpensive and usually not difficult to fit.

Buying a router

Apple produces two routers – AirPort Extreme and AirPort Express – both of which are wireless, nicely designed, fully featured and very easy to set up. However, any router should work with both PCs and Macs, so if you're on a budget you might want to investigate the wider market, dominated by Netgear, Linksys, Belkin and D-Link.

When looking around at the alternatives, the first decision to make is whether you want one with or without wireless capability. The latter cost slightly more, but not much, and they can save you money overall as you won't have to buy any Ethernet cables. And wireless routers give you the best of both worlds, as they typically have ports for connecting with cables, too.

Next, you need to decide whether you need a router with a modem built in: if you already have a cable or DSL modem with an Ethernet socket, then a standard router should be fine. If not – for example, if you have a USB ADSL modem – then it's neater and cheaper to choose a router with a built-in ADSL modem.

Other things to consider when choosing a router from Apple or any other company include:

▶ **AirTunes** Currently only available on the AirPort Express, AirTunes allows you to connect the router to a hi-fi and stream music wirelessly from iTunes and, with a little know how, other applications (see p.198).

▶ **Ethernet ports** Does it have Ethernet sockets as well as wireless capabilities? If so, how many?

▶ **External aerial socket** This is useful if you ever want to expand the range of your network beyond the couple of hundreds yards (depending on walls in the way) that a standard router will give you.

▶ **Firewall** A decent in-built firewall improves your network security.

▶ **USB port** A USB port, as found on the AirPort Express, allows you to connect a printer to the router – very useful if you use a laptop.

▶ **Wireless speed** Don't go for anything slower than AirPort Extreme (802.11n).

Top to bottom: AirPort Extreme Base Station, AirPort Express and a non-Apple wireless router (by Linksys).

AirPort & Wi-Fi

Historically, Apple branded their kit's wireless capability as "AirPort" (see below). The underlying technology, however, is Wi-Fi – just as with PCs – and these days even Apple have deferred to using the generic term "wireless". Whatever you want to call it, the end result is that Macs and PCs can connect to the same networks, and to each other.

Wi-Fi, also known by the less user-friendly name 802.11, is actually a family of slightly different standards, all of which work with each other. Recent Macs can handle 802.11n. This allows faster data transfer than the earlier 802.11g (aka AirPort Extreme) and 802.11b (aka "non-Extreme" AirPort).

Tip: If you're making a wired computer-to-computer network with two Macs, you could use a FireWire cable instead of a standard Ethernet cable.

(sometimes these two devices are combined in one unit) and each computer connects to the router, either with wires or, in the case of a wireless router, via Wi-Fi (AirPort).

Setting up a router can be as easy as plugging it in, switching it on and following a few on-screen instructions. Or it can be as unpleasant as a trip to the dentist – especially with a non-Apple router, and even more so if you're configuring a broadband connection at the same time. It's beyond the scope of this book to go into the details; follow the instructions that came with your unit and Internet account, and if you get stuck phone your ISP or look online for help (see p.301).

Computer-to-computer networks

Having a router for your home network is definitely the ideal option. But if you'd rather not spend any money buying one, or you want to quickly create an impromptu network – for example to share files between two laptops – you could opt instead for a computer-to-computer (or peer-to-peer) network.

In this arrangement, the two machines connect directly with one another. One of them connects to the Internet in the normal way, and its operating system (OS X or Windows) takes care of sharing the connection with the other computer (in effect acting as a "software router"). Again, you can do this with either a standard Ethernet cable or wirelessly.

Peer-to-peer networks work fine, though they're not great for more than two computers, and they can be inconvenient, as the computer that distributes the connection has to be switched on and connected to the Net in order for the other(s) to get online.

Setting up

Setting up a computer-to-computer network is simple. First, connect the two computers together using a standard Ethernet network cable. Or, if it's to be a wireless network, hit the AirPort menu on the Mac's menu bar, choose **Create Network...** and pick a name (and a password if you want extra security). Then go to the other computer and select the new network.

Another stage is required before you can share an Internet connection. First, choose which computer will connect directly to the Internet and get online in the usual way. If that machine is a Mac, open **Sharing** from **System Preferences** and check the **Internet Sharing** box; pick your Internet connection type (AirPort, Ethernet, etc) and also choose which type of network connections you are happy to share across. Alternatively, if you want a PC to connect to the Internet and share the signal with a Mac, get the PC online in the usual way and then launch the **Network Setup Wizard** or **Internet Connection Sharing Wizard**. You'll find this in the windows **Start** menu under **More Programs > Accessories > Communications**.

Wireless security

Most wireless routers will let you activate a WEP or WPA password. Do this, or anyone within a few hundred feet will be able to access your network. Note that in some cases you may need to prefix the password with a dollar sign (eg **$secret**) when connecting your Mac to the network.

Sharing files

To specify individual folders as being "Shared" and to choose who is allowed to access them across your network, open *System Preferences > Sharing*, check the *File Sharing* box and use the "+" buttons below the two windows on the right to browse for folders and set sharing "permissions" (see p.89) for different registered Users and the populous as a whole.

Tip: By default, your Mac will be called something like "Peter_Buckleys_Computer". Feel free to change it to something shorter and more user friendly in **Sharing**, within **System Preferences**.

Sharing files between networked OS X Macs is usually very simple. First, on each Mac that you want to share files between, open **System Preferences**, hit **Sharing** and check the **File Sharing** box. You should then be able to browse for **Public** and **Shared** folders on each machine via either the connected machine's icon on the Sidebar of a Finder window or the **Go** menu.

For more complete file sharing, however, you'll need to log in to one Mac via the other. To do this, highlight the other Mac in a Finder Sidebar and hit the **Connect As...** button to the right. From here, select the folder icon of the User you want to log in as, and then enter password details (see p.53) when prompted.

Once connected to another Mac in this way you can not only move files back and forth between machines, but also open files from the other Mac into an application on your Mac, edit them, save them and close them again without ever having moved them from their original location.

When you are finished with the connected Mac, disconnect by hitting the ⏏ icon next to its icon in the Finder Sidebar.

File sharing with PCs

In theory, sharing files between PCs and Macs on the same network should be as easy as sharing between Macs, though it doesn't always work out like that.

First, on the Mac, as before, open **System Preferences** > **Sharing** and check the **File Sharing** box. On the PC, run the **Home Networking Wizard** (which you'll find in the Start menu under **Programs** > **Accessories** > **Communications**) and then select folders you want to share, right-click them, select **Sharing and security** and check **Share these files on the network**.

From the Mac you should then be able to browse for shared files on the PC in exactly the same way as you do when browsing other Macs (see opposite). If you want to browse the Mac from the PC, start from **My Network Places**. However, if you want full access to the Mac files from the PC, you'll need to log in as a user. To do this, go back to the **Sharing** preferences on the Mac, highlight **File Sharing** again and make a note of the address supplied in the pane. Open **My Computer** (or any other Explorer window) on the PC, enter the Mac's address in the Address Bar and press Enter. When prompted, enter the user name and password of the Mac user account you want to access, and press **OK**.

Xgrid

Fancy turning your network into a super computer? OS X's Xgrid function allows you to combine the computational power of all the Macs you have connected together. See:

Xgrid apple.com/macosx/features/xgrid

Help!

To find out more about home networking, or if you're struggling to get yours up and running, try the following sites:

macwindows.com
practicallynetworked.com

10 Importing files & programs

There's something deeply pleasing about switching on a brand new computer – free from corrupt files, badly labelled documents, old software and other debris from years of use. But most people will want to import at least some data – applications, files, emails, bookmarks and the like – from their old computer. The process depends on the computer you're importing from…

From a Mac with OS X

Importing data – including files, applications, emails, preferences and settings – from a Mac with OS X (version 10.1 or later) is a breeze. All you'll need is a standard FireWire cable, which you can pick up in any computer store. Plug the cable between the two machines and, on the new Mac, open **Migration Assistant** from **Applications > Utilities**. You'll be asked to restart the old Mac while holding down the **T** key. This boots the old Mac in what's known as "Target Mode" (see p.296), in effect treating it as an external hard drive to the newer Mac.

The Migration Assistant will offer you a bunch of options about what you want to transfer. Importing **Applications** automatically imports the **Library** folders, which contain emails, fonts and other system- or application-related files. Finally, hit the **Migrate** button and things should start moving over (this can take a while).

If something isn't working properly after you've used Migration Assistant, repair permissions with Disk Utility (see p.279). If that doesn't help, try manually installing the problematic application.

Tip: If you used FileVault on the old Mac, turn this off before starting Migration Assistant, or you won't be able to import your account.

Manually copying files between computers

There are four main ways to move files between computers:

▶ **On a hard drive or key drive** Portable hard drives and keydrives, which plug in via FireWire or USB, are perhaps the easiest way to move (and backup) data. Once connected, the drive's icon will appear on the desktop (Mac) or in My Computer (PC), ready for you to drag files onto it. When you're done, eject the drive, connect it to the destination machine and drag the files to wherever you want them.

▶ **On an iPod** You can use an iPod as a portable hard drive. Just plug in the Pod, open **iTunes Preferences** (in the **iTunes** or **Edit** menu), check the **Enable FireWire Disk Use** box, and the iPod will appear as a drive on the desktop or in My Computer. If there's no room on the iPod, you could temporarily delete the music from it using iPod Software Updater (download it from Apple if you can't find it). Next time you connect to iTunes, the music will be copied back across.

▶ **On CDs & DVDs** If the machine you want to copy files from has a CD or DVD writer, you can burn data CDs with files and use that to move them to the destination computer. To learn about burning CDs, follow the instructions that came with your computer or CD writer.

▶ **Via a network** If the computer you want to copy files from has Wi-Fi (AirPort), an Ethernet port or a FireWire port, you can quickly network it together with the destination machine and copy the files across directly. See p.70 for instructions.

Tip: When copying files between a Mac and PC using any kind of external drive (including an iPod), the drive will need to be formatted on the PC. The reason is that OS X can recognize Windows-formatted drives but PCs can't recognize Mac-formatted drives.

From an older Mac

You can manually copy data from an old Mac using any of the standard techniques (see box on p.73). Besides any documents, photos, music and movie files, you need to think about moving…

Applications

Some applications can simply be copied over – take the relevant folder or file from **Applications** (on the old Mac) and drop them into **Applications (Mac OS 9)** in the top level of your new Mac's hard drive. If some applications won't work, you may need to reinstall them from the original CD or downloaded installer file.

Email

First, you need to get the emails from the old Mac to the new one. If you use Netscape or Eudora, you should be able to export (or simply drag) mailboxes out of the program. Copy the resulting files to the Desktop of your new Mac. If you're using Outlook Express, this won't work; instead, find your "Identity" folder (buried in your hard drive) and copy this folder to your new Mac's desktop.

Next, open Mail (or whichever email program you intend to use on the new Mac) and choose **File > Import Mailboxes…**. Follow the prompts, directing the program to your freshly imported folders on the desktop when necessary. If you can't get any of this to work, you could try transferring your mail via IMAP (see p.76).

Contacts

Open whichever program you use for contacts on the old Mac and look for an **Export…** option – it will usually be in the **File** menu.

> **Tip:** If you only need a few key emails on your new Mac, why not just forward them to yourself? This is quicker and easier than importing mail boxes.

If offered a choice, export them in the vCard or LDIF format. Move the resulting files to your new Mac, open **Address Book** from **Applications**, choose **Import…** from the **File** menu, and point the program to the relevant location.

Bookmarks

Open Internet Explorer on the old Mac, choose **Organize Favorites** from the **Favorites** menu, and then choose **Export Favorites** from the **File** menu. Move the resulting file to the new Mac, open **Safari**, press **Import Bookmarks…** from the File menu, and pick the relevant file.

From a PC

Again, you can copy files from a PC using any of the usual techniques (see box on p.73) or using a special transfer system such as Move2Mac (see right). Besides everything in My Documents, you may consider moving the following:

Program files

Don't bother. Macs can only handle Windows programs using an emulator (see p.12) and even then you'll need to install them from CD or installer files, not by just dragging the files across.

Outlook data

The easiest way forward is to spend $10 on Outlook2Mac (littlemachines.com), a little application that exports mail, contacts and calendars from Outlook (*not* Outlook Express) into formats that can be imported into Address Book, iCal and Mail or Entourage.

Import scripts

If you're having problems importing data into Mail or Address Book, try the relevant scripts under the AppleScript menu (see p.124).

Move2Mac ($50) combines software and a cable (either USB or parallel-to-USB) for moving files, contacts and bookmarks (but not mail) from PC to Mac. You might find it handy if the PC lacks a CD burner or an Ethernet port, and you don't have a portable hard drive. See: detto.com/move2mac.

IMAP mail transfers

If you can't export your mail in a format that your new Mac mail program can recognize, you could try setting up your email on the old machine via IMAP and moving your mail via a mail server. Your ISP may allow you to do this for free. For more details, search Google for **Apple 106778** or **Microsoft Q311129**.

Tip: If you want to export bookmarks from Firefox, you'll need to choose **Manage Bookmarks** from the **Bookmarks** menu before you can choose **File > Export**.

Non-Outlook email

If you use Outlook Express, there's currently no easy way to import your messages, but you could try IMAP (see box). Most other mail programs let you export your mailboxes – look in the **File** menu or drag the mailboxes and email folders directly from the application window to the PC's desktop. Then move the resulting files to your Mac, launch your new mail program, choose **Import** from the **File** menu and follow the prompts.

Address Book & bookmarks

Create a folder on the PC's desktop. Then open Outlook Express, choose **Tools > Address Book** and then press **Select All** in the **Edit** menu. Drag the addresses to the folder, then move that folder to your Mac, open Address Book and choose a **File > Import...** option. Alternatively, try the **Import Address** AppleScript (see p.124).

For bookmarks, open Internet Explorer, choose **Import and Export** from the File menu to export your "Favorites" as an HTML file. Move them over to the Mac, launch Safari, choose **Import** from the **File** menu, and select the relevant file.

Music

If you have music on your PC, copy the files to your Mac and drag them directly into iTunes. If some tracks won't import, the files may have DRM protection (see p.209). To get around this, return to the PC and try burning the tracks to CD; then rip the CD into iTunes. If this doesn't work, or you're worried about the negative effect on sound quality that will result from burning and ripping the tracks, look online for a program to strip off DRM protection. Be aware, though, that in some cases doing this may not be legal.

OS X tips
& tricks

The Dock

The icon-laden reflective shelf that sits (by default) at the bottom of your screen is the Dock, a useful one-stop shop for accessing frequently used applications, files and folders, and for controlling applications and windows currently in use. If you're coming to Macs from a PC background, you'll find the Dock a bit like a combination of the Start Menu and Taskbar in Windows. But it's far more versatile, and there's more to it than immediately meets the eye.

The Dock is split into two sections. On the left are frequently used applications. If an application is running, you'll see a small blue light below its icon; if it's not running, clicking on the icon will launch it. On the right are "Stacks" (see p.81) of icons for frequently used files and folders, the Trash (see p.47), and by default your **Documents** and **Downloads** folders. The two portions of the Dock are separated by a thin line called the Dock Separator.

It's important to understand that applications, files and folders don't actually live on the Dock. Rather, the icons are "shortcuts" to files and folders that reside elsewhere on your Mac (or to pages on the World Wide Web). Deleting something from the Dock *does not* delete the file or folder it points to. Equally, if you drag an item onto the Dock you are not making a copy of the file or folder, so don't then go and delete the original.

Tip: By default the Dock displays the applications that Apple thought you might like to be there. If you find yourself lumbered with Dock icons you never use, simply drag them off the Dock and they disappear in a puff of smoke.

Tip: To slide the Dock discreetly off screen when your mouse pointer has moved away, turn on **Hiding**.

Tip: Drag the Separator up or down to scale the Dock and its icons. Hold ⇧ down before you click and you can drag the Dock between the right, left and bottom edges of the screen.

Dock Preferences

The **Dock** pane of **System Preferences** lets you make a few changes to the way the Dock looks and works. For quick access to these options, use the **Dock** submenu of the menu, or right-click the Separator to reveal a context menu.

Mess around with the **Position on screen, Magnification, Minimize using, Animate opening...** and **Size** settings to see what you like. And don't worry about leaving room for future additions: the Dock will automatically re-scale itself as you add extra items.

For more Dock customizations, try the interface tweaking tools listed on p.119.

Add application icons

You will no doubt be keen to see your favourite applications permanently stationed on the Dock. Open your **Applications** folder (see p.87), pick a program and drag its icon to the left-hand side of the Dock, dropping it between two others. Once there, icons can be dragged around into any order you like.

(see p.87)

Tip: If you see a Dock icon jumping up and down, other than when a program is launching, it means that the application in question requires your attention.

Tip: If you launch an application that isn't already in the Dock, its icon will appear there until you quit the program. If you want it to stay there after you quit, click and hold the icon and choose **Keep In Dock** from the context menu.

◀ *Once an application is in the Dock, clicking and holding its icon reveals a menu of application-specific options, including a shortcut for making that program open when you are logged in at start-up.*

Stacks of files & folders

Similarly, you can add (and remove) shortcuts to any file or folder on your computer to the right-hand section of the Dock. This is great for items you need to access frequently – perhaps your home folder, or a document you're currently working on.

When folders are dragged onto the Dock in this way, they become so-called Stacks. When you create a Stack, rather than ending up with the icon of the folder on the Dock, a composite is created

Tip: To choose whether you want a Stack to appear by default as either a grid or fan, right-click its icon and choose an option from the **View as** submenu.

Tip: When you drag a file or folder onto a Stack icon on the Dock, the item is moved to the folder that was originally used to create the Stack.

Extra Docks

There are many tools available for download that take the Dock concept and run with it. Browse through the "System/Disk Utilities" section of apple.com/downloads and you'll find, among various others:

▶ **Popup Dock** ($20) Creates closeable, moveable Dock-like panels, to leave your main Dock free from clutter.

of all the icons in the folder – which can look rather odd. When clicked, however, it all makes sense and the stack unfurls to reveal the folder's contents as either a fan or grid (pictured below). If the original folder contains too many items to be displayed in this way, the **Show In Finder** button, found in both fan and grid stacks, is renamed to reflect how much is missing (for example, becoming **17 More In Finder**).

"Live" minimizing

The right-hand portion of the Dock is also used to keep track of any minimized windows (see p.103); click one to bring it back to life. These minimized items aren't just icons, but "live" miniaturized versions of the expanded windows. So if you minimize, for instance, a video window – such as a playing DVD or streaming QuickTime movie – the action will keep on rolling in miniature form.

Dock tips & tricks

▶ **Extra menu items** Click and hold an application to reveal its context menu, then hit ⌥ to see additional options, such as **Force Quit** (see p.294).

▶ **Show in Finder** Hold ⌘ while clicking any Dock item to reveal the original item in a Finder window.

▶ **Toggle Dock hiding** ⌘⌥D toggles between hiding and showing the dock.

▶ **Hide current application** Clicking an application icon while holding ⌥ will switch to that application and hide the current one.

▶ **Hide others** Hold ⌘⌥ and click on an application's icon to hide all other applications.

The Dock in context

In the mid-1980s, Steve Jobs, co-founder of Apple, was for a while extricated from the company after one too many run-ins with CEO John Sculley and the board of directors. During his time in the wilderness, Jobs set up a computer firm called NeXT, which produced the operating system that later developed into OS X, after Apple purchased NeXT in 1996.

The Dock is one of the most obvious remnants of NeXT in OS X – though the version Mac users know today is a far more shiny and fancy affair than the old, non-animated NeXT equivalent. And its usability has doubtless helped win many new Mac converts.

Certain features of the Dock have cropped up elsewhere. For example, Microsoft's Windows Vista features icons that enlarge when hovered over. And Google even developed a version of their search engine, GoogleX, with a Dock-style tool for choosing between different types of search. Interestingly, it was only live on Google Labs for a day or so, though it can still be found at: theplaceforitall.com/googlex2.

Files & folders

12

Whenever you save a piece of work on your Mac – whether it's a letter you've created, a photo you've downloaded, a spreadsheet, a movie or a piece of software – it is saved as one or more files. There are tens of thousands of files on your Mac even before you add any yourself. So to keep everything tidy, files are organized into folders.

This chapter provides tips on working with files and folders: how to browse, find, open, move, copy, arrange, delete and compress them. With this knowledge your Mac will be a tidier, more efficient and much less confusing place.

The basics

Folders, also known as directories, are usually represented by an icon that looks like a paper folder – either plain or featuring a graphic that says a little more about the folder's contents. Double-clicking any folder icon displays its contents in a Finder window.

Most files, by contrast, look like pieces of paper with a folded corner – though this isn't a golden rule. In many cases, the icon will be a tiny representation of the contents of the document. In other cases, however, the icon will reflect the application that your Mac would use to open the file (which is something you can choose, as we explain on p.87).

Current Work
1 item

Applications
95 Items

My Document.doc

My PDF

Creating files & folders

To create a new folder, make sure you're in Finder (by clicking the desktop) and then either choose the appropriate option from the **File** menu or use the shortcut ⌘⇧N. Alternatively, press the cog-style **Action** button in any Finder window. The folder will appear with the highlighted label "untitled folder", ready for you to type in a name for it, followed by **Enter**.

To create a file, you need to open an application, create some work and save it. Unlike Windows, OS X doesn't offer you a way to create a new blank file directly from Finder.

Renaming files & folders

You can rename any file or folder by clicking its text label and typing the new name. Alternatively, select a file, hit **Enter** and start typing. Note, though, that you shouldn't change the name of your home folder or any system or application files – it's bound to cause problems.

Deleting files & folders

To send a file or folder to the Trash (see p.47), either drag it to the Trash icon on the Dock or select it and press ⌘⌫.

Selecting multiple files & folders

To select more than one file or folder, hold the ⌘ key while clicking items. Or, to select a range of "adjacent" items, hold ⇧ as you click the first and last in the range. You can then hold down the ⌘ key and remove individual items from the selection. A final option is to drag over multiple files, starting in some blank space.

Special folders

As well as regular folders, the Finder file menu lets you create a couple of special folder types:

▶ **Burn Folders**
Use these for collecting files and folders that you want to burn to CD or DVD. When you're ready to write the disc, open the folder and hit the **Burn** button. Note that when you drag a file or folder into a Burn Folder you don't move the original but create an alias (see p.95) that points to the original.

▶ **Smart Folders**
These are essentially saved searches (see p.97). Their contents are determined by a set of parameters that you define in advance, and they stay up to date in real time as new or edited items meet the Smart Folder's criteria. To create one quickly, press ⌘⌥N (or press **Save** when you're searching Finder).

files & folders

Tip: If you select a music file within your iTunes folder, the associated album cover art is previewed both on the file's icon and in Quick Look.

Tip: When closing GarageBand projects, choose to create an "iLife Preview". This allows you to preview your project with Quick Look without having to open it into GarageBand.

Tip: Hit the ⬚ button to view your Quick Look selection in full-screen mode.

Tip: Quick Look sometimes also displays a special button for adding your selections to iPhoto.

Previewing files

If you'd like to swiftly view a file without opening an application, select it in Finder and click **File > Quick Look**. For even more speed, select the file and use the Quick Look keyboard shortcut: ⌘Y.

Try a few different file types out to see how it works. Most common files – from PDFs and Word documents to music and video files – are supported.

Multiple page documents can even be browsed from start to finish using the on-screen scroll bar. And if you leave the Quick Look window open while selecting different items in Finder, its contents refresh to reflect your selections.

You can also select multiple files to preview in Quick Look. This reveals extra controls at the bottom of the panel for playing a slide show and viewing an "Index Sheet" of the selections. In the pictured example, where several images have been selected.

Opening files

The obvious way to open a file is by double-clicking it. Assuming you have an application that can handle the file, things will spring into life. OS X will take a guess at which application you want to use to open the document, and set things in motion.

Pick the application

Most of the time this works fine, but very often more than one application is capable of opening the same file. For example, you could open a digital photograph in Preview, iPhoto, iMovie and various other applications.

To open a file in a different application from the one that OS X seems to favour, you can:

▶ **Right-click the file** and browse the **Open With** option in the menu.

▶ **Drag the file** directly to the icon of the application you want to use – either on the Dock or elsewhere.

▶ **Launch the application** you want to use and press **File > Open**.

If, however, you *always* want to open a particular file with a particular application, right-click the file, select **Open With > Other...**, choose the application you want to use, and check the **Always Open With** box.

Change the default application

You can also set the default application for a particular type of file – for example, if you wanted all PDFs to open into Abode Reader (see p.149), rather than Preview, when double-clicked. To do this, you'd select any PDF and click ⌘I (or choose **Get Info** from the **File**

Tip: If you want to open an application or file you have used recently, it can be accessed quickly from the **Recent Items** submenu of the menu.

Tip: To find out how to change the icon of any file or folder, see p.120.

This JPEG file would open into Preview if double-clicked. A quick way to open it in iPhoto instead is to drag it to iPhoto's icon.

Tip: If you drag a file over various application icons in the Dock, you can tell at a glance which applications will at least try to open the file by seeing whether each icon changes colour as the file hovers over it.

menu) to bring up the file's Info panel. From the **Open With** section, choose the application you want to associate with the file type and then hit **Change All…**. All the icons of that file type should change to reflect the new setting.

Files with blank icons

Files with blank icons are not associated with any particular program. When double-clicked, they'll elicit a dialog box with a **Choose application** button. If you have a hunch that a blank file contains an image, say, try a couple of image programs from the list. If that fails, select the file, press ⌘I and check the file extension (see box). If there's already an extension specified, search online to find out more about what it implies; if there isn't one, try adding one that relates to the type of file you suspect you might be dealing with.

File extensions

Every file has a file extension on the end of its name – a special identification tag, a little like a surname. In OS X, file extensions are frequently hidden to keep things tidy, though they can be revealed. To see the extension for an individual file, select it, press ⌘I and look at the name at the top of the info panel; to show extensions for all files on your Mac, choose **Preferences** from Finder's **Finder** menu and click **Advanced**, then tick the **Show all file extensions** box.

Even if file extensions are hidden, you can change the extension of a file simply by single-clicking its text label and adding the extension you want after a dot. This is occasionally useful if a file comes through in the wrong format after being transferred from another computer by email or some other means.

Using the Info panel

To find out more information about any file or folder, open its Info panel by selecting it and hitting ⌘I or choosing **Get Info...** from the Finder's **File** menu. As well as filling you in on various bits of information, Info panels let you make all sorts of changes to a file. The most useful options include:

▶ **The icon** You can click here and paste in a picture. See p.120 for more on customizing icons.

▶ **Spotlight Comments** By adding information or descriptive phrases to this panel, you can improve the efficiency of your Spotlight searches. See p.96 for more on Spotlight.

▶ **Stationery Pad** Check this box if you want to temporarily treat a file as a kind of template. When you double-click a stationery file, you actually open an untitled copy of the document, which you can edit and save without affecting the original.

▶ **Locking files** When a file or folder is locked, a padlock appears on its icon and it becomes "read only" – you can't edit or delete the file until the document has been unlocked.

▶ **More Info** Lists the metadata that Spotlight can use when searching for the file (see p.96).

▶ **Name & Extension** Lets you see and change the extension of the file (see p.88) and choose whether it should be displayed in Finder.

▶ **Open with** As we've just seen, you can use this panel to change the default application for a specific file, or for all files of the same type.

▶ **Sharing & Permissions** This panel lets you control which users on the Mac will be able to access the files or folders, as described on p.59.

Browsing files & folders

Though you can search for files (see p.96), you'll probably spend more of your time browsing for them using Finder. To open a Finder window, double-click any folder or drive, or use the ever-useful shortcut ⌘N.

Once you have a Finder window open, the most obvious way to navigate around is to double-click items within it. But there are various other tricks to browsing files and folders:

▶ **Back and forward** Use the back and forward buttons on the Finder window toolbar to move between views – just like browsing the Web.

▶ **Going up** Very often you'll want to move "up" a level: go to the folder that contains the folder you're currently viewing. Either use ⌘↑ or, even better, use the Path Bar (see Tip box) or right-click the title at the top of the window to go "up" as many levels as you like (see illustration). This also works in applications: click the document title at the top of a window to see the folders that contain it.

▶ **Select and open** Instead of selecting files and folders with your mouse and double-clicking to open them, try using the keyboard. With a Finder window open, you can jump to a file or folder by simply typing the first few letters of its name, or using the ↑ and ↓ keys. To open the selected file or folder, press ⌘↓.

▶ **New windows** To open a folder in a new window simply hold down the ⌘ key as you double-click it. Hold down ⌘⌥ if you want the current window to shut as the new one opens.

▶ **Ready, steady…** Finder's **Go** menu features links to various useful places – plus a submenu of recently visited folders. Also, get used to the menu's shortcuts, such as: ⌘⇧C (to see all the drives and discs in your computer) and ⌘⇧H (your home folder). Also try ⌘⇧U to open the **Utilities** folder and ⌘⇧A for the **Applications** folder.

Tip: To set what you see when you press ⌘N to open a new Finder window, open **Finder** > **Preferences** > **General**.

Tip: You can also move back and forward in Finder using the shortcuts ⌘[and ⌘].

Right-click the title of a window to see a dropdown of the folders containing the folder you're using.

Tip: Click **View** > **Show Path Bar** to reveal a useful strip at the bottom of Finder windows that can be used to navigate up through your Mac's folders.

The Sidebar

The Sidebar that appears by default in all Finder windows is one of the most useful features of the OS X interface. At its top, the **Devices** section displays your Mac's drives, discs and any connected iPods, digital cameras or other storage devices. When the Mac is connected to a network, the Sidebar may also display a **Shared** area with icons for other Macs and PCs on the same network. Click on a computer's icon to log in and share files (see p.57).

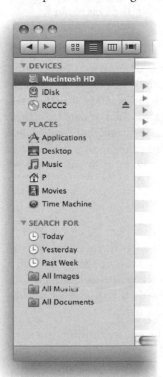

Next is the **Places** area, which contains useful shortcuts to folders, files and applications. By default, you'll find icons for Music, Desktop, Applications and so on, but you can drag any file or folder here to make it easily accessible (not only from Finder windows but also when saving or opening files). To remove an icon from the **Places** area, simply drag it off – this *won't* delete the original file or folder. You can also toggle the default items on and off using the check boxes within **Finder > Preferences** (see right).

Finally, at the bottom, is a list of saved searches, which you can easily add to – see p.97.

To change the width of the Sidebar, drag its right-hand edge, or to hide it, click the little oval-shaped button in the top-right of the window.

Tip: CDs, iPods and connected computers can be "ejected" using the ⏏ buttons to the right of each in the **Devices** and **Shared** areas of the Sidebar.

Tip: To create Sidebar links to your favourite websites, drag a site's address from the Safari address bar onto your Desktop to create a "Web link file" and then drag this into the Sidebar **Places** area.

▲

To change which default items appear in the various areas of the Sidebar, open Finder > Preferences and choose from the various options under Sidebar.

Change your view

OS X provides a number of options for letting you change the way things look when you're browsing through your files and folders.

Most obviously, each Finder window offers you four view options, which you can select from the trio of grouped buttons on the toolbar, or from the **View** menu. And you can tweak the settings for each view using **View Options**, also found in the **View** menu.

Icons view

In its default state, this view is a bit annoying and untidy, but open **View Options** and it comes into its own: you can set the icon size and have Finder automatically align items to a grid – or keep them organized by name, date modified, size or type. You can even change the background colour. As with the other two views, you can either apply your changes to the window you're currently viewing or to every window you open from now on.

List view

The great advantage of the list view is that it allows you to view all sorts of information about your files – and sort them accordingly. **View Options** lets you choose which columns appear in the window, and then you can click on the top of any column to sort by that "field".

The other useful feature of this view are the little triangles that appear next to each folder. Click these to "expand" and "collapse" the folder in question. Alternatively, select a folder and use the shortcuts ⌘→ and ⌘←.

Columns view

This view gives you a bit more perspective: when you click a folder its contents are displayed in the next column, and so on ad infinitum. It's often very useful for dragging files from one location to another, but the real beauty of this view is that when you select a file rather than a folder, a new "preview" column will appear. If it's a music or video file, you can play the track or watch a thumbnail of the footage without even leaving the finder window.

Cover Flow view

Inherited from iTunes, where it works brilliantly as a means of browsing album cover art (see p.211), Cover Flow is the latest addition to the OS X roster of views. Once in Cover Flow view, use either the ← and → or ↓ and ↑ keys to move back and forth through the racked up previews of files and folders. As with the List view (see opposite), the little triangles that appear next to each folder in the lower portion of the window can be "expanded" and "collapsed" in Cover Flow view using the shortcuts ⌘→ and ⌘←, allowing you to move up and down the Folder Tree.

View shortcuts

To switch views using the keyboard, hit:

⌘1 Icon view   ⌘3 Columns view
⌘2 List view   ⌘4 Cover Flow view

To open the View Options panel, use ⌘J.

Tip: If you have to perform a repetitive task involving copying and moving folders, explore Automator and Folder Actions (see p.124).

Tip: To cancel a drag that's in progress, hit **Escape**. This works in most applications – not just files in Finder.

Tip: If, when dragging an item, you hold it over the icon of a folder or drive (including those on the sidebar), the folder or drive will open up in a new window. This is very useful, as it means you can always drag to wherever you like, even without having multiple windows open: drag the item to **Macintosh HD** and drill down from there. Hitting **space** while hovering makes it open instantly.

Tip: You can open a folder into a new window by holding ⌘ while you double-click it. This can be handy when moving files around.

Housekeeping in Finder

It pays to keep all your files and folders as neatly organized as possible. Here's the least you need to know…

Moving & copying

In most cases, if you drag a file or folder from one location on your Mac's hard drive to another, it will simply be moved. However, if you drag something to a separate drive or server, or into some applications, it will be copied. And if you try to drag a whole drive, or drag a file onto a blank CD, you'll drag an alias (see box) rather than a copy. Your mouse pointer will display a green plus if the item is going to be copied, and a black arrow if an alias will be created.

If the default choice doesn't suit your purposes, hold down a key while you drag:

> ⌥   drag a copy (also works for text in most applications)
> ⌥⌘ drag an alias
> ⌘   move instead of copy; copy instead of alias

Of course, dragging isn't the only way to move and copy files in OS X. You can also:

▶ **Duplicate** Select one or more files or folders and press ⌘**D**. A copy will appear next to the original.

▶ **Copy and paste** You can copy and paste (though not cut) files and folders, just as you would text in a document. Select something, hit **Copy** in the **Edit** menu (or ⌘**C**); open the folder or drive where you want to put it and press **Paste** (or ⌘**V**).

Aliases

An alias, or "shortcut", is a file that exists simply to point to another file, folder or drive. There's less reason to create aliases manually in OS X than there used to be, since it's so convenient to drop shortcuts on the Dock (see p.79) and Sidebar (see p.91). Still, it can sometimes be useful – if you fancy having access to your home folder via the desktop, say.

To create an alias, select a file, folder or drive and hit ⌘L, or choose **Make Alias** from the **File** menu. Alternatively, drag the file while holding down ⌥⌘. If you want to delete a shortcut, you can do so safely: no harm will be done to the original file or folder.

Tip: You can set Finder to always open folders into a new window from the **General** pane of Finder's **Preferences**, though this does tend to make things a little cluttered as more and more windows appear.

Tip: Many of the options and functions mentioned on these pages can also be accessed from the **Action** button (the one with the cog graphic on a Finder window toolbar). Its contents relate to whatever's selected in the window or, if nothing is, the whole folder that you are viewing.

Labels

The Labels feature lets you mark up any file or folder as one of six colours, which can be useful for staying organized if you're working with lots of files and folders. In one project folder you might mark your unfinished documents in red, say, and finished ones in green. To pick a colour label, select one or more items, and choose from the **Label** section of the **File** menu – or in the context menu when you right-click.

If you like, you can edit the names of the labels – from "red", for example, to "unfinished" – in Finder's **Preferences**, which you can open from the **Finder** menu. That way, when you're using Finder's List view (see p.92), you can add Labels as a column and see your customized names.

Searching with Spotlight

One of the most significant features to be added to OS X in recent years was the Spotlight search tool. Spotlight searches fast – and not only for file and folder names and the contents of text documents, but also for so-called metadata: information *about* the files. Metadata includes everything from the exposure time of a digital photo to the recipient of an email.

Note, though, that not every application is supported. Spotlight will find emails in Mail but not Entourage, for example. But you can make many applications Spotlight-compatible with a plug-in from apple.com/downloads/macosx/spotlight.

Search for everything

To perform a complete system search, click the magnifying glass icon in the top-right of the screen or hit ^Space. Type in whatever you want to search for and a list of top results will appear. Click a result to open it, or hit **Show All** (or the **Enter** key) to open the results in a Spotlight window (basically a Finder window with an additional panel of Spotlight search options).

All regular Finder windows also feature a Spotlight search box on the top-right. Typing in this box instantly reveals the Spotlight panel and any results relevant to what you are typing. Click into the search box to get started; alternatively, choose **Find** from the **File** menu or hit ⌘F.

Refining your search

If you want to find files and folders while ignoring emails, metadata and other results, or perhaps home in on results relating to a par-

Tip: Spotlight works by "indexing" your hard drive, a bit like the way a search engine indexes the Web. Creating an index can take a few hours, so Spotlight may not work on a drive that's only just been added.

Tip: To go straight to a Spotlight window, hit ⌥^Space.

Tip: Applications, by default, appear as the highlighted top hit in the Spotlight menu; so, to quickly find and launch the Apple Web browser, for example, hit ^Space, type **Safari** and hit **Return**.

Tip: The Spotlight menu search box can also handle mathematical calculations – everything from basic addition and subtraction to logarithmic formulae.

ticular date, use the "+" button and dropdown menus in the window's Spotlight panel to add extra criteria. For oodles of choices, select **Other** from the first dropdown and you'll be offered criteria ranging from tempo and lyricist to exposure mode. Choose **Author**, for example, and you can search for all the files on your machine created by a particular person. None of this will work flawlessly, as not every application adds all the relevant metadata. But it can be hugely useful nonetheless.

In most cases you'll just want to type your search terms and specify the location you want to search. The grey locations strip will, by default, include options for your whole computer, your home folder and, perhaps, the folder you were viewing when you clicked ⌘F.

It's also worth noting that you can click the tops of each column to re-sort your results by **Name**, **Kind**, etc, and use Quick Look (⌘Y) to preview individual results.

Smart Folders

You can save a Spotlight window search, as described above, by clicking the **Save** button. Once you have named the search, it resides in the lower portion of the Finder sidebar as a Smart Folder (see p.85). This folder will automatically update as you add, edit or delete files on your Mac, allowing you to quickly reach fresh results without re-searching.

Essential search tips

▶ You can search for more than one word, including incomplete words. So Beet Conc, say, would find Beethoven's *Violin Concerto* in your iTunes Library.

▶ Type ! before a word to exclude it from the search. For example, Beet !Conc would find all your Beethoven recordings except concertos.

▶ Under **System Preferences > Spotlight > Search Results** you can: stop Spotlight finding any particular type of file; change the order in which results are displayed (by dragging items up and down the list); and set new search shortcuts.

▶ You can stop Spotlight searching a particular location (for security or performance reasons) within the Spotlight preferences **Privacy** pane.

▶ To see some of the metadata that a file contains, select it, hit ⌘I and look under the **More Info** section.

▶ When it can, the Spotlight menu also offers up a handy dictionary definition of your search term.

Compressed files

When you download software or other large files from the Web, you'll often find they arrive "zipped" or "stuffed" – saved in a special "compressed" format that your Mac has to decompress before you can do anything with the contents. This kind of compression serves two purposes. First, it reduces the overall size of files in order to make them quicker to transfer by email or over the Web, and to make them more space efficient on a hard drive, CD or any other media. Second, it allows you to bundle any number of separate files into a single "archive", again making them much more convenient to transfer over the Internet.

Opening compressed formats

There are many different compressed file formats. Your Mac can open most of the ones you'll come across – .zip, .dmg, .gz, .tar and .bz2 – without any extra software. Simply double-click the file and a new "unzipped" version will appear next to the original. However, at some stage you'll inevitably be sent a StuffIt (.sit or .sitx) file, in which case you'll need a free application called StuffIt Expander to open it up.

StuffIt Expander stuffit.com (free)

Creating compressed files

If you're sending files by email or trying to save disk space by far the easiest way to compress them is to make a ZIP file: select one or more files and folders, right-click and choose **Compress** from the context menu. If for any reason you want to create a DMG file, follow the directions on p.279, perhaps without adding a password.

follow the directions on p.279

StuffIt versus ZIP

StuffIt was once the most widely used compression format on Macs, and StuffIt Expander was included in OS X up to version 10.3. Compared with ZIP files, StuffIt archives are better at squashing data to the smallest possible size. However, StuffIt is now on the way out because: OS X can handle so many compressed formats itself; PC users can open ZIP files without downloading StuffIt Expander; and Mac users can create ZIP and DMG files with OS X. To create StuffIt files, you need to spend $49 on a special StuffIt application.

How lossless compression works

When a file is zipped up, or stuffed, the computer looks for repeating patterns that it can represent more concisely. Let's say that you've saved a document containing this text:

```
every land, every sea and every sky:
    here, there and everywhere
```

The compression program would notice that "here", "every" and "and" occur more than once, so would assign each of these collections of letters a more concise symbol. For example:

```
every = !, and = *, here = ^
```

Then it could write the same sentence as:

```
! l*, ! sea * ! sky: ^, t^ * !w^
```

In reality, of course, it's not quite this simple, and the computer would use numbers rather than symbols. But the basic principle is the same.

Images, music & video compression

The type of file compression discussed so far is known as *lossless* compression, meaning that the data that comes out when the file is unzipped or unstuffed will be identical to what you put in. This is distinct from the *lossy* compression widely used for shrinking sound, image and video files.

With lossy compression, the computer applies ingenious methods of picking out which bits of data our eyes and ears notice least, and discards them. Unlike lossless compression, this is a one-way process – you can't take a compressed music or image file and turn it back into the uncompressed original.

For more on compressing music, images and video, see p.207, p.241 and p.259 respectively.

Text as code

Sound, video and image files can withstand minor degradation through lossy file compression. But you could never perform the same techniques on a text or number documents. The reason is that words and numbers are really types of "code", so a minor change can completely alter the meaning.

Applications

An application is a piece of software that helps you perform a particular task or set of tasks. It might be something that came with OS X – such as iTunes – or something you installed yourself, such as Photoshop. If you're coming to Macs from a PC background, you might be used to calling applications "programs" – there's no difference between the two.

By default, all your applications live, logically enough, in a folder called **Applications**, which you'll find at the top of the folder tree in your hard drive. However, this is just a tidy and convenient storage place – you can put an application wherever you like on your Mac.

Within the **Applications** folder you'll also find another folder called **Utilities**. A utility is an application for techie tasks such as setting something up or diagnosing a problem. For quick access to your **Utilities** folder, press ⌘⇧U.

Launching & quitting

As we've seen, if you regularly use a particular application, you can drag its icon onto the Dock for quick access; likewise you could drag a shortcut to an individual application onto your desktop. But what if you want quick access to your whole **Applications** folder? A few other possibilities:

▶ **Via the keyboard** When in Finder, hit ⌘⇧A to jump to **Applications**.

▶ **Via the Dock** You can drag your whole **Applications** folder to the right-hand side of the Dock to create a Stack (see p.81).

▶ **Via the menu** Using a customization program (see p.119), you could add individual applications – or your whole **Applications** folder – to the menu.

> **Tip:** To quickly exit an application, press ⌘Q. Conveniently, the keys for save (⌘S) and close window (⌘W) live nearby. So when you've finished working in a particular application you can save and shut up shop with only the slightest movement of the thumb and middle finger.

The application menu

Once an application is up and running, you'll find all its menus at the top of the screen. The first one displays the name of the application and contains everything relating to it "as a whole": information about it; preferences for it; and options for quitting (closing) and hiding it.

The application menu also includes **Services**. Many Mac users ignore this feature of OS X, but it can be very useful, providing quick access to various tools and utilities. Let's say you're listening to a track in iTunes and you want to quickly look up the artist via Google. Simply highlight the name of the artist and click **Services > Search With Google**. Or if you're typing something in a program with no spell-check feature, select **Services > TextEdit > New Window Containing Selection** and the text will appear in TextEdit, where you can quickly check the spelling.

Switching apps & windows

If you're working in multiple applications and windows simultaneously, you may find yourself rooting around for a particular pane like a pig looking for truffles. Thankfully, there are a couple of tricks that make it much easier to quickly access the application, window or file that you're looking for...

The king of shortcuts: ⌘→

If there's one single keyboard shortcut that will transform the way you use your Mac, it's ⌘→ (**Command-Tab**). Hold down the ⌘ key, hit the → key and a bar will appear displaying all the applications you currently have open. Keep holding down ⌘ and you can cycle between the applications with repeated clicks of →. When you get to the application you want to access, release the keys.

Tip: While cycling through applications with ⌘→, hit **Q** to quit a highlighted program or **H** to hide one. This is a great way to quickly close lots of programs or clear the decks.

To cycle through the applications in the opposite direction, add ⇧ (**Shift**). Alternatively, keep holding down ⌘ and select one of the icons with your mouse.

To cycle between open windows in a specific application, swap → for ` (the key next to **Z**). Again, add shift to cycle through in the opposite direction. Note that this shortcut won't work in all applications, and it will ignore minimized windows.

Exposé

The OS X Exposé feature offers a quick way to "expose" open windows and the desktop using keyboard shortcuts. Hit one of these keys…

F9 See all open windows
F10 See windows in current application

… and then use the mouse to pick from the miniaturized windows. Or if you're after a file or folder on the desktop:

F11 Hide all windows

Hiding applications

Another useful way to cut through the clutter is to temporarily "hide" all the windows of a particular application (or all the other applications except the one you're working in). You'll find these options in the menu for an application, though it's more convenient to hold down ⌥ (to hide the application you are leaving) or ⌘⌥ (to hide all but the application you are selecting) when clicking to a different application via its icon on the Dock or via an open window.

Minimizing windows

To "hide" an individual window, minimize it to the Dock by pressing the yellow button in its top-right-hand corner. Or to minimize *all* the windows within an application (including Finder), hold ⌥ while clicking the minimize button. If you find the way windows "melt" down into their minimized state a bit too cute, change "Genie" to "Scale" in the **Dock** pane of **System Preferences**.

> **Tip:** From the **Exposé & Spaces** panel of **System Preferences** you can set up "Active Screen Corners" for the various Exposé commands. This way, simply moving your mouse pointer to one of the screen's corners does the same as pressing the shortcut.

> **Tip:** While using Exposé or minimizing windows, hold down the ⇧ key and it all happens in slow motion – good when you have a hangover.

Spaces

One of the more useful additions to OS X Leopard is the Spaces feature, which allows you to set up a number of different virtual working areas on your Mac for different applications and activities. The best way to understand it is to roll up your sleeves and have a go, but the basic idea is to cut down on clutter by limiting which active applications and windows are visible at any one time. You might create one "space" for work applications, say, another for music and video, and another for email and chat.

To get started, click the Spaces icon on the Dock (if it's there) or in the **Applications** folder, or alternatively open **System Preferences > Exposé & Spaces** and click the **Spaces** tab.

Once the feature is activated, you are ready to start adding spaces to your grid using the buttons in the top section of the panel and assigning different commonly used applications to always open into a specific space using the lower half of the panel.

Tip: Within **System Preferences > Exposé & Spaces**, check the **Show Spaces in menu bar** box; it offers a quick and easy way to switch between spaces and open Spaces Preferences.

Tip: You can create up to sixteen spaces (arranged 4x4), though anything more than six almost defeats the object of the exercise as it can become a drag to keep track of where things are and switch quickly between applications.

Create rows and columns of spaces

Associate applications with different spaces

Assign shortcuts for switching spaces

Once this is done, you can go back to using your Mac as usual, getting used to the idea that applications and windows move in and out of view as and when you need them. What's more, there are various different ways to move between your new spaces, either:

▶ Click **F8** (by default, see opposite) to reveal the so-called "bird's-eye" view (pictured below) and then either click the space you want, or use the arrow keys to navigate to the one you want and then hit **Return**.

▶ Click the **Spaces** menu bar icon and select a space from the list.

▶ Click the Dock icon of any application associated with a specific space to be whisked to that space. Note that if an application is currently closed, clicking its Dock icon will both launch the application and take you to the associated space.

▶ Use the keyboard shortcuts ^1, ^2, ^3, ^4, etc, (by default, see opposite) to go directly to a space.

▶ Use the keyboard shortcuts ^← and ^→ (by default, see opposite) to toggle between the various spaces.

Tip: When previewing all your spaces in the "bird's-eye" view, click and drag individual spaces to rearrange them on the screen.

Tip: In "bird's-eye" view you can drag individual Finder and application windows between different spaces, even where the application is already associated with a certain space – useful for keeping a space tidy when working with multiple documents from a single application.

Installing & uninstalling

Though some applications take you through a step-by-step installer process (a bit like on a PC), in the majority of cases installing software on Mac OS X involves simply dropping a single file or folder into your Applications folder – or somewhere else if you prefer. Uninstalling is just as simple: drag the file or folder to the Trash.

This ease of installing and uninstalling applications is one of the most user-friendly elements of OS X. It also makes it easy to share applications – copy a file or folder from someone else's **Applications** folder into yours, and in most cases it will work straight off. (Note, though, that in the case of commercial software, this might break the terms of the license agreement that your friend accepted when he or she originally installed the software.)

The only problem with all this is that when you drag an application to the Trash, you may be left with a few residual files (preferences and the like) in your Mac's Libraries. This is harmless, though if you're short of disk space, or you like to practise the Mac equivalent of Feng Shui, you may want to delete them. If the application came with a readme file, check that – it will often point you to all the relevant files. Otherwise, you could try using Spotlight (see p.96) to search for the name of the application to locate relevant files – but only delete the ones you feel sure aren't used by other applications.

If you find yourself becoming really obsessive about cleaning out residual files, consider downloading Allume's SpringCleaning tool.

SpringCleaning www.allume.com/mac/springcleaning ($50)

Downloading software

Though some data-heavy packages are only available on CD or DVD, most software these days can be downloaded from the Web. Simply go to a download site (see p.304) or the homepage of whoever produces the application you want, and look for a download link. Usually the download will start immediately, though in some cases you'll first be asked to choose a "mirror" site. These are simply various locations on the Internet where the file is stored. Software developers use mirrors because having too many people download large files from their websites can slow things down – and cost them money.

When the download is complete, you'll usually end up with a compressed file on your desktop. This might be a ZIP or a DMG file, or even a DMG file within a ZIP file. Also known as Disk Images, DMGs act like virtual disk drives: when double-clicked, the drive will be "mounted" on your desktop and Finder window Sidebars – just as if you'd plugged in an external hard drive.

Once opened up, the downloaded file will usually contain the application itself and possibly also a readme file. This is worth scanning as it not only provides general information about the software, but also typically gives some installation advice – such as which files will be installed where when you launch the application (useful if you later want to uninstall it).

Once the software is safely installed in your **Applications** folder, you can delete (or backup) the original downloaded file – and the uncompressed version of it, if there is one. If you installed from a DMG file, however, you'll need to "eject" the virtual drive – by dragging it to the trash or pressing the ⏏ icon next to its name in a Finder window Sidebar.

Dashboard

The OS X Dashboard feature provides a quick and easy way to do everything from checking the weather forecast to finding a phone number and searching a favourite website. The list is almost endless. Though Dashboard appears in the Applications folder (and on the Dock), it's not really an application as such – it's a "layer" of OS X that houses mini applications called widgets.

To quickly summon the widgets currently installed on your Dashboard – which range from a calculator to an international weather tool – simply hit **F12**, or click the Dashboard icon in the Dock. Have a play with what's available; you'll soon figure out what

Tip: If you always use the **F12** key to access the Dashboard, there's no need to keep its icon in the Dock. Click and hold it and choose **Remove from Dock** from the menu. If you ever want to put it back, drag the Dashboard icon from **Applications** onto the Dock.

Tip: You can change the key that reveals your Dashboard in the **Exposé & Spaces** pane of OS X's **System Preferences**.

does what and which widgets are only going to do their thing if you are connected to the Internet. To close the Dashboard, hit **F12** again or click on some empty space between widgets.

The few widgets that are laid out before you when you first call upon Dashboard are not the only ones in your OS X armoury. Click the "+" icon in the bottom-left corner to show the Widget Bar along the bottom of the screen.

To add widgets to your Dashboard simply drag them out of the Widget Bar and watch as they ripple into life. To remove a widget from the Dashboard, click the "**x**" icon that is visible at its top-left corner when the Widget Bar is open.

An alternative to the Widget Bar is the "Widgets" widget. Click the **Manage Widgets...** button when the Widget Bar is open to reveal a special widget that replicates the functions of the Widget Bar, displaying all your installed widgets. This tool can be used to activate and deactivate widgets and also features a button for accessing **More Widgets...** online.

Tip: To teasingly slow the Dashboard's animated blitz across the screen, hold down ⇧ while you click **F12**.

Tip: To close widgets without opening the Widget Bar, hold the ⌥ key as your mouse pointer hovers over the widget. This will reveal the widget-closing button.

Tip: If an individual widget becomes buggy or freezes, reload it with the keyboard shortcut ⌘R.

▲

When your mouse pointer hovers over a widget, you may see a little "i". Click here to get access to the widget's settings.

Always-on widgets

If you want to make a widget available all the time – not just when Dashboard is open, download the very handy DevMode widget from homepage.mac.com/neticen.

Once the DevMode widget is up and running, hit **F12** to reveal Dashboard. Then click and drag the widget you want to keep active, hit **F12** and hey presto – you have a floating widget. To put it back on the Dashboard, again press **F12** while dragging it.

Where widgets live

Each individual widget is a little application. But unlike "regular" applications, which tend to live in your **Applications** folder, widgets live in two special locations within your hard drive:

▶ **Macintosh HD > Library > Widgets** Widgets in here appear on the Widget Bar of all users on the Mac.

▶ **Your home folder > Library > Widgets** Widgets in here appear on your Widget Bar only – not those of other users.

Widgets don't have to live in these folders. As with other applications, you can keep them anywhere that's convenient and open them with a double-click. But if you want them in your Widget Bar, you have to use these folders.

Widget syncing

If you have a .Mac account (see p.34), you can synchronize your widgets across various Macs registered to your account – meaning you don't have to download new widgets multiple times to get them installed on all your machines. To do this, open **System Preferences > .Mac** on each machine and then check the **Dashboard Widgets** box under the **Sync** tab.

Tip: Be warned. Though a Mac is unlikely to be affected by malware (see p.111), small, easily installed applications such as widgets offer an obvious way in for malicious software, so avoid any widgets that look remotely suspicious.

Widget preferences

If you want full control over your Dashboard environment, including the ability to turn it off and set widget security levels, try the Widgets Preferences Pane application from ego-systems.com.

Active	Name	Version	Location
☑	Address Book	1.0.1	
☐	Amazon Search	1.0	
☑	Calculator	1.0	
☑	Calendar	1.0	
☑	DashBlog	0.7 Beta	
☑	Dictionary	1.1	
☑	Flidget	0.9	
☐	Flight Tracker	1.0.1	
☑	iPassword	1.6	
☐	iStarter	1.0	
☑	iTunes	1.0	
☑	Phone Book	1.0	
☐	Stickies	1.0	
☑	Stocks	1.0	
☐	Tile Game	1.0	
☑	Translation	1.0	
☑	Unit Converter	1.0	

Tip: Some users have found that over time widgets can hog large amounts of RAM (see p.39), making both Dashboard and other applications slower. As a remedy, try closing widgets you're not using, and restarting your machine from time to time.

Konfabulator

Dashboard was introduced with OS X Tiger, but the idea of widgets dates back to Konfabulator, which was a third-party product available for Macs and PCs that has since become Yahoo! Widgets. There are hundreds of free widgets available for Yahoo! Widgets, though they are not compatible with Dashboard so you will need to download the separate application to use them. For more information, see: widgets.yahoo.com

Get more widgets

The widgets that come with OS X are useful, but they're only the tip of the iceberg. There are thousands of widgets available online to download – and most of them are free. If you can think of a specific widget that you'd like, chances are that a developer somewhere has already thought the same and made it. As you might expect, your first port of call should be the Apple site, as their collection is vast and well organized:

Apple apple.com/downloads/dashboard

You can also go straight to this site from the **More Widgets...** option on the Dashboard bar. But it's not the only widget website:

DashboardWidgets.com dashboardwidgets.com/showcase
DashboardExposed.com dashboardexposed.com
WidgetDeveloper widgetdeveloper.com

Some widgets will automatically appear on your Widget Bar after you've downloaded them, but others may need to be dragged into one of the two widget folders already described.

Hidden features

Many widgets have fun extra features that aren't obvious from a first glance. Two examples, from the collection you already have:

▶ **The weather in Nowhere** Open the weather widget, hold down ⌘⌥ and click the widget a few times. You'll be taken to a mysterious city called Nowhere and shown all the weather systems the widget can describe.

▶ **Sort yourself out** If you've played with the Tile Game widget but got bored of the leopard image, try putting yourself in the picture. Pick an image in Finder and, while dragging the file, press **F12** – still holding down the mouse button. Keep dragging the image and drop it into the Tile Game.

Roll your own widgets

One of the reasons why widgets are so popular is the ease with which they can be created. The easiest way to create widgets is by using the Web Clip button (pictured) in Safari (see p.159), which lets you grab a section of an existing Web page (say a favourite site's search box) and save it as a fully functioning and live-updating widget.

Even widgets that are not derived from Web pages comprise little more than HTML code, JavaScript and a couple of images. If you know what that means, you could probably have a crack at building something a little more advanced. To find out how, visit:

Apple developer.apple.com/macosx/dashboard.html
Dashboard Development For Newbies dashdev.djupet.se

For more developer resources, tips and Dashboard hacks, see:

DashboardWidgets.com dashboardwidgets.com/links

dashboard

A few choice widgets

The following, all available via the Apple site, are some of our favourite widgets, and should give you an idea of the range on offer...

Asteroids widget

Play the classic arcade game. Your score is recorded online, and if you get into the top 100 chart of highest scorers everyone else who has this widget will know about it.

XwordLookup

Solve those impossible crossword clues by typing in any letters you have, along with the gaps. The widget reveals all the possible answers.

Wikipedia

One of many reference widgets, this provides instant access to the world's greatest wiki.

Air Traffic Control

Widgets are often quite geeky, so expect to see loads that delve into networking and the like. This one scans your area for available Wi-Fi networks.

TV Tracker

See what's currently playing on US TV channels. There are loads of similar widgets for everywhere from Australia to Sweden.

Panda Cam

See what's going down in the panda enclosure of the San Diego Zoo. For a completely customizable webcam widget, seek out SlothCam.

Ovulation Calculator

Find out the best time to make a baby during your monthly cycle.

Ceefax

The BBC's text-based information service, freed from the TV. News, listings and weather reports served up with a retro feel.

Customizing

15

We've already discussed various ways to customize how your Mac looks and works – by changing the Dock and Finder windows, for example. But there are many other tweaks that you can make, from picking a desktop image to installing techie tools for altering almost every aspect of the system. If you're happy to risk damaging your machine, and you don't care about details such as warranties, you could even try bypassing the software modifications and start hacking the hardware – see p.38.

Basic customizations

The desktop

The most obvious Mac customization is to substitute the rather corporate-looking abstract shape that, by default, occupies your desktop with something of your own choosing. This is easily done: either open **Desktop & Screen Saver** from **System Preferences**, or right-click the desktop and select **Change Desktop Background…**

Here you'll find a bunch of Apple-supplied pics, plus direct access to your iPhoto Library and albums, and a **Choose Folder…** option to pick an image from anywhere on your Mac. You can even cycle through a folder of images at a frequency of your choosing.

Cool desktop tools

▶ **Wallsaver** (free) Put a live screen saver on the desktop background. nwwnetwork. net/wallsaver

▶ **Desktastic** ($13) Scribble and type onto the desktop. panic.com/desktastic

▶ **Stattoo** ($13) "Tattoo" the desktop with a clock, iCal and Mail info, battery meter, etc. www.panic.com/stattoo

Next, tinker with your desktop icons. Click on the desktop and hit ⌘J to open **View Options**, where you can pick the icon size and sorting options. Further changes to what appears on the desktop – hard drive icons, discs, etc – can be made by opening **Finder Preferences**, accessible via the **Finder** menu (or with the shortcut ⌘,).

Windows

Besides changing the View Options and Sidebar in Finder windows – as described on p.91 – it's possible to make various other modifications to how your windows look. Right-click the toolbar (the bit at the top with the buttons on) and you'll find a number of options, including **Customize Toolbar**, which will reveal a palette of buttons that you can drag onto the top of your windows. The same technique also works in many applications.

A few other modifications – including the colour of highlighted text labels, scroll button layout, etc – can be made under **Appearance** in **System Preferences**.

Menu bar

The menu bar can quickly fill up with notification icons and other symbols and menus, probably not all of which you need or use. Each one can be switched on and off in a preferences panel somewhere, but the easiest way to remove something is to hold down ⌘ and simply drag them off – or reorder them as you like.

Tip: You can quickly remove an item from your Finder windows toolbar by pressing ⌘ while dragging.

Customizing hotkeys

It's possible to customize many OS X keyboard shortcuts in various System Preference panels – most obviously in **Keyboard & Mouse**. Many applications also let you add or change shortcuts (look within **Preferences**, or in the **Tools** menu). But for total control over shortcuts in all applications, spend $10 on **Menu Master**, downloadable from unsanity.com.

◀ *Holding down the ⌘ key lets you drag items around on the menu bar. The same technique works on Finder window toolbars and elsewhere in OS X.*

If there's something missing from your menu bar, look in the relevant pane of System Preferences, or the preferences panel of the application the item relates to, for a check box to reinstate it.

You can also enhance the menu bar with certain downloadable programs. iSeek (www.ambrosiasw.com/utilities/iseek, $15), for example, puts a customizable Google search box to the left of your menu bar icons. For more customization apps, see p.119.

Screen savers

Screen savers – animated displays that kick into action after your computer has sat unused for a set period – were first developed as a practical means of stopping static images "burning" into old-style screens. These days they're mainly for fun, though they also serve a security role, as you can set OS X to request a password when "awaking" after displaying a screen saver (see p.277).

To choose from the various screen savers that came with your Mac, open **System Preference** and hit **Desktop & Screen Saver**. There are a few good ones – including "RSS Visualizer", which displays headlines from any website newsfeeds you've subscribed to using Safari (see p.161). The design is over-clever, but the idea is great.

Obviously, you're not limited to the screen savers provided by Apple. There are hundreds more to be found online – some free, others pay-to-use, and ranging in style and concept from the sublime to the ridiculous. When you download and double-click a screen saver, you'll be offered the option of installing it only for your self or for all user accounts on the machine. Depending which

Tip: If you never see your screen saver because your Mac always goes to sleep before it appears, adjust the **Put the computer to sleep...** setting within the **Energy Saver** preferences pane.

Tip: The **Screen Savers** list holds options for using pics from your iPhoto Library as slide-show-style screen savers and also for subscribing to RSS (see p.161) and .Mac screen savers (see p.252).

Tip: Press the **Hot Corners...** button within the **Screen Saver** preferences pane if you'd like to be able to instantly activate the screen saver by moving your mouse to a corner of the screen. This is useful with screen savers that serve some function beyond looking pretty.

customizing

Tip: Nearly every screen saver lets you make various tweaks to how it looks and works. Select one, and hit **Options…** in the **Screen Savers** System Preferences pane.

you choose, OS X will drop the screen saver in either the **Library > Screen Savers** folder of your home folder, or the **Library > Screen Savers** folder of Macintosh HD. To uninstall a screen saver, find it in one of these two folders and drag it to the Trash.

Following are a few of our favourite OS X screen savers to get you in the mood. For more, look online, starting here:

Apple apple.com/downloads/macosx/icons_screensavers
OS X Screensavers macosxscreensaver.com

Cavendish

Generates a random set of celestial bodies and then accurately models their gravitational effect on each other.

OOOkTunes

Turns your Mac into a "now-playing" display for your iTunes – in a colour and font of your choice.

ClockSaver

"A simple but elegant analog clock." Say no more.

SnowSaver

Snowflakes falling against a blue background. Surprisingly mesmerizing.

Holding Pattern

Become an international jet setter without lack of leg room or climate-change guilt trip.

3D Desktop Aquarium

Watch as your Mac fills with water and fish. With the full version ($10) you get to choose whether you want fresh- or salt-water aquatic vertebrates.

Serious customizations

If you want to tweak the way OS X looks and feels beyond the tweaks discussed so far, you'll need to download some extra tools. There are all kinds of customization utilities out there, so if there's something you'd like to change, there probably is a way. A word of warning, though: some customization programs let you make deep system changes that should be handled with care.

Among the most popular and useful customization tools are:

▶ **FruitMenu** unsanity.com/haxies/fruitmenu ($10)
Let's you do practically anything with the menu and context menus: browse your hard drive, add and remove items, preview pictures and more. Great for quickly accessing files, apps and System Preferences panels.

▶ **TinkerTool** bresink.de/osx/TinkerTool.html (free)
Display hidden files, disable sound effects, add Quit to the Finder menu, and make scores of other little changes.

▶ **Visage** keakaj.com/visage.htm ($10)
Tweak the log-in and boot-up screens and the system alerts ("Peter, are you sure you want to shut down?").

▶ **Mighty Mouse** unsanity.com/haxies/mightymouse ($10)
Change the style and size of your mouse pointers.

▶ **Cocktail** www.macosxcocktail.com ($15)
Unlocks all kinds of techie features and offers a few interface customizations: the way windows minimize, the position of the Dock, etc. Also lets you tamper with Exposé, Mail and Safari. Make sure you download Cocktail 4.0 (Leopard Edition), as older versions won't work.

FruitMenu lets you access individual System Preferences panels and ferret through your hard drive, directly from the menu.

Cocktail
a perfect mixture for Mac OS X

InterfaceLIFT

Mac OS X Icons

Customize the look of ap
icons. You can even cha
by following our detailed
our icon FAQ.

Please note that we also offer icons for W

Icon Set Preview

Download (mac) | More Info

Download (mac) | More Info

Download (mac) | More Info

Download (mac) | More Info

Download (mac) | More Info

Customizing icons

Scalable, high-res icons are one of the things that make OS X such a nice-looking system. And they're completely customizable, too – you can replace any icon with one that you prefer, or even one that you've made yourself. Thousands of icon sets are available for free download, making it easy to either subtly change the style of your set up or to fully convert it into a shrine to anything from retro design to, urm, sushi and powertools. Among the biggest and best icon collections are:

Apple apple.com/downloads/macosx/icons_screensavers
InterfaceLIFT interfacelift.com
Icon Factory iconfactory.com

For even more, try:

Icons.cx icons.cx/icons
IheartNY iheartny.com/icons
Pixiland pixiland.de/osxicons
Pixelgirl Presents pixelgirlpresents.com

Changing icons

To replace an icon you don't like with one you've downloaded (or one that appears elsewhere on your system) first select the file or folder whose icon you want to use, and press ⌘I to bring up the Info panel. Click the icon at the top of the panel and then press ⌘C to copy it. Next, select the file or folder where you want to use the copied icon and, again, press ⌘I. Click the icon at the top of the Info panel, and press ⌘V to paste the copied icon into place.

This technique will work on all icons other than so-called System icons, such as the Trash and new folders. To edit those, you either need some in-depth technical know-how or the help of a tool such as Candybar, which lets you change not only icons but toolbar buttons in Finder, Mail and other apps. In case you change your mind, there's a one-click restore switch to put everything back.

Candybar panic.com/candybar ($15)

Icon managers

If you end up with a huge archive of downloaded icons, you might welcome the services of an icon manager such as Pixadex. Use it to browse your collection, create custom icon sets and save "iContainers" – packages of icons that can be installed with just a double-click.

Pixadex iconfactory.com/px_home.asp ($19)

Making your own icons

Making a basic icon is easy. Using any decent graphics program, create a 128 x 128 pixel image, draw your icon and save it as a TIFF, JPEG or PNG file. The resulting file should automatically have an icon bearing the picture you drew, which you can then copy and paste to any other file in the normal way. (If no icon is displayed, grab the free Pic2Icon utility from download.com.)

Creating a slick-looking icon with a transparent background is more fiddly. It's possible to do it by adding an alpha-channel mask to your icon in Photoshop and importing the result into **Icon Composer** (part of Xcode, which you can install from **Applications > Installers**). But it's far easier to use an icon-creation tool such as:

Iconographer mscape.com/products/iconographer.html ($15)

16 Automating

There's nothing more tedious than performing a repetitive task on a computer, be it a one-off pain (changing the names of a big stack of files, say) or a daily chore (such as downloading news headlines from the web, pasting them into a simple text doc and transferring them onto your iPod to read on the train). With a little effort up front, however, it's not difficult to get the computer to put in the legwork – leaving you free to do something more interesting.

Automating computers is nothing new. There are scores of programming languages designed expressly to create "scripts" for computers to follow – including Mac OS's own AppleScript (see p.124). But without learning a scripting language, we've traditionally been limited to the automation tools built into a few applications (such as "macros" in Word and "actions" in Photoshop). For Mac users, that changed with the introduction of Automator.

Automator

Automator, which you'll find in **Applications**, lets you program your computer without a hint of technical know-how. The basic idea is that you assemble a time-saving "Workflow" by combining various off-the-shelf "Actions" (individual tasks such as finding unread emails, converting file formats, importing files into an application,

In case you were wondering, the Automator robot is called Otto.

and so on). Workflows have the power to do some pretty complicated things – publishing a podcast, for instance, or harvesting
full-size images behind an online gallery of thumbnails and adding
them to your iPhoto Library.

Creating workflows

Automator comes installed with a large collection of
Actions, arranged down the left according to the application they relate to. To start a Workflow, drag an action
into the right-hand pane and, if necessary, tinker with its
settings. Then add another action, but make sure it makes
sense as a follow-up to the first. If it doesn't (if you try to
follow **Find iTunes Items** with **Crop Image**, for example) you'll
see red text where the two actions should link together.

When you've strung a few actions together, hit the **Run** button to see if your Workflow functions as planned. Don't be put off
if it fails at first; think logically through the Workflow from start to
finish, make some tweaks and try again. Once everything's working correctly, hit **Save As…** in the **File** menu and save a "Workflow"
file. Next, click **File > Save As…** and export your workflow as a
standalone application. This way, you can run it without opening
Automator – and you get to feel like a programming guru. You
could even give your application its own icon (see p.120) and drag
it onto the Dock.

Adding actions

You're not limited to the Action that came with Automator, as there
are loads of extra ones available to download and import (see box).
You could even have a shot at designing your own, though you'll
first need to learn some AppleScript…

> **Automator online**
>
> For extra Actions, ready-made
> Workflows and Automator
> tips and tricks, drop in to:
> apple.com/downloads/
> macosx/automator
> automatoractions.com
> automatorworld.com

AppleScript

To a certain extent, Automator is just a friendly interface for AppleScript, the long-standing Mac scripting language. Just like an Automator Workflow, an AppleScript is essentially a series of commands that can be opened and edited or exported as a mini application.

To see the sample scripts that came with OS X, open **AppleScript Utility** from **Applications > AppleScript** and check the box to activate the AppleScript menu. A new icon will appear up on your menu bar (near the clock), revealing scores of scripts when clicked. For thousands more, drop in to:

Apple apple.com/applescript
Doug's AppleScripts For iTunes dougscripts.com
MacScripter macscripter.net

Writing AppleScripts

If you fancy trying your hand at programming, and especially if you want to create your own Automator Actions, learning a bit of AppleScript is a good place to start. Compared with most programming languages it's very human-friendly, with code that even the uninitiated can make some sense of (eg `tell application "iTunes" to quit`). Yet AppleScript is also powerful, especially if you master AppleScript Studio, a development environment for building fancy graphical interfaces onto your scripts.

AppleScript Studio is part of XCode, an OS X programming toolkit that you can install via **Applications > Installers.** But don't try and run before you can walk. First download a basic tutorial (the starters' guide at applescriptsourcebook.com is excellent) and experiment with Script Editor, which you'll find in **Applications > AppleScript**.

Mac as office

Software for office & home

The Mac platform has long been the preserve of design and media professionals, so if you want to put something on paper – be it a simple letter, a glossy newsletter or a styled-up film script – there's plenty of software available to help you. And so it is with tools for presentations, number-crunching, note-taking, cataloguing and any other area of work and life management.

There isn't space here for in-depth articles on using word processors, DTP (desktop publishing) tools, spreadsheets and presentation packages. Instead, this chapter aims to give you an overview of which applications – and widgets – are best for which documents and which tasks.

Which office suite?

An "office suite" is a set of applications designed for work-related tasks. Most include a word processor for writing and editing text and a spreadsheet for manipulating numbers. Suites often add to this recipe a program for preparing and delivering presentations, a database app, and also email, calendar and organizing tools. The

software for office & home

Saving tips & tricks

⌘S is a standard shortcut for **Save**, while ⌘⇧S is often **Save As**. And when you're specifying where to save your work…

▶ Hit ⌘D to go to the desktop, or ⌘⇧H for your home folder.

▶ Use the ▼/▲ button to reveal or hide the file browser.

▶ If there's a search box, use it to find folders to save into. Or create a new folder using the button at the bottom-left.

▶ Just as in Finder, you can navigate back and forward, and change views, using the button on the top-right.

▶ You can drag the Sidebar pane on the left in and out.

various components of an office suite typically share the same look and feel, and a degree of functional integration.

Many Macs ship with Apple's own office suite – AppleWorks – which seems likely to be replaced soon by the newer iWork. Then there's the ubiquitous Microsoft Office as well as various freebies, such as OpenOffice. Each of these is described below.

Of course, you don't necessarily need an office suite. Even if your Mac didn't ship with AppleWorks, it will have come with **iCal** and **Address Book** for scheduling, **Mail** for email and **TextEdit** – a surprisingly decent word processor, capable of handling images and tables and offering detailed font control. TextEdit can even save – and in many cases open – documents in the Microsoft Word format.

Microsoft Office

$400/£300 standard; $150/£100 for students and teachers; $500/£480 for pro edition with Virtual PC: see p.12

This is by far and away the world's most widely used office suite, to the extent that familiarity with its various components – **Word**, **Excel**, **PowerPoint** and **Outlook** (known as **Entourage** on the Mac) – are prerequisites in many fields of employment. If you've used Microsoft Office before, you'll know what to expect: tools that are powerful but sometimes infuriating, especially the "helpful" features such as Word's determination to restyle your text as you type. If you want to be able to open every office document that you'll ever be sent, or to get good at using the applications found in practically every office, then this suite is essential. But if you only want to type the occasional letter or essay, don't go near it. You'll be paying for mail merge and pivot table tools that you'll almost certainly never use.

iWork

$79/£55; 30-day trial with many Macs; apple.com/iwork

iWork is Apple's attempt to reinvent the office suite according to its key design principles: ease of use and elegance. Currently, it consists of three applications. Pages is a word-processing and layout tool, which is particularly good for nice-looking letters, newsletters and the like. It's a bit like a stripped-back, user-friendly version of Word, but comes with a wide range of highly usable templates to base your projects on. Keynote is a similarly pared-back equivalent of PowerPoint. Again, what it lacks in features it makes up for in ease of use and elegant templates. Numbers, a spreadsheet application, completes the package.

OpenOffice & NeoOffice
Free; openoffice.org & neooffice.org

OpenOffice is a powerful and completely free office suite created by volunteer open-source programmers around the world. It's not yet quite as fully featured as Microsoft Office, but it's quickly catching up – and in many ways is easier to use. The project is partly funded by Sun Microsystems, who sell a version of the same software, but with various extra features, under the brand StarOffice. At the time of writing, OpenOffice is available in two versions for Mac, the easiest to use and install being NeoOffice. As well as word processing, spreadsheet, presentation and drawing programs, NeoOffice does a very good job of opening and saving all kinds of formats – including those of Microsoft Office. It's not as slick-looking as most Mac applications, but it's an astonishingly good freebie.

Publishing & design

Creating cards, newsletters, pamphlets – or even simple magazines – isn't too difficult on a Mac, as long as you have the right software. If all you want to do is print greetings cards bearing your own digital photographs, then select an image in iPhoto, press **Print** and use the **Greeting Cards** presets in the **Style** dropdown. But for anything combining text and pictures, you'll need a word processor or desktop publishing (DTP) package.

OS X's built-in TextEdit application lets you paste in pics and style up text. Microsoft Word provides much more flexibility, though it's far from ideal as a page-layout program – learning to use it properly, and to circumvent its annoying habits, can take quite a while. Instead, for foolproof professional-looking results, try Apple's Pages (see p.129), which comes with scores of template sets – from

The Pages approach to desktop publishing. Pick an Apple-designed template, such as this one, replace the text and images with your own and tweak the layout to fit.

"Personal Resume" to "Non-profit newsletter" – ready to adapt to your requirements.

If you're wanting to create a specific kind of layout, however, look online to see whether there's a tool devoted to exactly what you have in mind. Comic Life, for example, let's you easily pull snaps out of iPhoto, apply filters, drag on some speech and caption buttons – maybe a Batman-style "ka-blam!" – and the job's done.

Comic Life plasq.com/comiclife ($25)

Likewise, if you want to produce business-style reports, with slick-looking tables and charts, RagTime beats any standard office suite – and it's free for personal use.

RagTime www.ragtime-online.com

No animals were harmed during the production of this page. Created with Comic Life.

Or maybe you're a wannabe screenwriter. Of course, you can type a script in a simple text editor, but if you're serious about getting noticed you'll want to lay things out properly. FinalDraft, makes it easy to align columns for instructions and dialogue, and will even export text to Keynote (see p.129) to create storyboard slides. Wannabe producers, meanwhile, may want to try Gorilla – for managing film budgets, schedules, crew and more.

FinalDraft finaldraft.com ($229)
Gorilla junglesoftware.com ($129)

For really serious magazine or book layouts, however, you'll need some professional tools. The industry standards are **InDesign** (used to create this book) and **QuarkXPress**, which provide more flexibility and features than anything else on the market. Combine either with a copy of Photoshop (see p.249) and Illustrator (see p.237), and you'll have the software kit used in most publishing houses. But put aside a few months to learn how to use it all properly.

InDesign adobe.com ($700)
QuarkXPress quark.com ($300)

Organizing life & work

If there's one thing that computers are good at, it's creating order out of chaos. So no surprise, then, that there are scores of programs available to help manage the various parts of your life. We cover contacts and calendars separately (see p.140), but that only scratches the surface of what's available. Some pointers…

Notes & journals

OS X comes with a Stickies widget (see p.108) for scribbling notes and ideas. But you can't fit much text on each note and too many notes will quickly clutter your Dashboard. Instead, try Notepad Widget which lets you add multiple sheets on one "pad" – or WikityWidget, a wiki-based tool that automatically creates links between notes. Both are available from: apple.com/downloads/dashboard

Naturally, note-taking and journalling don't have to be confined to the Dashboard. You could also investigate some standalone applications such as:

▶ **MacJournal** marinersoftware.com ($30)
Purported to be the world's most popular journalling software for the Mac, this great program lets you easily create a daily (password protected) log of text and images.

▶ **ToDo X** nomicro.com ($15)
A great little notepad and "to-do" list organizer. Its very clean design makes it a dream to use.

▶ **myJournal** dereksoft.com ($10)
Another password-protected journal tool which this time supports multiple journals – so the whole family can have one. It also features blogging tools to help you publish your thoughts online.

Money & business

There are many personal finance tools available for Mac OS X, including **Quicken**, the powerful package popular in the US. But there are also many free alternatives, such as **SpendThrift**, which lets you keep accounts, import Quicken data, create graphs and much more.

Business widgets

There are loads of Dashboard widgets specifically aimed at business users – many are little more than corporate-looking notepads, but there are also real-time stock trackers, currency converters and more. Check out the listings at: apple.com/downloads/dashboard/business

Quicken quicken.intuit.com
SpendThrift blackllamafaction.org/spendthrift

If you run a small business – or you're thinking of starting one – look online to see whether there's any software related to your specific field of activity. There are specialist tools for managing everything from dance schools (TanzProfi) to medical centres (Med-Center Office), as well as more general tasks such as time-billing and invoicing (iBiz) and project management (Merlin).

All of the aforementioned, and many more, can be found via the Business & Finance section of:

Apple Downloads apple.com/downloads/macosx

Catalogue madness

You probably already have a spreadsheet or database tool as part of iWork or Microsoft Office. Though designed primarily for business use, these tools are also indispensable to the obsessive computer home user, as they can be used for cataloguing anything from recipes to film collections. But before you start creating any catalogue with Excel, AppleWorks or NeoOffice, search the Web to see whether there's a specialist option for whatever you're trying to achieve. For example:

▶ **About Wine XT** wine-software.net ($55)
This wine-lovers' software will help you manage the contents of your cellar and also provides tasting notes.

▶ **Readerware** readerware.com ($40)
A great cataloguing tool for book collectors. Enter an ISBN and it will grab the rest of the data from the Internet.

▶ **DVDpedia** bruji.com ($18)
Catalogue your DVDs using an intuitive and stylish interface. The same company also makes tools for cataloguing CDs and books, and offers a free widget to search all three simultaneously.

Fonts & special characters

If you want to create professional-looking documents or presentations, it's essential to choose appropriate typefaces – or fonts as they're known in computer-speak. OS X comes with a decent selection of fonts built in, but you can also add your own, and switch your various fonts on and off to stop them slowing down your system. Equally important when dealing with text is to use all the suitable special characters, such as accents, umlauts and other diacritics.

Fonts

Though you might think of fonts as things that are hardwired into your computer, each font is actually just a file (or a set of files). When you open an application and look in the font menu, what you see is a list of all the font files residing in various special folders on your Mac. These folders are:

▶ **Your Home > Library > Fonts** Fonts in this folder are available to you only – not to other users on your Mac.

Apple typography

If you're into Macs and fonts, you might find yourself wondering which typefaces are uppermost in Apple's own font sack. They are:

▶ **Myriad** On ads, product literature (and the menus of some iPods).

▶ **Lucida Grande** The system font in OS X, used in menus, windows, etc.

▶ **Garamond** The Mac branding font before Myriad.

▶ **Chicago & Charcoal** Widely used in pre-OS X Macs and many older iPods.

▶ **Macintosh HD > Library > Fonts** Fonts in this folder are available to every user on the Mac.

▶ **Macintosh HD > System > Fonts** The fonts used by OS X. Never meddle with these or your system might crash and refuse to boot up again.

Managing fonts

If you've downloaded, purchased or been sent new fonts, you can add them to your system by simply dropping them into either of the first two folders listed above. Likewise, you can remove fonts you don't want by dragging them out of those folders. But, especially if you regularly deal with fonts, you'll find it much easier to use a font-management tool – such as **Font Book**, which is built in to OS X. Open it from **Applications**.

Font Book is a tool for browsing, previewing, adding and removing fonts, arranging them into sets, exporting them and more. Here's a quick breakdown of how it works…

▶ **Add fonts** Double-click any font file on your system and it will open into Font Book. If you like the look of it, click the **Install Font** button. It will be dropped into the User collection unless you change this in **Preferences**.

▶ **Preview** Font Book is great for browsing and choosing fonts. Choose **Custom** in the **Preview** menu, type some sample text in the right-hand pane and then click on different fonts to compare. Use the slider on the right to change the size.

▶ **User, Computer** These icons at the top of the Collection pane show you which fonts are available to only you and to all user accounts. You can drag fonts from the main list to these icons.

▶ **Collections** Just like playlists in iTunes and albums in iPhoto, collections in Font Book are for grouping fonts together by project, by style or by any category you like. This makes them easier to browse, enable, disable and export. To create new collections, press the "+" button.

▶ **Enable/Disable** If you've got too many fonts "active" on your machine, font menus become impractically long and your computer will run more slowly. To get around this, select fonts or collections you're not currently using and choose one of the **Edit > Disable…** options. This can also be done with the keyboard shortcuts ⇧⌘D (to disable selected fonts) and ⇧⌘E (to disable selected collections). You can always enable them again later.

▶ **Resolve duplicates** If you have more than one copy of a font installed on your system, the font in question will have a little dot next to it. Select the font and choose **Edit > Resolve Duplicates**. Duplicate fonts can cause system instability.

▶ **Delete fonts** To send a font to the Trash, select it and press **Remove Font** in the **File** menu.

Tip: Font file icons also offer a two-letter preview in Finder (best seen in Icons view, see p.92), while the whole font can quickly be previewed using Quick Look (⌘Y).

Tip: Click the arrow next to a font family name to reveal the individual styles, such as **bold**, *italic* and so on.

Tip: Automator (see p.122) includes all sorts of options for Font Book, allowing you to filter, find and otherwise speed up your type management.

Tip: If you get seriously into typography, you may want to replace Font Book with a third-party tool such as:

Suitcase extensis.com

Accents & special characters

Anyone who's worked on a PC will be used to the astonishingly bad Windows system for entering accents, diacritics and other special characters. Unless you're in Word, which features the **Insert Symbol** option, you have to hold down ⌥ and type the character's four-digit code on the number pad. Macs make it much easier, with a special-character input panel and a logical set of shortcut keys.

Character palette

OS X's built-in Character Palette lets you browse, find and insert all kinds of special characters (in your various fonts) into most applications. Simply put your cursor where you want the character, select the character you want from the palette and press **Insert**.

To open Character Palette, click the flag icon near the clock in the menu bar and choose **Show Character Palette**. If no flag is there, open **System Preferences** from the menu, select **International**, then **Input Menu** and check the boxes next to **Character Palette** and **Show input menu in menu bar**.

> **Tip:** To find a special character to match the font you're using, select **Glyph** from the Character Palette's **View** menu and then choose the font in question from under **Glyph Catalog**. Or to browse characters in all fonts, select **All Characters** from the **View** menu and browse by category.

138

Special character shortcut keys

Once you get used to the common special-character shortcuts, you'll never look back. First, you hit the keyboard combination relating to the type of accent you require. The common ones are:

´	⌥E
`	⌥`
¨	⌥U
^	⌥I
~	⌥N

Then simply press the key of the letter that you want to add it to. So, to create the accent ï, for example, you'd hit ⌥U followed by I. For é, you'd key ⌥E followed by E. Simple. And capitals work just as you'd expect. To create É, say, you'd hit ⌥E followed by ⇧E.

Note that these shortcuts will only work if the character in question exists in the font that you're using. So while you'll almost always be able to create common characters such as ñ, you might not be able to muster more unusual variations such as ŭ.

Here are a few other useful special character shortcuts:

ç	⌥C
ø	⌥O
å	⌥a
•	⌥8
–	⌥-
#	⌥3
¢	⌥4
€	⌥2

Word

In Microsoft Word, if you're so inclined, you can use the in-built character palette. Simply select **Symbol** from the **Insert** menu.

Tip: If the font you're using doesn't feature the special character you need, you could try to combine two separate characters if the application you're using lets you alter the spacing ("kerning") between them. For instance, you could create ĝ by typing ˚ and g, and then altering the spacing between the two characters. Alternatively, use a different font. Try Lucida Grande for a particularly wide range of characters.

19 Contacts & calendars

Tip: To learn how to import your contacts and calendars from an old Mac or PC, turn to p.74.

Tip: If your Mac's date or time are wrong, correct them in **System Preferences** under **Date & Time**.

There are various Mac applications designed to help you keep your appointments and contacts organized. Some, such as Microsoft's Entourage (see p.75), are built into office suites and offer a wealth of tools useful in a big office environment. But for home use, OS X's built-in organization programs – iCal and Address Book – are difficult to beat; they combine ease of use and plenty of features with the potential for syncing with other Macs and expansion via downloadable plug-ins.

This chapter briefly explores what iCal and Address Book have to offer, and shows you how to use them in conjunction with iSync and iTunes to keep your contacts and calenders synchronized with PDAs, mobile phones, iPhones and iPods.

Have you ever noticed that while iCal is running, its icon in the Dock displays the correct date? ▶

iCal

iCal is essentially a computerized diary. You change the view in the main panel by clicking the **Day**, **Week** and **Month** buttons at the bottom (⌘1, ⌘2 and ⌘3 respectively), and add "events" by either double-clicking anywhere in the grid – or, in the Week and Day views, by dragging over a period of time.

You can also maintain a list of tasks in the To Do panel on the right (if it's not visible, hit the drawing-pin button). Again, a double-click will do the trick.

To make changes to an event or To Do item, double-click it and then hit the **Edit** button. Here you can change the name, make events recur every day, week or year, add an attachment, and also assign an alarm and a calendar…

▲

The buttons on the bottom-right and bottom-left let you display and hide the various iCal panes.

Calendars

The real beauty of iCal is the way it lets you organize events in separate colour-coded calendars – for holidays, work, school, sport or whatever you like. By default, your various calendars are all visible, but using the check boxes in the left-hand Calendars panel, you can be selective about what you see. You could view just "Work"

Alarms

In the info panel, you can assign an alarm to any event (or a To Do item, though you'll first need to pick a "due date"). Besides a flash-up message and sound, you can have iCal send you an email reminder, run an AppleScript (see p.124) or open a file. The AppleScript option is full of potential – for example, you could have iCal fade out whatever you're listening to in iTunes and speak a reminder – though for this sort of thing it's probably easier to use the "open file" alarm option and choose an application you've created in Automator (see p.122).

Tip: iCal's built-in **Birthday Calendar** automatically displays birthdays from your Address Book as iCal events. Turn it on or off from the **General** pane of iCal **Preferences**. You have absolutely no excuse for ever missing granny's birthday again.

Key iCal shortcuts

New event	⌘N
New calendar	⌘⌥N
New calendar group	⌘⇧N
New To Do	⌘K
To Do panel	⌘⌥T
Go to today	⌘T
Go to date…	⌘⇧T

*iCal can import events in iCalendar, vCal and Entourage formats. To import a calendar you've downloaded or been sent double-click it or choose **File > Import…***

Tip: You can also drag a calendar into the main panel of iCal (to combine it with the currently selected calendar) or to the Calendar list (to be given a choice).

and "Travel" calendars in the office, say, and "Social", "Sport" and "Family" calendars at home. To add a new calendar, hit the "+" button at the bottom of the window. To delete one, select it and press backspace.

If you end up with lots of calendars, use the option in the **File** menu to create some calendar groups ("work" and "life", for example). Once you've dragged a few calendars into a group, you can turn all of them on or off with one click.

Subscribing to & importing calendars

The best thing about this modular approach to time management is that you can import calendars that other people have created. Even better, people can publish calendars online in such a way that you can "subscribe" to them, with iCal regularly checking to make sure you have the latest version.

There are scores of freely available calendars covering everything from sports fixture lists and band tour dates, via public holidays and meteorological events, to political and academic timetables. If you know the address of a specific one, click **Calendar > Subscribe**. Otherwise, browse the thousands on offer at:

iCal Share icalshare.com

Sharing your own calendars

If you'd like to send a calendar to friends or family, simply select it, press **File > Export…** and send it by email. The recipient will be able to import it as long as he or she uses a calendar program that supports the iCalendar format. These include Outlook (not Outlook Express), Entourage, Mozilla Calendar and Lotus Notes.

To publish your calendars online so that other people can subscribe to them, you'll need an account with either .Mac (see p.34) or some other service, such as iCalx (icalx.com). If you're technically inclined, you could try publishing calendars on your own website, but you'll need webspace on a server that supports WebDAV. That's pretty rare, so your best bet may be to try setting up your own Mac to function as the server. For instructions, see:

Enabling WebDAv on OS X gregwestin.com/webdav_for_ical.php

Invitations

If you want to invite friends to take part in an event using iCal, select the event, type their email addresses in the **attendees** field of the **Edit** panel, and hit the **Send** button at the bottom. The recipients will receive information about the event in an email and, if they use iCal and Apple Mail, the invitation will flash up in their iCal Notifications pane.

You can also add attendees – and create new meeting events – by dragging names from iCal's **Address Panel**, opened from the **Window** menu or with the shortcut ⌘⌥A.

Tip: iCal features a superb printing palette that lets you print nicely presented calendars in any number of ways. Choose **File > Print…** (or hit ⌘P) to explore the options.

Tip: Exporting calendars is also useful for backing them up, but if you want to back up all your iCal events and information at once, use **File > Back up iCal…**

Extra iCal tools

As with all Apple programs, there are plenty of downloadable tools to extend iCal's capabilities. For example:

▶ **iCal Events** (free) A widget that lets you view upcoming iCal events via the Dashboard. benkazez.com

▶ **MenuCalendarClock** (free, or $20 for full version) view iCal events via the menu bar. www.objectpark.net/mcc.html

Address Book

Address Book does what it says on the tin, though it also has a few fancy tricks up its sleeve. For example, you can wirelessly move names and numbers back and forth from a Bluetooth phone (see p.146).

The basics

To add a contact, press the "+" button below the **Names** panel. Edit the details as you like, clicking the ⬍ icons and the green and red circles to add and remove data fields. To add a little picture, double-click the small frame to the left of the contact's name and hit the **Choose...** button. Alternatively, drag an image directly into the square from Finder, iPhoto or even a webpage. (If you edit the picture on your own entry, it will apply to your user account pic, too.)

When you're done, click out of the **Edit** mode using the button at the bottom of the window.

Essential shortcuts

New card	⌘N
Edit card	⌘L
New Group	⌘⇧N
New Smart Group	⌘⌥N
View card only	⌘1
View card & columns	⌘2
View directories	⌘3
View next card	⌘]
View previous card	⌘[

Tip: You can edit the default card set-up settings in the **Template** pane of Address Book **Preferences** (⌘,).

Tip: Click a phone number's label and choose **Large Type** from the pop-up menu – guaranteed to stop you miss-keying phone numbers.

vCards

Each contact in Address Book is stored as a vCard – basically a virtual business card that contains their name, address, email, phone numbers, etc.

Groups & Smart Groups

You can organize your contacts into groups in the left-hand pane. This not only makes your address book easier to browse but also allows you to quickly send emails to a selection of people – and to export multiple contacts as a single vCard.

Press the "+" button to create a new group, and then drag contacts onto its icon. Note that (like iTunes playlists and iPhoto albums), you can add each contact to more than one group. Once the group is populated, right-click it to either email everyone it contains, or export a group vCard.

Smart Groups, like other "Smart" items in OS X, populate themselves automatically according to conditions that you define. You might create one based on a dialling code to assemble everyone you know in a certain district, for instance, or one based on email addresses to group together people from a certain company. Select **File > New Smart Group...** to give it a go, or hold down the ⌥ key and hit the cog button at the bottom-left of the window.

Import & export

Address Book uses the common vCard format, and can also import various other formats, so even if your friends are using a different address-book application it's highly likely they'll be able to export contact cards (for themselves or for mutual friends) in a form that you can import. And vice versa.

To import contacts that you've been sent, simply double-click them or look under **File > Import**. Likewise, to get a contact out, choose **File > Export** or drag it straight onto the desktop or into a folder. You can even drag a contact directly onto your email program's Dock icon to quickly forward it to a friend.

Tip: Single-click a contact to view it in the main panel; double-click to view it in a new floating window.

Tip: Most labels – "work", "home", etc – reveal relevant options when clicked: an online map for a US address, say, or a "send message" option for an email address.

Tip: With a .Mac account (see p.34), you can access your Address Book contacts via the Web. Set it up under **Sync** within **.Mac System Preferences**. You can even share your online address book with other .Mac users. In Address Book open **Preferences**, tick the **Share...** box and add contacts.

Prefer it on paper?

Address Book's print options are nearly as good as iCal's. Select a contact, group or "All", choose **File > Print** and output labels, envelopes, or even a pocket address book.

Syncing

Modern life is a complicated beast, and it tends to get more complicated as you accrue extra gadgets. Say you bump into an old friend and they give you a new number: you add it to your mobile phone, but what about your Mac, your PC at work, your PDA or iPod? And it's not just phone numbers – addresses, calendars, bookmarks, passwords and files also end up strewn over multiple devices. You can get away with organizing things manually, but the ideal solution is to sync everything automatically – especially if you regularly use more than one Mac.

▶ **Multiple Macs** By far the easiest way to sync data across multiple Macs is to sign up for a .Mac account (see p.34). Once you've set things up under the **Sync** tab of the **.Mac System Preferences** pane, you can add contacts, bookmarks, appointments and passwords to any of your Macs – or via the Web at mac.com. As long as you choose to "merge data" whenever prompted, all locations will be kept up to date.

▶ **Phones & PDAs** If your phone/PDA and Mac both have Bluetooth, you can sync your contacts and calendars wirelessly; otherwise, it may be possible to connect them via a USB cable (ask in a phone shop if you don't have one already). With the device connected – or in discoverable mode if you're using Bluetooth – open **iSync** from **Applications** and choose **Add Device…** from the **Devices** menu. A picture of your phone or device should appear. Click the icon to view device settings and, when you're ready to sync, hit the big metallic button.

▶ **iPods & iPhones** To add updated Address Book and iCal data to an iPod or iPhone every time you attach it to your Mac, open iTunes and connect your iPod or iPhone. Select the device in the Sources area, and set your options under the **Contacts** tab.

Tip: In iSync > Preferences choose to show syncing status in the menu bar. From the icon that will appear you can manage iSync and .Mac synchronizations and conflicts.

Tip: To get more than just calendars and contacts onto your iPod or PDA, download a third-party synchronization tool such as Jax (joesoft.com) or PocketMac (pocketmac. net). Also explore Automator (see p.122).

Printing & faxing

Whether you use your Mac for work or pleasure, at one time or another you're going to want to print your handiwork. OS X makes setting up printers a doddle, and offers useful tools for previewing your printouts and "printing" to PDFs. Furthermore, many Mac applications feature handy print presets, from greeting-card layouts in iPhoto to a pocket-sized contacts list in Address Book. And with OS X's built-in fax feature you can say goodbye to that noisy, cumbersome old monster that lurks under your desk…

Setting up a printer

Most printers with a USB or Bluetooth connection will work fine with OS X (if you have an old model with only a long "teethed" parallel plug, it's probably time to upgrade). In most cases, there's no need to install the software that came with the printer, as your Mac has hundreds of printer drivers pre-loaded. Just plug it in, hit **File > Print** in nearly any application and the new printer should appear in the **Printer** dropdown.

If this fails, the **Printer** dropdown should at least contain an option to **Add Printer…**. This opens OS X's Printer Setup Utility, which can also be found in **Applications > Utilities**. The utility scans

Buying a printer

There are hundreds of consumer printers on the market. The first choice is whether to go for an office-style laser model (fast and high quality), a special photo printer (the only way to get that glossy photo-lab look) or a cheap-and-cheerful inkjet. Also consider resolution, speed, number of inks and refill costs. Visit these sites before opening your purse:

macreviewzone.com
printscan.about.com

You should encounter few set-up issues with a machine from one of the big names (such as Epson, HP or Canon), but to find out exactly which models are supported natively by OS X, look here:

apple.com/support/leopard/printing

Tip: From the **Print & Fax** pane of **System Preferences** you can set a default printer and view your printer's "print queue" – a list of not-yet-completed print jobs.

Tip: From the **Printers** menu of the Printer Setup Utility, choose **Create desktop Printer...** (⌘⇧D) to place an icon on your desktop that you can then drag files onto to print them straight from Finder.

Tip: If your printer stops responding, visit the **Printing** pane of **Print & Fax** in **System Preferences** and try removing and re-adding the offending printer – this often does the trick.

for connected devices; select the one you want and click **Add**. If it's a Bluetooth printer, or a printer that's connected to another computer on your network (see below), you may have to click the **More Printers...** button to browse for it. From the dropdown at the top, choose the type of connection you're trying to make – Bluetooth, Windows Printing, etc and see what appears.

Sharing printers on a network

If you have two or more computers, one of the best reasons for connecting them together into a network (see p.66) is that you can easily share one printer between them all. The ideal set-up is to connect your printer to the network's router. This is often impossible as most routers lack a USB port and most printers lack an Ethernet port. However, you can plug a USB printer to an AirPort Extreme Base Station or AirPort Express (see p.67); if it doesn't work straight off, launch the AirPort Utility from **Applications > Utilities**.

The more common setup is to attach the printer directly to one of the computers and to tell the computer to "share" it over the network. On a Mac, tick the **Printer Sharing** box on the left of the **Sharing** pane of **System Preferences**. On a PC, run the Network Setup Wizard (within **Accessories > Communications** in your list of programs) and follow the prompts. Obviously, the computer the printer is connected to will need to be switched on in order for the others to print through it.

Printing & presets

In most applications you can print by choosing **Print** from the **File** menu or using the shortcut ⌘P. This will usually elicit a box where you can mess about with lots of customizable layout options and effects. If you create a configuration that you think you'll want to

Printing to PDF

PDF (Portable Document Format) is a file format, first developed by Adobe, that is widely used for everything from product manuals to press releases, as well as for sending publications (such as this book!) to a printer. The beauty of PDFs is that they combine text, fonts and images in a convenient bundle that can be viewed on practically any computer – regardless of which applications or fonts it has installed. Hence the "portable" tag.

Even better, the file size will be comparatively tiny compared with the original document, so PDFs are ideal for sending by email. The only downside (and this isn't always a downside) is that PDFs aren't editable – at least not to any useful degree.

Traditionally, to create PDFs you need a special application (such as Adobe Acrobat), but OS X lets you create PDFs from any application. Just hit **File > Print** and use the **PDF** button at the bottom of the box. The feature is placed here as the process of creating a PDF is akin to preparing a document to send to print. But rather than sending the information to a "real" printer, your Mac sends it to a "virtual" printer that renders your work as a PDF.

PDFs are a great way to send documents to other people, since you know they'll be able to open them, and that they will look on their machine exactly as they did on yours. When you press **Print**, you can even choose to create a PDF and attach it to an email in one fell swoop (look under the **PDF** dropdown). All the recipient will need – and they probably have this already – is either a Mac with OS X or a PC with a copy of the free Adobe Reader program:

Adobe Reader adobe.com/reader

PDFs can also be very useful for your own records. For example, when you register with a website, or book a holiday over the Internet, instead of copying out all the on-screen information and reference numbers, simply print a PDF of the webpage straight from Safari.

OS X opens PDFs with Preview, though there's also a version of Adobe Reader for Mac. It's worth having as occasionally it will display a PDF that Preview is struggling with.

*With OS X you can annotate PDFs with text labels and circles, as shown. Furthermore, it's possible to password protect a PDF: hit **File > Print** and choose **Encrypt PDF** from the **PDF** button's dropdown in the print dialog box.*

Print scheduler

You can set a document to print or fax at some point later in the day (useful if you want to appear to be in the office, busily faxing, when you're actually out for a long lunch). Hit **File > Print**, choose **Scheduler** from the **Copies & Pages** dropdown menu and then set a time.

Tip: You can let other computers on your network send faxes through your Mac's modem by ticking the **Let others send faxes through this computer** box from the **Sharing** pane of **Print & Fax** preferences.

use again, choose **Save As…** from the **Presets** dropdown. Then you'll be able to quickly access that recipe of settings in the future, from almost any application. Finally, use the **Preview** button to get an accurate idea of how a printed page will look, and then hit **Print**.

Mac as fax machine

Faxing directly from a computer is *much* more convenient than using a fax machine. Instead of printing a document and then feeding the hard copy into another device, simply send the fax directly from your word processor, email or any other application – and have faxes you receive appear in your email inbox.

To send and receive faxes you need to connect your Mac's built-in dial-up modem to a phone socket using the supplied cable (if you can't find it, pick up another at any computer shop). A broadband connection won't get in the way, but neither will it handle faxing – you have to use the dial-up modem.

▶ **Sending faxes** Click **File > Print** in any application, and choose **Fax PDF** from the **PDF** dropdown. Enter the number of the recipient (or use the "silhouette" button to choose a contact from Address Book), add a cover page, if you want one, and hit **Fax**. The fax will be sent straightaway, unless you're already using your modem to connect to the Internet, in which case OS X holds the fax until the next time you disconnect.

▶ **Receiving faxes** If you'd also like to receive faxes on your Mac, open the **Print & Fax** panel of **System Preferences**. In the **Faxing** pane, check the **Receive faxes** box, enter your phone number and choose how you'd like your Mac to handle whatever arrives. You can have faxes automatically printed, or even forwarded to an email account so you can view new arrivals away from home.

Online

The Web

21

If you're coming to Macs from a PC background, you'll probably be used to surfing websites with Internet Explorer, the Web browser whose blue "e" icon is inseparable from the World Wide Web in many people's minds. OS X comes with a different browser: Safari. In most ways, this is a far superior piece of software to Explorer, with lots of useful features that we'll highlight in this chapter. You'll find Safari's compass-style icon in Applications, and probably also on your Dock.

Other browsers

Safari is an excellent browser, but it's not the only player in town. There are scores of other Mac browsers available to download for free, and you may find one you prefer. The most tempting option is Firefox, a superb application created by volunteer programmers from around the world. Firefox is better than Safari in some ways and worse in others – for example, there are more free plug-ins available for it, but it's generally a tad slower. In this chapter we'll discuss Safari and Firefox, so you get a sense of what each can offer.

Firefox getfirefox.com

Default browsers

If you do choose to use something other than Safari as your main browser, you'll want to let OS X know, so that when you click on a link in an email, say, the right browser opens up. To do this, open Safari, click **Safari > Preferences** and you'll see the option in the **General** pane.

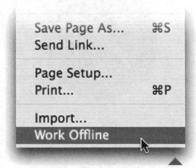

The Firefox File > Work Offline option lets you browse and click between pages that you've recently visited without being connected to the Internet. Great for reading the news on the train, for example. You can increase the number of offline pages you have access to by upping the cache size in Firefox Preferences.

There are many other browsers out there – Opera, Mozilla, Netscape, Camino and OmniWeb to name just a few. They all have something to offer, but few Mac users choose them over Safari. For the lowdown on just about every Mac browser ever released, see:

Mac Browsers darrel.knutson.com/mac

Browsing tips

There isn't room here for a step-by-step guide to surfing the Web – and you probably don't need that anyway. Instead, the next few pages focus on some of the cool features of Safari and Firefox that you may not be aware of.

Windows & tabs

One thing that marks out experienced Web users is that they very often have multiple webpages open simultaneously. It makes sense to work this way: you might have your webmail open in the back-

Tip: In Safari, when you visit a webpage by typing its address or hitting a bookmark, the page is marked as a "SnapBack" point. If you then browse to other pages by clicking on links, you can return to the last SnapBack point by clicking the little orange button next to the current page's address.

ground, for instance, while you read a blog in the foreground. Or you might fire open all the interesting-looking stories from the homepage of a news site; by the time you've read one, the others will have loaded, so you won't have to wait around. To open a link in a new window, right-click it and choose **Open in New Window**.

An even better option is to open multiple pages within a single window, with "tabs" at the top to let you switch between them (see above). In Safari, right-click a link and choose **Open in New Tab** to get started.

More useful still is to use keyboard shortcuts for new windows and tabs. Open **Safari > Preferences > Tabs** and use the three check boxes to toggle between the various keyboard combinations. For example, if you favour tabbed browsing with new tabs appearing in the background (great for opening lots of links from one page), check the **⌘-click opens a link in a new tab** box and uncheck the **Select tabs and windows as they are created** box. With this configuration, simply hold down ⌘ as you click links to open them as new tabs in the background or hold both ⇧ *and* ⌘ to open a new tab in the foreground.

Tip: In Safari, tabs can be reordered by simply dragging them to the left or right. To detach a tab to create a new window, hold down ⌥ and drag.

Tip: If you visit a webpage all the time, drag its icon (to the left of its address in your browser) to the right-hand section of the Dock for 24/7 easy access.

Tip: When viewing a PDF in Safari, a single click of the page reveals on-screen PDF controls for zooming, opening in Preview and downloading the file.

Tabs

General Appearance Bookmarks Tabs RSS AutoFill Security Advanced

☑ ⌘-click opens a link in a new tab
☐ Select tabs and windows as they are created
☑ Confirm when closing multiple pages

⌘-click: Opens a link in a new tab.
⌘-Shift-click: Opens a link in a new tab and selects it.
⌘-Option-click: Opens a link in a new window behind the current one.
⌘-Option-Shift-click: Opens a link in a new window and selects it.

Retracing your steps

Obviously, you can move back through the pages you've just been looking at using the **Back** button. But it's often quicker to click and hold on the **Back** (or **Forward**) button to choose the page you're looking for from a list…

Even with this technique, however, the menu will only show you a certain number of pages that you've viewed in the current window. To jump back to any page that you've viewed in the last week or so, use the **History** menu (or the **Go** menu in Firefox).

Bookmarks

When you find a page that's worth another visit, add a "bookmark" so you can quickly return to it later. You can do this via the **Bookmarks** menu – from where you can also access your bookmarked sites – or using the shortcut ⌘**B** (Safari) or ⌘**D** (Firefox). Get into the habit of using folders to group bookmarks together or you'll end up with a huge menu in which it's hard to find anything. You can create folders, and delete unwanted bookmarks, by choosing the **Show All…** or **Manage…** option in the **Bookmarks** menu.

If you visit a page all the time, drop it onto the Bookmark Bar, located below the **Back** and **Forward** buttons. If it's not visible, you'll find an option for it within the **View** menu. Either drag page icons directly onto the bar (as shown below) or save/move bookmarks into the Bookmark Bar folder, which lives with your regular bookmarks. You can even create sub-folders within your Bookmarks Bar folder to generate dropdown menus of your favourite sites.

Browser plug-ins

Whether you use Safari, Firefox or something else, there are bound to be various downloadable "extensions" available for adding extra functions and options to your browser – adblocking being one example (see below). For Safari, you can find the best extensions (some free, others commercial) via the wonderfully named:

PimpMySafari pimpmysafari.com

Firefox has scores of extensions available, and they're nearly all free. Either choose **Tools >**

Extensions and click **Get More Extensions**, or simply pop in to:

Mozilla Update addons.mozilla.org

Online bookmarks

If you'd like to be able to access your bookmarks via any computer, and you don't want to pay for .Mac (see p.34), use a free online bookmarks manager. Google and Yahoo! both offer one but even better is the "social bookmarks manager" del.icio.us (http://del.icio.us). The social aspect lies in the fact that you can view other people's bookmarks and they can see yours. It's a great way to discover – and help promote – interesting sites.

Tip: Besides plug-ins, you can make some tweaks directly to Safari by entering code into the Terminal application. For example, you can change the page-loading indicator from a blue swathe to a little pie-chart-esque disc. To find out how, see: maconlysource.com/?m=20070622

Searching

Safari (and Firefox) let you search Google directly from the toolbar, which saves you going to Google's homepage in order to search. When searching this way, all the regular Google tricks work, including:

Googling this:	Finds pages containing:
apple mac	the terms "apple" and "mac"
"apple mac"	the exact phrase "apple mac"
apple OR mac	either "apple", "mac" or both
apple -mac	"apple" but not "mac"
~mac	"mac" and related words ("Apple", etc)
"apple * macs"	"apple produce macs", etc
site:www.apple.com "safari"	"safari" within the Apple website

Being able to search Google directly from Safari or Firefox is great, (especially in Firefox, where you can search from the address bar to go straight to the top Google hit). But if you become a real search addict you might want to be able to search without even first opening your browser. You could use a search widget, so many of which are available that you'll find a whole category of them at:

Apple Downloads apple.com/downloads/dashboard

However, Dashboard can be slow to open, and you don't want to waste time clicking into the right widget. Better, then, is a tool for searching from anywhere with a shortcut key (Huevos) or even via a Google box on your menu bar (iSeek):

Huevos ranchero.com/huevos (free)
iSeek ambrosiasw.com/utilities/iSeek ($15)

Tip: In Safari, use the shortcut ⌘⌥F to send your cursor straight to the toolbar search field when you want to type a search term.

Tip: In both Firefox and Safari, right-click any highlighted text on a webpage and choose the option to search the Web for that term. You can also search Google for selected text in nearly any application using Services (see p.101).

Find something on a page

To search for a word or phrase within a webpage using either Safari or Firefox, choose **Edit > Find** or use the shortcut ⌘**F**. You can then jump forward and back between occurrences of the same word or phrase by clicking ⌘**G** or ⌘⇧**G**, respectively.

Tip: To resize any webpage text field in Safari – such as a search box – simply grab its bottom-right corner and drag.

Tip: As an alternative to bookmarking, you can turn any part of a webpage into a handy widget to use in Dashboard (see p.108) by simply clicking the Web Clip button and dragging around the area you want to use– brilliant for providing quick access to a commonly used search field or online tool.

Keyword searching

One of the best things about Firefox is the way it lets you set up customizable searches. Let's say you regularly use MultiMap to view street maps, but its homepage is slow to load. Go to the site, right-click the search box and choose **Add a Keyword for this Search**. When prompted, choose "map" as the keyword.

Next time you want to search for a map, you don't need to open the MultiMap homepage. Simply type the keyword, along with whatever you want to search for, straight into the bar where you usually type Web addresses. If you wanted a map of the London postcode W1D 6HR, for example, you'd type: map W1D 6HR.

You can do the same thing in Safari with the Safari SIA plug-in from horneddragon.com.

Parental Controls

If you'd like to limit your child's browsing to certain approved websites, create a user account for him or her and enable Parental Controls (see p.54).

Alternatively, try a special children's browser, such as KidBrowser, which makes browsing fun and easy as well as safe. KidBrowser, which costs €19, is available from:

app4mac.com

Privacy

Anyone who can access your account can easily see all the sites you've recently visited. If that thought bothers you, clearing your history isn't enough, as your cookies, cache and auto-fill entries also show where you've been. Instead, click **Safari > Reset Safari…** to go back to a completely clean slate. Alternatively, choose **Safari > Private Browsing** to prevent Safari from recording any traces of your surfing. In Firefox you'll find controls for clearing such data selectively within **Firefox > Preferences > Privacy**. To delete everything in one fell swoop, choose **Tools > Clear Private Data….**

Kill the ads

There's nothing more annoying than pop-up ads and flashing banners offering you too-good-to-be-true deals. Fortunately, there are measures you can take to reduce the number of online ads you see.

▶ **Pop-ups** can be easily blocked: click **Safari > Block Pop Up Windows.** The only problem is that Safari doesn't let you allow pop-ups on certain sites (such as webmail systems that use pop-ups for messages). Firefox offers a better pop-up blocker, with warnings when a window has been blocked and the option of adding sites to an "allow list" (open **Firefox > Preferences > Content**).

▶ **Banners** If you download the right extension, it's possible to stop some banner ads appearing on webpages. For Safari, visit the "Adblocking" section of pimpmysafari.com; for Firefox grab the AdBlock extension from addons.mozilla.org. With Adblock you can simply right-click an ad and choose **Block ads from….** Banners from that server should no longer appear in webpages you view.

RSS

RSS (Really Simple Syndication) is one of the best things to happen to the Web in recent years. In short, RSS allows blogs, news services and other websites to produce "feeds" or "newsfeeds" containing headlines and short descriptions of each new or updated article, complete with links to the full story. You can scan a feed at a glance and see if something's been added or changed without even having to visit and browse the website. Even better, you can "aggregate" the feeds from your favourite sites, in effect creating a totally personalized online magazine or newspaper.

Safari has RSS tools built right in. When you visit a site (or a section of a site) that offers a feed, an RSS button should appear to the right of its address; click this to view the feed. Occasionally, Safari fails to find a feed, in which case you'll need to find a link to the feed and click it (the link will often be an orange button labelled "XML").

To combine RSS feeds from various sites, bookmark each feed and put the bookmarks into a folder, perhaps on your Bookmark Bar. Then click the folder and select **View All RSS Articles**.

Another way to view RSS feeds is as a screen saver. Open **System Preferences > Desktop & Screen Saver > Screen Saver,** and choose **RSS Visualizer**. Click **Options...** to pick from your Safari feeds.

Firefox doesn't currently feature full RSS support, but it does let you view feed headlines via the Bookmarks Bar. To create one of these "live bookmarks", go to any site with an RSS feed and click the orange button at the bottom-right corner of the Firefox window. For full RSS functions in Firefox, grab an extension (see p.157).

Tip: If you'd like to be able to browse your newsfeed collection from any computer, sign up with an online aggregator such as:

bloglines.com
feedlounge.com
google.com/reader
my.yahoo.com

The free version of RealPlayer – not to be confused with the trial version of the all-singing-and-dancing RealPlayer Plus.

Video & music online

Video and music can be made available over the Internet in two ways. They can be "streamed" (played straight off the Web in real time) or downloaded (saved to your hard drive and enjoyed at your leisure).

Streaming

Streaming is most commonly used for online radio stations, TV replays, YouTube clips, concert broadcast, movie trailers and more. Usually, the quality isn't brilliant (especially with video), as the files are very compressed, and it's not possible to save the streams – at least not without special software (see bitcartel.com/radiolover).

Many streaming audio and video will play back using Apple's QuickTime format, but some links require you to install a software freebie. Download the free OS X versions (not the free trials) of:

RealPlayer real.com/freeplayer
Windows Media Player windowsmedia.com/download

Downloads

Though a huge amout of music and video downloading still takes place illegally via P2P file-sharing (see p.190), there's plenty of legal stuff available too – pay-to-download services such as the iTunes Store as well as freebies from labels and up-and-coming artists. Aside from iTunes, few of the major online music services offer Mac-friendly files, though some specialists do. As a rule of thumb, any service that offers MP3 files should be fine; any that offers DRM-protected WMA files will be incompatible.

As for movie and TV downloads, there's not much available on the legal side beyond the selection found at the iTunes Store. Most full-length movie downloading happens via P2P networks such as BitTorrent, with the files typically arriving in MPEG or AVI formats. Depending on the "codec" (eg DivX) used to create the compressed video file, you may need a special program to play them back. Of course, downloading copyrighted movies for free in this way is illegal.

Email

Email on a Mac works in much the same way as on any other computer. You get an account – most commonly from your Internet Service Provider, or an online company such as Yahoo! – and then send and read messages either through a special email program or via a webpage.

If you've already got an email account that you want to use, skip ahead to p.165. Otherwise, have a think about what type of address you want; it pays to do this now, as it can be a real pain to switch accounts once you've given your address to everyone you know.

Pick an email account

When it comes to scoring an email address, there are three main options. You can get your address from…

▶ **An Internet Service Provider** Most ISPs provide at least one email address as part of any Internet access package. The advantage of these accounts is that they won't cost you anything extra, they're reliable and you don't have to view any ads along with your messages. The disadvantages is that if you ever switch ISP, you'll lose the address.

◀ *Andy Bouchard's wonderfully lo-fi reworking of the Mail icon (and others) can be downloaded from: andybouchard.com.*

POP3 & webmail

There used to be a clear distinction between "POP3" email accounts (with which you send and receive messages using an email program such as Mail or Outlook) and webmail accounts (such as Hotmail and Yahoo!, which you access via a website). These days, however, the boundaries are blurred: decent POP3 services offer web access and decent webmail services offer POP3 access. Only accept an account that offers both.

email

▶ **A webmail provider** The advantage of signing up with a web-based email provider is that they don't tie you to your ISP. Furthermore, the better services, such as Yahoo! or Gmail, provide so much online storage for your messages – up to 2.5 gigabytes at the time of writing – that you can leave all your emails permanently online (allowing you to access them from anywhere) as well as downloading them to an email program on your Mac ("POP3 access"). On the downside, when you're viewing your messages via the Web, you may have to view banner adverts on the page; there's no guarantee that the service will remain free forever; and, if you have a common name, you may end up with an address as catchy as johnsmith2972@yahoo.com.

Gmail gmail.com
Yahoo! yahoo.com

▶ **A domain registrar** One problem with both the above options is that you can't completely design your own address. Even if you can get the first half of the address you want – such as john@my-isp.com or john@gmail.com – you're still stuck with the email provider's name after the @ sign. But if you register your own domain name (web address) you'll get control of all addresses ending in that domain. If you registered www.johnsmith.com, for example, you could use the email addresses mail@johnsmith.com, work@johnsmith.com, john@johnsmith.com, etc. Addresses such as these demand plenty of kudos and are also very practical (they don't lock you to any individual ISP or email provider). The only downside is cost: you'll have to pay an annual fee to control the domain and usually a hosting fee to get your mail up and running properly (you need POP3, not "email forwarding"). For more on registering a domain name, see p.186.

If your domain name of choice isn't available, you could try NetIdentity, which offers email accounts (and web addresses) based on the many domains that they own. For example, they might offer john@smith.net.

NetIdentity netidentity.com

Which mail program?

Though it's sometimes handy to access emails via the Web, there's no substitute for using a decent email application – or "client" – to compose, read, sort and organize your emails on your computer. There are many mail applications available, but none are better-suited to the majority of Mac users than Apple's own Mail. Mail is stable, user-friendly and has some very cool features – as we'll see over the next few pages. It also offers unmatched integration with Address Book (see p.144) and iCal (see p.140).

If you don't get on with Mail, or you require a specific feature that it doesn't offer, check out the alternatives. The best-known option is Microsoft's Entourage – essentially the Mac version of Outlook (not to be confused with Outlook Express). Entourage comes as part of Microsoft Office and is worth trying out if you've already paid for the Office suite or are familiar with Outlook on a PC. Otherwise, it's probably not worth the money, for while it does provide certain extra tools, most of these are designed for a big-office environment and are less useful than the features it lacks – such as seamless integration with iCal, iTunes and iSync.

Entourage mactopia.com

Of the various other options, Thunderbird (see box) is probably top of the list, though tiny minorities of Mac users swear by alternatives ranging from Opera Mail (built into the Opera browser window, see p.154) to feature-packed clients such as Mailsmith and PowerMail.

Mailsmith barebones.com
PowerMail ctmdev.com

Tip: To get Entourage to sync your mail with a mobile device using iSync, grab PocketMac GoBetween from: isyncentourage.com.

Thunderbird

The sister application of the Firefox Web browser (see p.153), Thunderbird is a powerful, completely free open-source mail application with some unique tools (such as a built-in RSS reader) and excellent spam filters. It doesn't integrate with other elements of OS X as smoothly as Apple's own Mail, but it's worth test-driving nonetheless. Download it from: mozilla.org/thunderbird.

Using Mail

Apple's Mail application (also known as Mail.app to differentiate it from the generic term "mail") should already be visible on your Dock. If not, you'll find it in **Applications**.

Setting up accounts

You may have entered your mail account details when you first turned on your Mac, or when you first launched Mail. If not, or if you want to set up Mail to send and receive extra email accounts, head for the **Accounts** pane of Mail's Preferences panel (⌘,). Either hit the "+" button to add an account or edit what's already in place within the **Account Information** pane. Here you'll see:

▶ **Description** Can be whatever you like (eg ISP Account)

▶ **Type** In most cases this will be POP3, though if you're using a .Mac, IMAP or Exchange account, specify accordingly.

▶ **Name and password** These are nothing to do with your OS X name and password; they're for your email account only.

▶ **Incoming mail server** The name of the computer (owned by your email account provider) where you messages live until you download them. It usually takes the form: mail.yourprovider.com or pop.yourprovider.com.

▶ **Outgoing mail server** The name of the computer that routes your sent mail in the right direction. It usually takes the form SMTP.yourprovider.com.

Those are the only essential settings, but before closing the Preferences panel, have a look through **Mailbox Behaviors** and **Advanced** pane, where you'll find extra options to temporarily disable accounts, set "sent" and "junk" mail to be deleted, and choose whether you'd like to leave copies of your messages on the server after downloading them (see box above).

Now you're ready to start sending and receiving. All email programs are pretty much alike, so you shouldn't struggle with Mail if you're used to Outlook Express or any other tool. Even so, it's worth working through the following step-by-step guide to pick up a few tips.

Email on more than one computer

If you use more than one computer – your Mac at home and your PC at work, say – you can easily set up your mail account on both. However, with the default settings in place, you'll usually find that if you download messages to one machine, they'll be deleted from the server and will no longer be available to download to the other. You'll end up with your mail archive spread across two computers.

One workaround is to set up Mail to leave a copy of the messages on the server after downloading. To do this, uncheck the **Remove copy from server...** box on one computer. You'll find this within **Mail > Preferences > Accounts > [the account] > Advanced**. On the other computer, choose to delete the server copy after, say, two weeks. That way, as long as you use both computers every fortnight, you'll always have a complete and up-to-date mail archive on both machines.

Other options are to choose an IMAP email account (whereby all your mail will live on the server); to use the syncing features of a .Mac mail account; or to grab a Gmail or Yahoo! account that provides enough server space to leave a copy of all messages online.

Outgoing servers

Some ISPs only let you access their outgoing mail server when you're online using their connection. But you can use any functioning outgoing mail server for any email account, so if you're setting up multiple accounts, you may want to use your ISP's outgoing mail server for all of them. Likewise, if you're not at home and can't get Mail to send messages, it's likely to be an Outgoing Mail Server problem. Either try a different server, contact your mail provider for advice, or send mail via your mail provider's website when out and about.

Creating messages

To create a new message hit **New** (or ⌘N) and enter one or more addresses in the **To:** and **Cc:** fields. You can either type these manually or pull contacts in from Address Book (see p.144).

Hit the **Address** button, select a contact and either hit the **To** or **Cc** button, or drag the contact into your message.

Add a subject, type your message and, if you like, click the **Fonts** and **Colors** buttons to change how things look. You might also want to add an attachment (see below) and a signature (see opposite). Finally, click **Send** or, if you'd like to come back to the message later, **Save as Draft**.

Responding

The other way to create a message is to respond to one that has been sent to you. You have various options, all of them accessible via the **Message** menu and in the menu that appears when you right-click a message.

▶ **Reply** (⌘R) Responds to the sender alone.

▶ **Reply All** (⌘⇧R) Responds to all the recipients of the email.

▶ **Forward** (⌘⇧F) Sends the message on to someone else. Note that you can forward more than one message at once: simply highlight various emails (by clicking on them one while holding down the ⌘ key) and when you press **Forward** the text and attachments of them all will be combined in a single email.

Tip: The **View** menu and button let you add two fields when creating messages:

▶ **Bcc** Lets you copy in recipients without the other recipients of the email being able to see. Useful for sending group email when you don't all the addresses to be public.

▶ **Reply-To** Add an address here and any replies will go to that email account rather than the one you're sending from.

▶ **Redirect** (⌘⇧E) Forwards the message in such a way that it will appear to have come from the original sender (and at the original date and time). Useful when someone sends you an email in error.

▶ **Reply with iChat** (⌘⇧I) If the person who sent you the message is in your iChat Buddy List (see p.176) *and* in your address book, you can use this option to start a text, voice or video conversation. When the sender of a message is available for an iChat reply, you'll see a green dot next to the message; if they're logged into iChat but "away", you'll see a yellow dot.

▶ **Bounce** (⌘⇧B) The original email will be returned to the sender, to whom it will appear as if the message never got through. Useful for replying to unwelcome correspondents and for creating an excuse when you forgot to reply.

When you reply to or forward a message, the original text is quoted at the bottom of your email, coloured and styled to differentiate it from your reply. To change how quoted text looks, or to change how this feature works, look within the **Fonts & Colors** and **Composing** panels of Mail Preferences.

Stationery

If you want a message to make a particular impact click the **Stationery button** to select from various Apple-created HTML templates with graphics for birthdays, announcements and so on.

Attachments

You can include a photo, document or any other file along with your email. Just click the **Attach** button (or hit ⌘⇧A) and choose the file you want to send. Even simpler, drag and drop the files into the message window. Note, however, that you shouldn't send attachments of more than a few megabytes – at least not unless you know the recipient has broadband and won't mind. Big attachments can take an age to download on a slow connection, and may even crash the recipient's email account. One way to lessen the load is to compress files before attaching them (see p.98). If they're still too big, send them via the web at:

MailBigFile mailbigfile.com
YouSendIt yousendit.com

Signatures & vCards

You can add a personal touch at the end of your emails in the form of "signatures". Most people include their address, phone number and job title, sometimes rounding off with a recycled witticism.

To create or edit signatures, open **Preferences** from the **Mail** menu and look in the **Signatures** panel. You can create as many as you like and choose which to use case-by-case with the **Signature** menu (underneath the "Subject" in blank messages).

You can change the text style via the **Format** menu or even drag in a file such as your vCard from Address Book (which the recipient could then import into their own contacts list). If you do this, however, your recipients will end up with multiple version of your vCard in their inboxes, so you might consider putting your vCard online instead and then linking to it in your signature. Add some text, such as "Download vCard", then select the text, right-click it, choose **Edit Link...** and enter the relevant URL (eg www.mysite. com/vcard.vcf).

When the lightening icon appears, it means Mail can't access the server for the account in question.

Sending & receiving

When you're connected to the Internet, mail will dispatch messages as you send them; otherwise, they'll sit in the **Outbox** until next time you connect. Likewise, when you're online, Mail will check for new emails at regular intervals. You can specify the frequency that this happens under the **General** panel of Mail Preferences, or check for messages at any time using the **Get Mail** button.

When new messages arrive, you'll hear a sound (if the default tone annoys you, change the **New mail sound** under the **General** panel of Mail Preferences). You'll also find that Mail's icon in the Dock displays the number of unread messages in a little red star. Within Mail, each mailbox also displays a number, referring to the number of unread messages it contains.

Individual unread messages are marked with a blue dot; if you'd also like to have them display in bold type, look within the **Viewing** panel of **Preferences** (in the **Mail** menu).

Spam

Most email users receive a certain amount of "spam" – unsolicited messages – offering anything from links to porn sites to get-rich-quick schemes. Needless to say, such messages are invariably scams of some sort, so never reply to them and *never* follow links from them to websites to take up their "offers". To reduce your risk of landing lots of spam, avoid making your email address too public. Consider using a second account, or an alias (see p.95), for anything such as signing up to mailing lists, publishing online or giving out to customers or clients. If the new address gets too bogged down in junk, you can simply stop using it and set up another.

If the spam's already arriving thick and fast to your main address, however, you'll need to "train" your email application to filter out the junk as it arrives. In Mail, suspected spam messages are automatically marked in brown. If a legitimate message has been marked, select it and press **Not Junk**; likewise, if a spam message has been missed, select it and hit **Junk**. Do this for a month or two and you should find that Mail does an increasingly good job of spotting junk. Once you're happy with its success rate, open **Preferences** and, under, **Junk Mail**, choose to have junk messages automatically moved into a separate folder. This should cure the headache, though it's worth scanning through the junk folder occasionally for legitimate messages.

If Mail's junk-filtering doesn't do the trick, you may want to download some other anti-spam tools. You'll find plenty via:

Apple Downloads apple.com/downloads/macosx/email_chat

A good last resort against junk mail is to sign up with SpamArrest. Emails from unknown senders are kept from your inbox until their identity is confirmed. It's foolproof, but not free.

Managing mail

Incoming mail arrives in the inbox, which, if you have more than one account set up, breaks down into sub-inboxes. But to keep things organized, you may want to sort messages into "mailboxes" – essentially folders. To create a mailbox press the "+" button at the bottom-left or use the **Mailbox** menu, and then simply drag messages into it. If you want a message in more than one mailbox, hold down ⌥ as you drag.

Following are a few other useful techniques for viewing and organizing your mail:

▶ **Sorting** You can sort messages in any mailbox according to any column – "From", "Subject", "Date Received", etc. Simply click the text at the top of the relevant column. To add more columns, right-click any column header and choose from the list.

▶ **Rules** You can set up "rules" so that when something happens (a message arrives from Uncle Jim, say) Mail does something (such as putting the message in your "Family" mailbox). To set up rules, open **Preferences** from the **Mail** menu and look under **Rules**.

Though most commonly used for shunting messages around as they arrive, rules can be run at any time on existing messages by clicking **Apply Rule** in the message window (or hitting ⌘⇧L).

▶ **Threading** The **Organize by Thread** command in the **View** menu lets you view your emails as nested "conversations" – with a message at the top and all the replies to that message underneath. You can expand or collapse individual threads using the little triangles to their left; or deal with them all at once using the options in the **View** menu.

▼	Lockett, Andrew	Did you get that la...	17 Mar 2005
	Lockett, And...	RE: Did you get th...	17 Mar 2005
↩	Lockett, And...	RE: Did you get th...	17 Mar 2005

Other Mail features

RSS

Most people keep track of RSS feeds though their Web browser but it's also possible to view them in Mail. For feeds that you always want to stay abreast of, this is an excellent option – you'll spot new articles or posts every time your check your email, and you can delete, sort and search stories, or mark them as read or unread, just as you would with messages.

To add an RSS feed to Mail, use the "+" button or click **File > Add RSS Feeds**. Then either choose from feeds already bookmarked in Safari or simply paste the URL of one or more feeds into the **Custom** box. To find the URL of a feed, visit the website in question and look for an XML, Feed or RSS link.

To-Do lists

Another useful feature added to Mail in OS X Leopard is the To Do list – a useful way to keep on top of upcoming tasks. Click the **To Do** button (or key ⌘⌥Y) to add a new entry to the list. You can right-click (or Ctrl-click) the entry and assign various attributes to it – including a priority rating, deadline, reminder alert and an associated iCal calendar (see p.140). To change which of these attributes are visible in the list, right-click the header of any column.

23

Phone, video calls & chat

With a Mac and an Internet connection, it's free and it's easy to communicate in real time with other computer users around the world – in text, voice or even video. Even better, with the right software you can call "regular" telephones – both landlines and mobiles – for a fraction of the cost that your telco would charge. This chapter explains how.

Computer-to-computer messaging and calls

Messenger applications let you exchange typed messages, as well as voice and video calls, between computers. Once you build up a list of contacts – or "buddies" – you'll be able to see at a glance which of them are at their computers and ready to communicate. Then just click a button to send an instant message, to call them or to start a video conversion – Star Trek-style.

iChat & other messengers

Macs come with an excellent messenger built-in. It's called iChat, and it lets you communicate with other iChat users, plus anyone who uses the following alternative messengers popular among PC users:

AIM (AOL's instant messenger) aim.com
Google Talk google.com/talk
Jabber See box, below

The only problem is that millions of PC users who you might want to chat with use different messaging tools such as MSN, Yahoo! and ICQ. iChat can talk to these programs but it requires a techie work-around using Jabber (see box). Instead, you might prefer to download the relevant messenger:

MSN Messenger for Mac microsoft.com/mac
Yahoo! Messenger messenger.yahoo.com
ICQ icq.com

Jabber

Jabber is an instant messaging system used in many universities, companies and elsewhere. iChat doesn't let you set up a Jabber account, but if you already have one, you can use iChat as a Jabber messenger. Enter your details in the Accounts pane of iChat Preferences, and then open the **Jabber List** from **Window** menu (⌘3) to see who's online and exchange messages.

One clever thing about Jabber is that it can use so-called "gateways" to log on to IM networks such as MSN and Yahoo!. And since Jabber is built in to iChat, it is possible via a slightly round-the-houses route to chat to MSN and Yahoo! buddies within iChat. To find out how, see: allforces.com/2005/05/06/ichat-to-msn-through-jabber.

Tip: If you get sick of switching between multiple messengers, try a multi-network tool such as:

Adium adiumx.com

*The Buddy List shows a name and picture for each of your contacts. To change your own picture, go to **System Preferences > Accounts** or take a snap in Photo Booth (see p.236) and hit **Buddy Picture.***

▼

Tip: If you want to log in to iChat but not be seen by even your closest buddies, choose the **Invisible** status option.

Using iChat

Before you can use any instant messenger, you need to get yourself an account – basically a "'screen name" (username) and password. You'll be prompted to do this the first time you launch iChat, which you'll find in the Applications folder, or perhaps already sitting in the Dock.

If you already have a .Mac, AIM, Jabber or Google account, you can log in to iChat with these details. Otherwise, choose Get an iChat Account… and you'll be taken to a page where you can sign up for a free .Mac trial (for more on .Mac, see p.34). At the end of the trial period, you'll get to keep your account name and password to use in iChat even if you don't sign up for .Mac. Alternatively, you can grab a username and password from either AIM (aim.com) or Google (google.com/accounts).

Adding buddies

Once you're logged in, you're ready to add some contacts and start messaging. If your friends already use iChat, Jabber, Google Talk or AIM, email them and ask for their screen names. Next, open the Buddy List from the Window menu (or by pressing ⌘1) and hit the "+" button at the bottom of the panel to add a contact. If they're not already in your Address Book, click New Person.

From that point on, it's hard to go wrong. A glance at your Buddy List will show you which of your contacts are online and ready to communicate with. To get started, highlight a name and hit the Ⓐ button at the bottom to start a text conversation or the ⑧ and ⑯ buttons for phone calls and video calls respectively.

Audio & video calls with iChat

iChat enables you to make voice and video calls to other iChat and AIM users. You can "conference" with up to ten other people using audio, or three others using video. If your Mac has a built-in mic and camera, everything should work automatically; but if you're adding external equipment you'll need to set things up in **iChat > Preferences > Audio/Video**.

You can tell from your Buddy List which of your contacts is set up for

What you'll need for audio & video calls

To make computer-to-computer voice calls, both parties simply need some kind of microphone and speakers, either built-in or attached to their computer. However, a headset or USB handset (see p.180) will drastically improve the sound quality.

For video calls, you'll also both need a webcam. Most recent Macs have a built-in iSight camera; if your model doesn't, invest in one of the many USB Video Class (UVC) webcams that OS X supports. Logitech are a sound brand, while the sleek XBox Live Vision camera (pictured) is another good choice. Alternatively, you could use a FireWire camcorder as a webcam, if you have one.

Finally, for decent quality voice or video calls, both parties will need to have broadband. Dial-up connections can be used, but the sound will be bad and the video will be more like an inch-wide slideshow, updating every second or so – worth it, perhaps, for a glimpse of a loved one on the other side of the world, but not a real means of communication.

Tip: To enter full-screen mode when video conferencing, use the option in the **Audio** menu, hit the button at the bottom of the video window, or use the keyboard shortcut ⌘^F.

voice and video calls – you'll see a phone icon when audio chat is possible, and a camera icon when video is possible. To start chatting or conferencing with someone, double-click the camera or telephone icon next to their name, or highlight them and use the buttons at the bottom of the list.

iChat tips & tricks

That's the basics covered, but there are various other functions and tricks that are worth knowing about:

▶ **Status menu** Below your name at the top of your Buddy List is a dropdown where you can choose how you want to appear to others whose Buddy List you appear on – "Available", "Away", "Offline", etc. You can also use this menu to type custom status messages ("At the shops, back in 5", etc).

*Under the **Messages** tab of iChat Preferences you can set the way text messages appear.*
▼

▶ **Current iTunes Track** The same menu also offers the option of showing all your buddies what you are currently listening to in iTunes along with a link so that they can click through to the Apple Music Store and preview the track for themselves.

▶ **Groups** Select **Use Groups** from the **View** menu to divide your Buddy List into collapsible categories – Work, Family, etc. Groups can be added and edited using the "+" button at the bottom of the Buddy List, while individual buddies can be dragged from group to group within the list. To add a person to more than one group, hold down ⌥ while your drag.

▶ **Send files** Drag any file onto a name in your Buddy List – or into an open conversation – and, once the recipient has chosen to accept the file, it will make its way to their desktop. Unlike email attachments, this technique is great for sending large files.

▶ **Insert smilies** Using either the **Edit** menu option or the dropdown menu at the right-hand end of a chat box, you can add "emoticons" (emotion icons) or "smilies" to your messages. How much fun can you handle?

▶ **Blocking** To prevent a specific person from messaging you or seeing when you're online, open **Preferences** from the **iChat** menu and, under **Accounts**, click **Security**. Check **Block specific people**, click the **Edit List...** button and add your nemesis using the "+" button.

▶ **Parental controls** If you have children and you'd like to make sure they only chat to approved contacts, set them up with a "managed" OS X user account, and enable and configure iChat parental controls (see p.54 for more information).

▶ **Tabbed chats** Allows you to easily and tidily hold several chats at one time by arranging them under tabs, as with Safari. Simply choose **iChat > Preferences > Messages > Collect chats into a single window**.

▶ **Record your calls** Using the option in the **Video** menu, you can record audio and video conversations – great for interviewing or recording podcasts (see p.224). iChat requests permission of the person you're chatting with starting the recording.

▶ **Special effects** You can choose to add special effects to your iChat video conversations and also background images. The results are a little gimmicky, but if you fancy looking like you're chatting from a mid-80s pop promo, investigate the options under **Video > Show Video Effects**.

▶ **iChat Theater** This tool lets you display PowerPoint, iPhoto slideshows and most other file types to people you're chatting with. To get this started use the **Share a File** or **Share iPhone** options in the **File** menu.

▶ **Screen sharing** With a click of a button, two iChat participants can share and control one of the participants' Macs, all the while communicating via an audio chat. Great for providing technical support to technophobe relatives and friends. Just select a buddy in the list and then choose **Share My Screen** or **Ask to Share Remote Screen** from the **Buddy menu**.

Tip: To start a group chat, select multiple contacts in your Buddy List (by holding down ⌘ while you click), hit the "A" button and type a message. Each person who accepts can chat with everyone else in the session.

Tip: To quickly add a person to your "blocked" list, click the **Block** button that appears in the window when you receive a message.

Bonjour

iChat usually works over the Internet, but it also lets you chat to other users on your office or home network – even when you're not connected to the Net. This is useful if, for instance, you want to quickly send files between laptops when you're out and about. Simply open the **Bonjour** panel from the **Window** menu (or hit ⌘2) to see all available buddies on your network with iChat running. For more information about setting up networks, see p.66.

Calling telephones

Not everyone is a broadband user who spends their life glued to their computer, ready to receive incoming calls. Good news, then, that it's also possible to use your Mac to call regular phones – landlines and mobiles – via your Internet connection. Doing so can save you money, especially if you regularly call long distance. It can also be very useful if your home phone is often in use, effectively providing a second line with no monthly charge.

The technology that allows computers to connect to normal phone lines is called VoIP (Voice over Internet Protocol), though various companies use an alternative term such as "Internet telephony" or "broadband phone".

Skype & other services

Many of the messengers listed on p.174 allow you to call telephones, but by far the most popular VoIP service, partly thanks to its ease of use and reliability, is Skype. It's like a regular instant messaging program, with free computer-to-computer calls between users, but it also allows you to buy "SkypeOut" credit for calling regular and mobile phones around the world. The prices are very low: roughly 2¢/1p per minute to landlines and mobiles in most of Europe, North America and Australasia, regardless of

If you want to improve the sound quality of your Skype calls, or to make VoIP feel a bit less like Star Trek, connect a USB handset, such as this TipTel 116, to your Mac.

your location (note, though, that calls to UK mobiles cost more like 25¢/15p per minute). You can also receive calls to your Mac from regular phones, though you have to pay a monthly "SkypeIn" subscription.

Skype skype.com

Other pay-as-you-go computer-to-telephone calling services worth exploring include:

Gizmo gizmoproject.com
Rebtel rebtel.com
Jajah jajah.com

Subscription plans

An alternative to a Skype-style system is a VoIP service that offers unlimited calls for a fixed monthly charge. These typically let you connect a regular telephone to your broadband router, missing out your Mac altogether. Services include:

BT Broadband Voice btbroadbandvoice.com (UK)
VoicePulse voicepulse.com (US)
Vonage vonage.com (US) • vonage.co.uk (UK)

24 Your own website or blog

Publishing a website with your Mac is as easy or as hard as you choose to make it. If your sole aim is to put a few pictures online to show your friends and family, then your best bet may be to avoid the nuts and bolts of site creation and employ some simple photo-sharing tools (see p.252) or iWeb (see below). Likewise, if you just want to plot your daily thoughts in a blog or publish a podcast, then there are plenty of uncomplicated options available. If you're after more flexibility and kudos, however, you'll want to use your Mac to create a proper website…

Using iWeb

The simplest way to build a website with a Mac is to use Apple's iWeb application. iWeb is part of the iLife suite and, at the time of writing, comes pre-installed on all Apple computers except the Mac Pro. If you have a .Mac account, iWeb is also the easiest way to create a blog or podcast.

Compared with other such programs, iWeb is supremely easy to use, but be aware that the results can look a bit prefabricated and that you are prompted at every turn to publish your pages to a .Mac account. If you don't want to pay for a .Mac account (see p.34), you can still use iWeb to build your site, but you'll need to manage the hosting of your pages separately (see p.187). Another drawback of iWeb is that its simplicity masks the mechanics of how webpages actually work – so if you want to learn Web design properly, there's no substitute for learning some HTML and building something from scratch.

iWeb basics

To get started, open iWeb from the Dock or Applications folder. When prompted, choose a design theme and pick what kind of page you want to create first – Welcome, Blog, Photo and so on.

A pre-fab page will appear, ready for you to customize with your own text, photos, videos and so on. Click the **Media** button to browse and then drag items straight into the existing placeholders – or anywhere else on the page.

As you add new pages, they'll appear in the left-hand sidebar, where you can also rename each page, should you wish. Links will automatically be created between each page in your site.

Web Widgets and tools

▶ **HTML Snippets** Click the **Web Widgets** button and choose **HTML Snippets**. A dialogue box will appear that can be used to paste HTML code into your webpage. With a basic understanding of how HTML works, you can borrow code from pretty much any page you can find (in Safari, choose **View > View Source** to see a page's HTML code). Some sites, such as YouTube, even offer code up on a plate – you'll find it next to each video.

Tip: iWeb can also be launched from several other Apple applications, allowing you to publish galleries of images to the Web direct from iPhoto and publish iMovie clips and films direct from iMovie.

▶ **Google AdSense** Also found in the Web Widgets menu, this option allows entrepreneurial iWeb users to set up an account with Google's popular AdSense service. Google feed through ads appropriate to the content of your page and you earn a small fee if and when visitors click the ads. Take into account, however, the clutter you will be adding to your page, and also consider that if your site is doing little more than making photos available to distant aunts and uncles, on-screen advertising is neither particularly appropriate or likely to make you any money.

▶ **Google Maps** This Web Widget option embeds a Google Map tool in your page. By default, you'll probably be offered a map displaying your address from your Mac's Address Book (see p.144), but you can replace this with any location you want before clicking Apply to place the map on your page.

▶ **Inspector** To fine-tune elements of your page, select an item and hit the **Inspector** button on the toolbar at the bottom. In the panel that pops up, you can, for example, alter the line spacing of text, tweak links and so on.

Publishing your site

When you're happy with your results, simply hit the **Publish** button to upload the pages to a .Mac account. Files that have been success-fully uploaded appear in blue until further changes are made and you need to upload them again.

If you don't have a .Mac account, choose **File > Publish to a folder...** to export the site to your hard drive. The resulting folder can then be uploaded via FTP to your Web space (see p.187).

Tip: With a .Mac account your site address is likely to be something like http: web.mac.com/username/ Site/Photos/Welcome.html. Not exactly snappy. If you would rather use your own Web domain address (say www.peter.com), but in conjunction with iWeb's one-click publishing to a .Mac account, you can set this up by choosing **File > Set Up Personal Domain** and following the prompts.

Other ways to create a website

Using iWeb and .Mac isn't the only way to create a website. Other techniques are far trickier and more time consuming, but they offer more control.

Though you wouldn't know it from using iWeb, most webpages consists of a bunch of separate files – a text-only HTML document written in a simple computer language called hypertext markup language, plus a file for each image or other element used within the page.

Preparing images for the Web isn't too difficult (see box), but creating HTML documents and assembling them into an interlinked site is much more tricky. The best way to start is to work your way through an online HTML tutorial – for example at w3schools.com.

HTML editors

Since HTML files contain nothing but text, it's perfectly possible to create a webpage in an application such as Text Edit. However, most people prefer to use a more advanced tool, which automates some of the process and generally speeds things up.

There are scores of HTML editors out there. Some, such as Freeway and RapidWeaver, use templates to make the process simple – just like iWeb. At the other end of the scale are professional level packages such as Adobe Dreamweaver:

Freeway Express softpress.com ($99)
RapidWeaver realmacsoftware.com ($40)
Dreamweaver adobe.com/dreamweaver ($399)

Preparing images

Before dropping an image into your webpage, prepare it for online use – make sure it downloads as fast as possible and behaves itself on-screen. Use an image editor (see p.249) to:

▶ **Reduce its dimensions** Make the image the size you want it to appear on the page by shrinking its dimensions in pixels.

▶ **Compress it** Only use compressed image formats such as JPEG, GIF and PNG on your website. Your digital photos will probably already be in JPEG format, but you may want to shrink the file size further by saving a copy at a slightly lower quality.

Some site building tools, including HomePage, take care of all this automatically.

Tip: For a simple site, create and save all your images and HTML pages in a single folder. This makes everything easier to manage and keeps the links between pages short and sweet.

Get a domain name

If you'd like a personalized Web address, you'll need to register a "domain". You pay a fee and that gives you exclusive use of the address for a set period (usually a year or two at a minimum) after which you can renew it.

If someone else has already taken your ideal name – eg www.peter.com – you'll have to try changing the end (.net, .info, etc) or the name itself (eg www.peteronline.com). Any domain registrar will instantly confirm what's available and let you bag your domain. Major registrars include:

123-reg.co.uk (UK)
domaindirect.com (US)
domainmonger.com (US)
uk2.net (UK)

When you register a domain name you'll usually be offered a hosting package for an extra fee. If you don't accept this, you'll need to either set up the domain to "forward" all traffic to some other address (your webspace or blog, say) or associate the address to a server – either a third-party host or your own Mac.

It's even possible to create a website using Microsoft Word. Simply create a "standard" document with text and pictures then choose **File > Save As Webpage**.

When you've created your pages, it's best to save them with short lowercase names without any spaces or special characters (for example, pictures.html or contact.html). Most importantly, save your homepage as index.html. This way, when someone types yoursite.com into their browser, the homepage will automatically appear.

Publishing webpages without .Mac

When your webpages and images are ready to go live, you'll need to make them available on the Internet, which means putting them on a server computer – a "host" – with an address where people can find them. There are three main options:

▶ **Free webspace** If your budget is tight, you could plant the files in some free space, perhaps thrown in by your ISP as part of your Internet connection package, or from a free webspace provider such as tripod.com or geocities.com. The problem is that you'll end up with an address such as webspace.myisp.com/peter. If you want something more like www.peter.com, you could register a domain name (see box) and use that as a front page to your free webspace. People will type, say, www.peter.com, which will redirect them to webspace.myisp.com/peter. Note, though, that some registrars will display – unless you pay a small surcharge – an ad banner at the top of your site to anyone who reached it via the new address.

▶ **A proper host** If you want to register a domain name and have it function properly, not just as a front door, you'll need to pay a small fee per month to house your pages on a "proper" Web host. By far the easiest option is to buy a hosting package and domain name at the same time, and from the same company – such as dreamhost.com.

▶ **Host it yourself** If you have an always-on broadband connection with a static IP address (ask your ISP if you're not sure), you could consider setting up your Mac as a Web host. OS X makes this very easy, as it comes pre-installed with the world's most popular server software, Apache. All you need to do is open **System Preferences** > **Sharing** and turn on **Personal Web Sharing**. Then put your webpages and images in the **Sites** folder of your home folder and they'll be accessible from anywhere at your-IP-address/~yourshortusername. If you'd rather have a non-numeric address, register a domain name and set it up to point all traffic to your Mac; visitors to your site will never know that you're hosting it yourself.

Uploading your site

Unless you're hosting your own site on your Mac, you'll need to upload your pages, images, etc, to wherever they're going to live on the Interet. To do this, you'll need some log-in details from whoever is providing your Web space. This will usually include a username, password and an FTP address for your space on the server.

It's possible to upload to an FTP address directly from OS X, but the easiest technique is to download a dedicated FTP program, such as the free and simple-to-use Cyberduck:

Cyberduck cyberduck.ch

Once you're logged in to your server space, you're ready to drag you website into it. Note that folder become part of the URL. So if you have a page called mypage.html and you put it in a folder called mywebsite, then the web address would be something like: mywebspace.com/mywebsite/mypage.html..

Tip: Many site-building tools also feature an FTP tool – so see what you already have before downloading a standalone tool.

Tip: Cyberduck offers a Dashboard Widget that makes it easy to quickly drop a file on your Web space.

Tip: For more detailed help with Web publishing, buy *The Rough Guide to The Internet*.

Blog hosts and tools

A blog, or weblog, is a special kind of frequently updated webpage consisting of short "posts", arranged with the most recent at the top. Many major sites feature blogs, sometimes written by teams of people. But the archetypal blog is composed by an individual – a daily log of a person's life, thoughts and online discoveries.

As we've seen, one easy way to create a blog is to use iWeb in association with .Mac. But it's just as simple – and entirely free – to sign up instead with a blog host.

Once you've created an account (a simple process that should only take a few minutes), choose a template to determine how your blog will look. Then log into the host's website from any computer and type a new post. People will access your blog via a sub-domain or your blog hosts's address – eg peter.blogger.com.

A few of the best-known blog hosts include:

Blogger blogger.com
GreatestJournal greatestjournal.com
Sparkpod sparkpod.com

If you have your own domain name and site already, choose a host that will let you display your new blog at your own address – or download some tools that will allow you to manage your blog direct from your Mac. One example would be the easy-to-use iBlog application:

iBlog lifli.com ($20)

iBlog. Desktop blogging for Mac OS X.

Tip: You can find more blogging software at Apple Downloads:

Apple Downloads apple.com/downloads/macosx

Publish a podcast

Podcasts are short audio or video "shows" made available via the Internet, usually via a free subscription in iTunes. Podcasting started as a craze but today is widespread, employed by everyone from school kids to politicians, multinational companies to comedians.

If you're a .Mac subscriber, probably the easiest way to create a podcast is to use iWeb. However, it's perfectly possible to create and publish a video or audio podcast manually. The process goes something like this:

▶ **Prepare your episodes** Use an audio or video editor (such as GarageBand, see p.223, or iMovie, see p.268) to record and mix your shows. Then export the files as MP3s (for audio) or MPEG-4 (for video).

▶ **Create an RSS feed** If you want people to be able to "subscribe" to your podcasts, via the iTunes Store or elsewhere, you need to create an RSS feed – the same technology used for online newsfeeds. The easiest way to do this is to use an RSS feed provider, such as feedburner.com, or an application like Feeder ($30), available from reinventedsoftware.com/feeder.

▶ **Publish your podcast** This basically means planting your shows and RSS feed somewhere online and registering your feed with a podcast directory where people will find it and be able to subscribe. The easiest way to do this is via iTunes (head for the iTunes Store and follow the links).

For more on podcasting, visit apple.com/itunes/store/podcaststechspecs.html, and sign up for the seminars and tutorials found at: seminars.apple.com.

Tip: You can record audio and video of yourself to use in an audio or video podcast using OS X's Photo Booth application and even interview and record friends on the other side of the world using iChat.

Tip: When recording your podcast in GarageBand, look in the Track Info panel for the vocal podcast presets to get the best sound from your voice recordings.

25 P2P file sharing

P2P ("peer-to-peer") file-sharing is a technology that allows computer users all over the world to "share" each other's files via the Internet. Even if you've never heard of P2P, you've probably heard of some of the programs that have made this kind of file sharing possible, such as KaZaA – and, historically speaking, Napster. And you've probably also heard people debating the legal and moral ins and outs of the free-for-all that file-sharing applications facilitate. If not, don't worry – the next few pages will bring you up to speed.

As we've already seen (see p.66), one of the reasons why people set up home and office networks is to allow each user some degree of access to the files stored on the other computers. P2P file-sharing applications apply this idea to the whole of the Internet – which is, of course, simply a giant network of computers. In short, anyone who installs a P2P program can access the "shared folder" of anyone else running a similar program.

With literally millions of sharers online at any one time, an unthinkably large quantity of files is available – from music and movies to images, software and documents. So, whether you're after a drum'n'bass track, a Web-design application, a Chomsky speech or an episode of your favourite sitcom, you're almost certain to find it. But that *doesn't* mean that it's legal. If you download or make available any copyright-protected material, you are breaking the law and, while it's still unlikely, you could be prosecuted.

Did you know…

In 2004, according to a study by Michael Goodman of The Yankee Group, five billion music tracks were downloaded via P2P, compared with only 330 million from online services selling legal, DRM-protected tracks.

The legal battle

Continuous legal action saw Napster – the first major P2P system – bludgeoned into submission (it has now resurfaced as a legitimate online music service, though it's not compatible with Macs). A similar fate befell Scour, this time because of movie rather than audio sharing, and in 2005, the Recording Industry Association of America (RIAA) and the Motion Picture Industry (MPI) were successful in closing down the company behind the Grokster program. But these casualties just paved the way for others, such as KaZaA, which stands by some margin as the most downloaded program in the history of the Internet.

These new-generation P2P tools are genuinely decentralized: they don't rely on a central system to keep tabs on which files are where. Which means that, though the programs are mostly used for the illegal distribution of copyrighted material, the companies producing them can't easily be implicated in this breach of the law (just as a knife manufacturer couldn't easily be sued for a stabbing).

The music, film and software industries have instead gone after the people who clearly *are* breaking the law: individual file sharers. Quite a few individuals have been prosecuted – mostly in the US – but with many millions sharing files each day, it's pretty inconceivable that anyone could attempt to sue all of them.

Whether or not it's ethical to use P2P to download copyrighted material is another question. Some people justify it on the grounds that they only download material they're considering buying; others believe that intellectual property is akin to theft; others still that they only download non-controversial material, such as recordings of speeches, freeware software or music that they already own on CD or vinyl. It's a heated debate – as is the question of whether file sharing has damaged legal music sales, something the industry insists on, but which many experts claim is questionable.

▲

As this spoof poster (available from modernhumorist.com) shows, many on the "free distribution" side of the DRM debate see their adversaries – led by the Recording Industry Association of America – as draconian authoritarians committed only to profit, power and an outmoded and unsustainable business model. Unsurprisingly, many musicians disagree. For both sides of the argument, see riaa.com and eff.org, or to keep up with recent happenings, keep an eye on theregister.com/internet/rights.

BitTorrent

The BitTorrent P2P system is hugely popular for large files – especially movies and television shows. Indeed, according to some estimates, it accounts for as much as a third of Internet traffic. As with the other networks, however, using BitTorrent to download copyrighted material is against the law.

To use BitTorrent, you first have to download the actual program, from:

BitTorrent bittorrent.com

Once that's done, you can search the Web for a "torrent file" of the music or video that you're after. BitTorrent search-sites (such as torrentz.com) come and go frequently, as many get closed down for legal reasons.

The tiny torrent file, once downloaded, will cause the program to swing into action and download the music or video in question from other BitTorrent users who are online. The more people who are currently downloading the file, the faster the download will be.

Mac P2P applications

There are various P2P "networks" – among them eDonkey2000, FastTrack SoulSeek and Gnutella – each of which can be accessed via various different applications ("clients"). Some of these clients are very sophisticated, with features such as the ability to download a single file from more than one source simultaneously or to import downloaded tracks directly into a playlist in iTunes. Following are the most popular Mac P2P clients and the networks they can access:

Acquisition acquisitionx.com (Gnutella)
LimeWire limewire.com (Gnutella)
MLMac mlmac.org (eDonkey, BitTorrent, FastTrack, Gnutella, KaZaA)
Poisoned gottsilla.net (Gnutella, FastTrack, OpenFT)
Soulseex chris.schleifer.net/ssX (SoulSeek)

There are many other programs and networks out there, as well as other ways of sharing files, such as via newsgroups, chat and BitTorrent (see box). For reviews of all the available programs, plus news and links to download sites, see:

Mac-P2P.com mac-p2p.com
Slyck slyck.com
ZeroPaid zeropaid.com

Sound

Sound basics

Macs handle sound in numerous ways. On the most basic level, they chirp on start-up, grunt when you hit a wrong key and offer congratulatory whistles when you save documents. More usefully, they allow you to play CDs and digital music files through programs such as iTunes, produce your own compositions and record your own performances and speak to friends and family around the world. You can even talk directly to your Mac.

All this will most likely happen effortlessly, but it's still worth taking a few minutes to understand how to control sound on your Mac – especially if you intend to augment your setup with additional mics and a breakout box or audio interface (see p.222).

Volume

You can change the overall volume on your Mac using the dropdown slider on the menu bar (by the clock). If it's not there, open **System Preferences** from the menu, choose **Sound** and check the box at the bottom of the panel. Most Mac keyboards include keys for quickly changing the volume and muting the sound altogether – look for the three little speaker symbols along the top of your keyboard.

Tip: When you're using your keyboard to change the volume, holding down ⇧ mutes the feedback sounds. Or, to avoid these sounds ever happening, uncheck the **Play feedback when volume is changed** box under the **Sound Effects** pane of the **Sound** section of **System Preferences**.

Tip: If you use a dial-up modem and you don't like the noises it makes when it connects to the Internet, turn off "modem sounds" within **System Preferences** > **Network** > **Modem**.

Inputs & outputs

Unless you have special additional hardware, your Mac will deal with one incoming sound source (eg a microphone) and one outgoing sound source (eg internal speakers) at a time. So if you have more than one input or output, you need to specify which you want to use. This is done within the **Output** and **Input** panes of the **Sound** section of **System Preferences**.

By default, you'll have one output set up – **Built-in Output** – which covers your built-in speakers or headphone socket (the name will change depending on whether there's anything plugging into the latter). All recent Mac models have an **Audio line-in port** listed within the **Input** pane. This socket encompasses both optical digital audio (which you are unlikely to encounter) and regular analogue audio sources (such as a radio or hi-fi connected using a mini-jack cable).

All recent Mac laptops and iMacs also have an integral microphone that can be selected within the **Input** pane. If you have an older Mac, you may have no input sources listed, or just the in-built mic.

If at some point you add external audio devices – such as a USB mic, or a full-on audio interface (see p.222) – you may need to open this preferences panel and select the device before you can get it to work.

Tip: Alerts can also be signalled visually instead of audibly. This is done using Universal Access (see p.51).

Tip: If you have more than one sound output set up, you can have your system alerts and sound effects play through one, and everything else (music, video, etc) through the other. You'll find this option under the **Sound Effects** tab in **System Preferences > Sound**.

Tip: If you intend to work on your Mac while listening to music through headphones, it's worth turning the volume of alerts down, as they can give you a bit of a shock, suddenly ricochetting across your ear drums at high volume.

Alerts & effects

The **Sound** preferences panel also contains the settings for **Sound Effects**. From the **alert sound** list, you can pick the noise you'll hear when you try to do something impossible. To toggle whether you hear sounds every time you copy or delete a file or folder, use the **Play user interface sound effects** check box.

Hi-fis & speakers

If you listen to music or watch DVDs on your Mac, you may find the internal speakers quiet and tinny, in which case consider hooking up your computer either to a hi-fi or a set of external speakers.

Connecting to a hi-fi with a cable

To get the sound from your Mac into your hi-fi, the latter will need an available line-in channel – look on the back for an unused pair of red and white RCA sockets. They may be labelled "Aux" or "Line In", though any input other than "Phono" (which will have a built-in preamp) should be fine.

Next, pick up an RCA-to-minijack cable (pictured). When buying a cable, check all the plugs are "male" not "female" (they probably will be) and, if you want true high-fidelity, spend extra to get gold-plated jacks – they deliver a slightly cleaner sound.

Run the cable from the Mac's headphone socket (or Line Out socket if your Mac has one) to the hi-fi's Line In.

---

iPod to hi-fi

One problem with running your Mac through your hi-fi is that you need to have the computer on to hear anything and, unless you have an AirPort Express, you may need to run a cable across the room. An alternative, if you're mainly hooking up the stereo to listen to iTunes, is to attach an iPod to the hi-fi. This doesn't give you quite the same ease of use and flexibility, but it's often more convenient. Simply run an RCA-to-minijack cable between your hi-fi's line-in and your Pod's headphone socket or, better still, the Line Out on the back of an iPod Dock. The Dock solution can be made all the more convenient when combined with a wireless iPod remote control.

Tip: If no signal seems to be getting to your stereo from iTunes, or whichever program you are using, and with whichever method you use to connect, make sure that your volume is turned up both in the program and on your selected output device's master volume.

Tip: Under **iTunes** > **Preferences** > **Advanced** > **General** panel within you can also choose to "Disable iTunes volume control for remote speakers". This allows AirTunes to stream your music at a continuous line level to your Airport Express, which can be preferable when it is connected to a hi-fi or amp with its own volume controls.

Airfoil

Connecting to a hi-fi with AirTunes

If your hi-fi has a line-in socket, but you don't want to be limited by cables – perhaps you have a MacBook, or your desktop Mac is in a different room from your stereo – investigate Apple's AirPort Express wireless base station (see p.67), with its so-called AirTunes feature. With this set up, your alert noises and other sounds will come through your Mac's speakers as usual, but you can stream music wirelessly from iTunes (see below) to the hi-fi.

The AirPort Express plugs into any power socket and can be attached to the hi-fi with a standard RCA-to-minijack cable. It communicates with your Mac wirelessly – so you'll need to buy an AirPort or AirPort Extreme card if you have an older Mac that doesn't have wireless built-in.

Once everything's in place, open iTunes Preferences and check **Look for remote speakers connected with AirTunes** under the **General** pane of the **Advanced** tab. Your hi-fi (which you will have given a name during the setup process) will automatically appear in a dropdown menu at the bottom of the iTunes window.

An AirPort Express can also beam an Internet connection around your home and allow you to connect to a printer wirelessly (for more information, see: apple.com/airportexpress). However, it doesn't allow you to stream music wirelessly from any application other than iTunes. Thankfully, this limitation can be easily circumvented with the help of a $25 application called Airfoil:

Airfoil rogueamoeba.com/airfoil

The solution isn't perfect, however, as you have to manually select whichever program you want to send through the ether, and there is a significant delay between the time the sound is played by whichever program you are using and the time that it actually gets to your hi-fi speakers. This means that the system is useless for watching DVDs or videos, or playing in sync with a backing track when using a multitrack recording application (see p.221).

Computer speakers

If all this talk of cables and sonic wirelessness smacks of overkill, but you're still unhappy with the sound that comes out of your Mac's internal speakers, the obvious solution is a pair of computer speakers. Most connect via a standard minijack plug, which will connect to the headphone/line-out port of your Mac, though a few models use a USB connection, in which case they take care of the digital-to-analogue conversion internally – which may be good or bad news depending on the quality of the speakers.

There are various speaker models designed specifically for Macs, with shapes and colours to complement Apple's computer aesthetic. Among the most striking examples are JBL's Creature II combo (pictured) and Harman Kardon's translucent SoundSticks – both of which feature a subwoofer for base and two "satellite" speakers for treble. Systems such as these provide a sound to rival medium-range home hi-fis, though you have to pay for the privilege. If you're on a budget, any pair of plain old PC speakers should work fine.

Tip: Airfoil can be used to stream audio from Dashboard widgets as well as regular applications – useful when using radio station widgets rather than having to stream from a station's website. For a list of available widgets, visit: apple.com/downloads/dashboard/radio_podcasts

HiFi-Link

If you are after a really clear sound through your hi-fi, consider Xitel's HiFi-Link. Essentially a pared-back audio interface designed specifically for connecting to a hi-fi, it connects to one of your Mac's USB ports (bypassing the built-in sound processors and sockets), converts the digital signal to analogue and pumps it through 30 feet of high-quality audio cable. Not bad for $50/£30. Find out more from:

HiFi-Link xitel.com/USA/prod_hflpc.htm

Tip: If the Queen's English is your first language, you might find that speech recognition works better if you adopt a slight American twang.

Tip: Perhaps the most fun to be had with Macs and speech is with the "Tell me a joke" command. A simple "knock knock" gag becomes surprisingly entertaining when delivered by a white plastic box in a deadpan monotonal drawl.

Tip: For more speech access features look under Universal Access (see p.51).

Speech

Human to Mac

Though the technology is still in its infancy, computers are beginning to be able to interpret human speech with a degree of reliability. In OS X, you can use this technology to give commands in certain applications, hide the Dock, switch between programs, open an Address Book contact, and so on. First, open the **Speech** pane of **System Preferences** and under the **Speech Recognition** tab click the **Calibrate...** button to teach your Mac to recognize your pronunciations.

Next, turn **Speakable Items** on to reveal a floating little speech tool, and decide how you'd like to tell your Mac that you're about to issue a command. Either define a "listening key" (by default **Escape**), or have your Mac permanently listen out for a spoken keyword (by default "computer"). Finally, look under the **Commands** tab to get a feel for the kind of commands that your Mac will recognize, and start speaking.

Mac to human

Beside speaking to your Mac, you can have the computer speak to you – reading out alerts, selected text and so on. Hit **System Preferences > Speech > Text to Speech** and pick a voice (avoid Albert, who will give you nightmares). If you'd like to have the Mac read selected text – useful if you have difficulty reading small type onscreen – you'll need to set a key combination to tell the computer when to start speaking. Pick something that's unlikely to clash with a key combination in another program. ⇧**Tab** is as good a choice as any.

iTunes & iPods

iTunes is OS X's built-in application for managing and playing music and video files. It's also used for moving digital media from a computer to an iPod or iPhone, but you don't need such a device to use iTunes. If you're mainly interested in creating a digital music collection to listen to at home – rather than carry around with you – you can do this using iTunes alone. After all, your Mac can do everything an iPod can do, including being hooked up to a hi-fi (see p.198).

Another function of iTunes is to provide access to Apple's iTunes Store, which is one of various Internet-based services from which you can legally buy and download music. Currently the only way to access the Store using your Mac is via iTunes: you can't shop there by visiting the Apple website using a regular Web browser.

But you don't have to buy your music from the iTunes Music Store. You can use iTunes to play music copied from CD or other computers, or downloaded from elsewhere on the Internet (though music files from certain online music stores may not be compatible).

The following provides plenty of information to get you up to speed with iTunes, digital music and iPods. But for the full picture, check out the bestselling *Rough Guide to iPods, iTunes & Music Online*. And for the lowdown on the Apple iPhone, track down *The Rough Guide to the iPhone*.

Tip: You can also access the iTunes Store when out and about using either an iPhone or iPod touch.

Zeros & ones

Clever though computers and iPods are, they only deal with numbers: digital, rather than analogue, information. In fact, their vocabulary is limited to just zeros and ones: the "binary" number system.

So music on your Mac – regardless of whether it's a song or a symphony – is reduced to a series of millions of zeros or ones. Or, more accurately, to a series of millions of tiny magnetic or electronic charges, each representing a zero or a one.

A typical song stored in your iTunes collection would consist of around 30 million zeros and ones, while a 80GB hard drive in a Mac or iPod could hold around 600 billion zeros and ones – 100 for every person on the planet.

The idea of reducing music to zeros and ones is nothing new: CDs, MiniDiscs and every other digital format also store music as binary code. But none of these other formats combines the capacity, flexibility and editability of the hard drive found in a computer or iPod.

An iPod primer

What is an iPod?

An iPod is like a cross between a Walkman and the hard drive used to store files in a computer. Instead of playing from cassettes, CDs or other media, an iPod holds music and video internally as digital data, in just the same way as a computer stores word-processing documents and other files. iPods aren't unique in this respect: many devices do roughly the same. They're collectively known as digital music players or MP3 players. But the iPod is by far the most popular brand.

High-capacity digital media players, including the iPod classic, have a hard drive, or "hard disk" – just like the one found in a home computer, but a bit smaller. Lower-capacity players, however – such as the iPod nano, iPod shuffle and iPod touch – store their music using "flash" memory: tiny chips of the kind found in digital-camera memory cards.

The models

At the time of writing, there are four types of Pod available:

▶ **iPod touch** Like the iPhone, the iPod touch features a huge display and touch-screen interface. It offers Internet access via Wi-Fi, for Web and email, and provides decent PDA functions.

▶ **iPod classic** The iPod classic replaced the fifth-generation iPod (also known as the "video iPod") in 2007. It has a search feature, comes in black or silver and has a massive capacity – either 80GB or 160GB.

▶ **iPod nano** Now in their third generation, nanos look very similar to the classic, only smaller – both physically and in terms of their capacity. They come in a choice of five standard colours or the special-edition crimson (PRODUCT) RED nano, a portion of the profits from which go towards the fight against AIDS in Africa.

▶ **iPod shuffle** The smallest and least expensive iPod is eminently portable but lacks a screen and doesn't allow any browsing of the music stored on it. It can hold just one playlist – of up to around 250 songs – at any one time.

How much space?

Choosing between the various iPod models is above all a matter of choosing how much storage capacity to go for – as measured in gigabytes (GB). Bank on around 1GB for twenty albums. However, bear in mind that you don't need an iPod capable of storing all your music. You can store your collection on your Mac and just copy across to your iPod the albums you want to listen to at any one time.

Note also that if you plan to use the iPod as a portable hard drive as well as a digital music player, you'll need enough extra space available for the kinds of files you're planning on storing. Word and Excel docs and the like are almost negligibly small, but backing up your whole system or storing image, video or program files quickly fills up space.

More than music…

iTunes and iPods aren't just for music. Here are some of the things you can do with them – all of which are covered in this book's sister volume, *The Rough Guide to iPods, iTunes & Music Online*…

▶ Transfer or store any kind of file

▶ Record voice memos

▶ Read emails and news

▶ Create a universal remote control

▶ Download photos directly from a camera

▶ Navigate the road network

▶ Listen to a new poem each day

▶ Deliver a PowerPoint presentation

Left to Right:
iPod touch, iPod classic, iPod nano, iPod shuffle. For more on using an iPod with iTunes, see p.201.
▼

Import music from CD

The best way to get your head around iTunes is to plant some music in your Library and play. Let's start by copying some tracks from a CD to your Mac's hard drive. This process is usually known as "ripping". iTunes, however, calls it "Importing".

You can't really go wrong. Load a CD into your Mac and it will appear in iTunes as an icon in the Sources area (on the left); click the icon and the CD's contents are displayed in the main panel.

Stage 1: Download the track names

If, when you first ran iTunes, you agreed to let it connect to the Internet whenever it likes, you'll probably find artist, track and album information for your CD automatically appear in the Song List. If not, make sure you're online and select **Get CD Track Names** from the **Advanced** menu.

This info is *not* pulled from the CD, which contains nothing but music, but downloaded from CDDB – a giant online CD database hosted by a company called Gracenote (gracenote.com). If you get no info from CDDB – or you get the wrong info – then you'll have to input the track info manually…

Stage 2: Edit the track info

You can enter information directly into any editable field of the Song List by clicking on its name twice (not too quickly). Any existing text will become highlighted and you're ready to type. Alternatively, to view, add or edit all kinds of information about one or more tracks simultaneously, select them in the Song List and hit ⌘I.

Selecting tracks…

To select multiple tracks in iTunes, either:

▶ Hold down ⌘ and click tracks selectively.

▶ Hold down ⇧ and click the first and last in a series of adjacent tracks. You can then deselect any individual tracks by clicking them with ⌘ held down.

▶ Open the Browser (see p.213) and click on an Artist, Album and Genre to select all the tracks they contain.

Tip: iTunes will also attempt to find album artwork for your CD to display in the iTunes Cover Flow view (see p.93). Album artwork can also be added by choosing the Get Album Artwork option from the iTunes Advanced menu. If that doesn't find what you want, it can also be done manually once the tracks have been imported (see p.211).

Stage 3: Join tracks

Before importing the tracks from a CD, it's possible to "join" some of them together. Then, when they're played back on your computer or your iPod, they'll always stay together as one unit, and iTunes won't insert gaps between the tracks. This is useful if you have an album in which two or more tracks are segued together or if you just think certain tracks should never be separated – even in Shuffle mode. Select the tracks you want to join and then click **Join CD Tracks** from the **Advanced** menu. In the short term you can change your mind by clicking **Unjoin CD Tracks**, but once you've pressed **Import**, the songs will be imported as a single audio file that cannot be separated without the use of audio-editing software (see p.220).

Tip: iTunes only allows you to join tracks before you import. If you want to join them after importing, seek out Track Splicer from Doug's AppleScripts For iTunes: dougscripts.com

Ripping services

It can take just a few minutes to rip a CD into iTunes – and you can listen to the music and/or do work in another application while this is happening. But if you have more money than time, there are services that will take away your CDs and rip them into a well-organized collection for around $1/£1 per CD. See, for example:

PodServe podserve.co.uk (UK)
DMP3 dmp3music.com (US)
RipDigital ripdigital.com (US)

Lose the hard copy?

Unless you're a sound-quality connoisseur or a fan of sleeve notes, you might find that once your CDs have been copied onto your Mac, the discs start to seem like a waste of space. Some have advocated selling them: many will go for $10/£5 through online auctions such as eBay, so if you sell enough you can end up better off than before you bought your Mac. Strictly speaking, the moment you sell the CD you are no longer the owner of the music, so this is legally dodgy. But it's a tempting idea nonetheless.

Converting formats

It's easy to convert existing tracks in iTunes into a different file format. First, pick a format and bitrate under the **Import** tab of the **Advanced** pane of iTunes Preferences. Then select the relevant tracks and choose the **Convert** option in the **Advanced** menu. Converted versions will appear alongside the originals.

At that point you can delete the original versions, but be sure to first check the sound quality of the new versions. Converting between compressed formats (eg MP3 to AAC) can result in a noticeable deterioration in fidelity.

Which format?

iTunes allows you to import your CDs in the following formats:

MP3 [Moving Pictures Experts Group-1/2 Audio Layer 3] MP3 no longer provides the best sound-quality/disk-space balance. But its ubiquitousness means that, if you import your music as MP3, you can be safe in the knowledge that it will be transferable to any other player or software that you might use in the future, or which friends and family may already own.
File name ends: .mp3
Best for: importing music you want to be able to share with non-iTunes people and players, and for burning special MP3 CDs.

AAC [Advanced Audio Coding] iTunes' default import format, AAC is liked by Apple for two reasons. First, it sounds noticeably better than MP3 when recorded at the same bitrate. Second, it allows Apple to embed DRM protection into most files downloaded from the iTunes Music Store, to stop people freely distributing them.
File name ends: .m4a (standard), **.m4p** (when DRM is included)
Best for: importing music you don't expect to share with non-iPod people and players.

Apple Lossless Encoder A recent Apple innovation, this format offers full CD quality, but only consumes around half the disk space – expect to fit between three and five albums per gigabyte. Currently the format only works on iTunes and iPods.
File name ends: .ale
Best for: importing music at the highest quality for computer or iPod use. Note, though, that it won't work with an iPod shuffle.

AIFF [Advanced Interchange File Format], **WAV** [Wave] These uncompressed formats offer the same quality as the newer Apple Lossless Encoder but take up twice as much disk space (and won't play back on an iPod shuffle). In their favour, they can be played on nearly any computer software and also imported into audio-editing programs. They also tend to rip more quickly than Apple Lossless.
File name ends: .aiff, .wav
Best for: importing music for burning onto CD and then deleting, or for editing with audio software, not for general iTunes/iPod playback.

Stage 4: Set the format & bitrate

Before importing your CD collection into iTunes, think about which file format and sound quality you want to use. iTunes offers various options, which you can access via the **Import** tab of the **Advanced** pane within iTunes Preferences (opened with the shortcut ⌘,).

The default setting (AAC format at 128kbps) is fine for listening via headphone or computer speakers, but if you want to put your music on a non-Apple's MP3 player, then AAC won't do (see box opposite), and if you're bothered about sound quality you might want to up the bitrate.

This is the total amount of data (the number of "bits", or zeros and ones) used to encode each second of music. The relationship between file size and bitrate is basically proportional, but the same isn't true of sound quality – a 128kbps track takes half as much space as the same track recorded at 256kbps, but the sound will be only marginally different.

Most people will be satisfied with AAC 128kbps (which is roughly equivalent to MP3 at 160kbps), but if you listen to high-fidelity recordings of acoustic instruments, and if you connect your Mac to a decent hi-fi, you may find this setting leads to a distinct lack of

Song Name ▲	Bit Rate	Artist
☑ Mozart Sound Check – 128 ACC	128 kbps	Hagen Quartet
☑ Mozart Sound Check – 160 ACC	160 kbps	Hagen Quartet
☑ Mozart Sound Check – 192 ACC	192 kbps	Hagen Quartet
☑ Mozart Sound Check – 224 ACC	224 kbps	Hagen Quartet
☑ Mozart Sound Check – AIFF	1411 kbps	Hagen Quartet

Tip: It's sensible to mix different file formats and bitrates in your Library, as some kinds of music receive less benefit from high-bitrate encoding. Sludgy, stoner-type rock, for example, may not require the same fidelity as a carefully regulated Fazioli grand piano.

Tip: In the bitrate dropdown, click **Custom** for extra options. **Mono** (under channels) halves the file size when you're importing mono recordings. And if you're recording in MP3 format, **VBR** (which stands for Variable Bitrate) varies the bitrate in real time, according to the complexity of the sound, potentially saving lots of disk space.

◄ *The best way to determine the right sound quality for your own ear, headphones and hi-fi is to pick a particularly clear and detailed track and rip it at various bitrates and/or formats. Then do some comparative listening either on headphones or, ideally, connected through a decent hi-fi or speaker system (see p.198).*

presence and brightness in your favourite recordings. If so, either opt for the Apple Lossless Encoder (see p.227) or stick with AAC and up the bitrate.

Stage 5: Import…

Now you've sorted out the track details and file format, it's time to import your CD into the iTunes Library. To the left of each song title in the Song List you'll see a checked tick-box; if you don't wish to import a particular track from a CD, uncheck its box. Now hit the Import button in the lower-right corner of the iTunes window and watch as each of your selections is copied to your Library.

> **Tip:** You can't "rip" video from DVDs into iTunes in the same way that you can music from CDs. Instead you need to use a third-party application such as HandBrake (see p.258 for details).

Where does the music go?

Unless you change the settings, each song is saved as a sound file with a folder for the album, within a folder for the artist. All these folders live within the **iTunes** folder, which lives in your **home > Music** folder. So the file for The Beatles' "Dig A Pony", for example, could be tracked down via:

iTunes ▶ iTunes Music ▶ The Beatles ▶ Let It Be ▶ Dig A Pony

Other ways to import

Apart from ripping music from CDs, you can expand your iTunes music collection by grabbing songs from…

▶ **iTunes Store** Apple's flagship music service offers more than two million tracks for ¢99/79p per shot. Simply hit the **Store** button, set up an account, and it's all quite self-explanatory from that point on.

▶ **Elsewhere online** You can download from other music services but only if they offer MP3 or WMA files *without* embedded DRM copy protection. For free downloads, try P2P (see p.190), though be aware that downloading anything copyrighted this way will put you on the wrong side of the law.

▶ **Sounds files** If you have music files on your computer, or an external hard drive, you can import these tracks into iTunes by simply dragging them into the main window – or directly into a specific playlist.

▶ **Vinyl or cassette** With sound recording and editing software, and the right cables, you can record music in from any source, including vinyl, cassette, MiniDisc and radio. For more information on how to do this, see p.219. You'll usually end up with a WAV file, which you can import into iTunes and convert to any format you like.

▶ **Another computer** If you want to import iTunes music from another computer, you'll need to find the relevant files on the source computer and move them across to the destination folder. This can be done using file sharing (see p.57) or some external media such as a portable hard drive, CD or DVD. Once the files are on the destination computer, drag them into the main iTunes window or a specific playlist and they will be copied into the destination Mac's iTunes Music folder.

▶ **From GarageBand and iMovie** Most music and video packages will let you export WAV files of your compositions or soundtracks, which can be imported into iTunes and converted into something more space efficient. GarageBand and iMovie make it particularly easy – see p.228 and p.272.

Tip: If you want to stop your kids either accessing the Music Store entirely or having their tender ears exposed to explicit material, look under **iTunes > Preferences > Parental**.

Tip: iTunes will import standard WMA (Windows Media) files, though in doing so they'll be converted into AAC format, so the sound quality may be slightly degraded. If the WMA files have embedded DRM protection then iTunes won't import them – unless you burn them to audio CD and re-rip them in another format.

Tip: If there's more than one computer on your network running iTunes, you can share each others' Libraries. Open iTunes Preferences on each machine and under the **Sharing** tab check the relevant tick boxes; then look in the Source List for the links to the music on the other computers.

Playing, browsing, deleting

In its default state, iTunes will play the tracks in the main window, in the order shown, and then stop. That might be your entire library, a CD, a playlist or whatever. But there are various other options. From the **Controls** menu, or using the buttons to the bottom-left of the window, you can choose from:

▶ **Repeat All** Plays whatever is in the Song List around and around forever.

▶ **Repeat One** Plays one track around and around forever.

▶ **Shuffle** Plays back whatever is on the Song List in random order.

Alternatively, choose **Party Shuffle** from the Sources list on the left. This generates a random mix of tracks drawn from either a playlist or your entire Library. When you hit the icon, a new panel appears where you can set parameters for how the list looks and where the tracks are drawn from, though you can also add selections from anywhere in your Library by dragging them onto the Party Shuffle icon in the Sources list.

Tip: When a song is playing but you've browsed elsewhere, use the SnapBack arrow in the right of the status window to reveal the track currently playing.

You can access a menu of the most useful iTunes controls by clicking and holding the mouse over the iTunes icon on the OS X Dock.

View modes

One of the best additions to iTunes in recent years were the three view modes, accessible via the View menu or using the set of buttons next to the Search box.

▶ **List View** presents your music, video, podcasts and so on as a sortable list with many columns. You can sort the list by any column by clicking on the header of that column. Click a second time and the order is reversed. To add new columns and remove others, either summon the View Options box from the Edit menu or use the keyboard shortcuts ⌘J. Alternatively, try right-clicking the header of any of the columns to reveal a dropdown menu of columns.

Tip: You can jump to a particular point in the list by pressing a letter or number: if you sort by artist and press "R", say, you might jump to The Rolling Stones.

▶ **Album View** works just list List View, except that no matter how you sort the list, the tracks are bound together within their respective albums, complete with album artwork where available.

▶ **Cover Flow View** Cover Flow view is a superb feature, allowing you to flick through your music collection by album artwork. It's like rummaging through an old stack of LPs, or browsing in a record store. You browse using the on-screen scroll bar or the left and right arrows on the keyboard. Tap Enter or double-click a cover to start playing.

Adding artwork

Both Cover Flow and Front Row are pretty dull unless your iTunes library is well stocked with album artwork. iTunes will grab a lot of artwork automatically, leaving you to find those it misses online; they can then be added manually.

▶ Select one or more tracks and drag or paste an image into the iTunes Artwork panel, revealed using the ▲ button below the Sources area.

▶ Select a track and choose **File > Get Info > Artwork > Add...**

▶ Select multiple tracks, choose **File > Get Info** and double-click the white **Artwork** box.

Most sleeves can be found online via a Google Image Search. However, bear the following in mind:

▶ When searching with Google, don't use the thumbnail; click through to the full-sized version.

▶ Try to find images at least 300x300 pixels. Google displays dimensions below its thumbnail previews.

Front Row

Front Row is OS X's full-screen media-player mode. You can use Front Row to access music and video from your iTunes library, play DVDs, browse your iPhoto collection – even to access online movie trailers.

The system is designed to be used with a remote control. However, if you have an older Mac without a remote, you can use the following keyboard shortcuts. Combined with a wireless keyboard this can be almost as useful.

⌘↺ Show and hide Front Row
↑ **and** ↓ Scroll through menus
⌥↑ **and** ⌥↓ Adjust volume level
Enter or Space Select/play/pause/resume
↺ Back to previous menu or screen

Combining multiple computers with Front Row and an AirPort Express (see p.67) can allow you to control your music in many different ways. For example, you might have an iMac in the study which houses your iTunes Library. If you enable iTunes sharing (from the **Sharing** pane of iTunes Preferences), you could access this collection via Front Row on a Mac laptop in the kitchen and have the music streamed to a pair of speakers in any room you like via an AirPort Express.

Browse & search

Though some people use iTunes for months without ever noticing it, the Browser is a very important feature, allowing you to see tracks arranged by genre, artist and album. To open Browser, enter List View or Album View and hit ⌘B. The Browser panel that appears automatically includes Artist and Album columns; if you also want a Genre column, visit the **General** pane of **iTunes Preferences**.

The Search box, on the right-hand side at the top of the iTunes environment, lets you find a track by typing all or part of the name of the artist, album, track title, grouping or composer. You can search more than one field at once, so typing **Whi Elep**, for example, would bring up The White Stripes' *Elephant*. To limit your search to artists, albums or genres, use the triangle dropdown menu.

Note that iTunes will only search those tracks currently displayed in the main window. So if you want to search your whole collection, make sure that the Library icon is selected in the Sources area before you start to type.

Deleting music

To delete music in iTunes, first click **Music** in the Sources list (as deleting tracks from a playlist does not really delete them). Then select one or more tracks, artists, genres or albums and…

▶ **Hit Backspace** on your keyboard.

▶ **Select Clear** from the iTunes **Edit** menu.

▶ **Right-click** and select **Clear** from the context menu.

▶ **Drag** the selections straight to the Trash.

Hit the green button to turn iTunes into a mini player.

Deleting from a Pod

Many new iPod users have spent hours trying to delete unwanted music from their Pod. The solution is simple: you do it via iTunes…

▶ Delete a track from iTunes and the next time you connect your iPod, it will disappear from there, too.

▶ If you want a track in iTunes but not on the Pod uncheck the box next to its name in iTunes and choose **Only update checked songs** in iPod Preferences.

▶ If you don't want to uncheck the songs (since this will stop them playing in iTunes), choose to manually manage the iPod's contents to take more direct control over what gets transferred to your iPod.

Playlists

A key feature of any computer jukebox software is the ability to create playlists: homemade combinations of tracks for playing on your computer or iPod; for burning to CD; for sending to friends; or even for publishing online. The first thing to understand about playlists is that they don't actually contain any music. All they contain is a list of pointers to tracks within your Library. This means you can delete playlists, and individual tracks within them, without deleting the actual music files; likewise, you can add the same track to as many playlists as you like without using up extra disk space.

Creating & editing playlists

To create a new playlist, hit the "+" button at the bottom of the iTunes window or press ⌘N. Give the new playlist a name, click on Music in the Sources area, and drag tracks onto the playlist's icon. You can also create a new playlist by dragging songs, artists, albums or genres directly into some blank space at the bottom of the Sources area – iTunes will even try to name it for you.

You can sort the contents of a playlist automatically by clicking the top of the columns in the Song list. Or, to arrange them manually, first sort by the number column (by clicking at the top of that column) and then drag the tracks around at will. To delete tracks from a playlist, simply select them and press backspace – this *won't* delete them from your Library.

Smart Playlists

Smart Playlists are just like normal playlists but, rather than being compiled manually by you, iTunes does the work on your behalf, collecting all tracks in your Library that fulfil a set of rules, or

Tip: Adjust the iTunes volume level using the keyboard shortcuts ⌘↑ and ⌘↑, and mute the program with ⌘⌥↓.

To rename a playlist, click its name once and then again. To delete one, highlight it and press backspace – or drag the icon into the Trash.

Smart Playlist ideas

Smart Playlists give you the opportunity to be creative with the way you organize the songs in your Library; they can be both a lot of fun and very useful. So much so, in fact, that there are whole websites devoted to the subject (such as smartplaylists.com). Following are a few examples to give you an idea of the kind of things you can do:

Functional...

Tracks you haven't heard
> Play Count is 0
All the music you've ripped or downloaded but not yet played.

On the up
> Date Added is in the last 30 days
> My Rating is greater than 3 stars
> Play Count is less than 5
A playlist of new songs that you like, but which deserve more of a listen.

The old Johanna
> Grouping contains piano
If you use Grouping or Comment fields to tag tracks by instrument, mood or anything else, you can then create Smart Playlists based on this info.

...or inspirational

Compilation of questions
> Song Name contains "?"
For days with no answers.

Space songs
> Song Name contains "space"
> Song Name contains "stars"
> Song Name contains "moon"
> Song Name contains "rocket"
For those who love their sci-fi as much as their music.

Tip: iTunes probably came with a few Smart Playlists labelled "60's Music", "My Top Rated", etc. Don't be scared to delete them.

Tip: If you want more space in your Sources area for playlists, consider hiding the icons for the Music Store, Party Shuffle, etc. You'll find these options under **General** and **Store** in **iTunes Preferences**. Also try using folders (**File > New Folder**) to organize your playlists within the Sources area.

Tip: If one song in a playlist is recorded more quietly than the next, select it, choose **File > Get Info** and use the **Volume Adjustment** tool in the **Options** pane.

"conditions", that you define. It might be songs that have a certain word in their title, or a set of genres, or the tracks you listen to the most – or a combination of any of these kind of things. A Smart Playlist's contents will automatically change over time, as relevant tracks are added to your Library or existing tracks meet the criteria – by being, say, rated highly.

To create a new Smart Playlist, look in the **File** menu or hold down ⌥ and click the "cog" button at the bottom of the iTunes window. Next, select your parameters in the Smart Playlist box, clicking "+" and "–" to add and remove rules. It's a bit like a bizarre kind of musical algebra. To edit the rules of an existing Smart Playlist, select it and choose **Edit Smart Playlist** from the **File** menu.

And then…

So you've created a dream playlist, and it's just too good to keep all to yourself. What next? You could:

▶ **Burn it to CD** Insert a blank CD into your Mac, select the playlist and click the **Burn Disc** button.

▶ **Design the artwork** Highlight a playlist and select **File > Print** (⌘P). A box will pop up offering you options for printing the track details as either a regular document or an insert for a CD jewel case. This is all very handy, but rather limiting artistically. Another option is to hit **File > Export Playlist…** and export the track names as a text document, and then paste them into another program that will allow you more creativity over the cover.

▶ **Publish it as an iMix** on the iTunes Music Store for others to admire. Select the playlist and choose **File > Create an iMix**.

▶ **Send it to us,** using the address playlists@roughguides.com, and we might just publish it in the next edition of *The Rough Guide Book of Playlists*.

Extra tools

There are a number of third-party tools and scripts that can help you create CD covers. For example, the free iTunes Publisher (available from trancesoftware.com) lets you export playlists in various formats, including tabbed text and HTML. Or try the useful "Playlist to papercdcase.com" script from Doug's AppleScripts For iTunes: dougscripts.com

Radio & podcasts

iTunes offers access to a number of radio streams (hit the **Radio** icon in the Sources area) but it's a pretty feeble selection compared with what you can access with RealPlayer and an online radio directory:

RealPlayer real.com
About Radio radio.about.com

Much more interesting is the podcast option. Unlike most online radio, which is streamed across the Net in real time, podcasts are audio "shows" made available as downloadable files, ready to listen to in iTunes or transfer to an iPod. Podcasts are usually free and often consist of spoken content (current affairs, poetry, etc). There are many musical podcasts, too, though there's a grey area surrounding the distribution of copyrighted music in this way.

It's usually possible to download an individual podcast "show" directly from the website of whoever produced it, but the idea is to use iTunes (or some other "aggregator") to subscribe to podcasts that you're interested in. iTunes will then automatically download any new episodes at regular intervals, so you always have fresh news, debates, poems, music and more.

To start subscribing, click **Podcasts** in the Sources area and hit the **Podcast Directory** link at the bottom. When you find one that looks like it might float your boat, hit **Subscribe**. Then return to the podcasts icon in the Sources area to find your downloaded shows. While you're there, click **Settings...** to choose how you'd like iTunes to deal with old episodes and how often it should check for new ones.

> **Tip:** Unplayed podcast episodes appear in iTunes with a blue dot next to them, and the total number of unplayed episodes in your library is displayed in the Sources area.

Using an iPod

By default, an iPod will automatically synchronize itself with your iTunes Library, making an exact match of all your songs and playlists whenever you connect. However, there are alternatives…

▶ **Automatically update selected…** If you connect the iPod and look under the various tabs of the Options panel, you can customize exactly which portions of your iTunes library you want in your pocket. This is useful if you have an iPod without the capacity to hold your whole collection; you want to save time when updating your iPod; or you're using multiple iPods with a single copy of iTunes (each user can choose what they want and don't want).

▶ **Manually manage music and videos** This option, found within the Summary tab of the iPod Options panel, gives you complete control over the contents of your iPod – you update your Pod by dragging tracks, albums, playlists, TV shows, videos, genres, etc, from the iTunes Library onto the iPod icon.

If you manually manage your iPod, you'll have to "eject" it on screen each time you want to physically disconnect it. Either click the ⏏ next to its icon, or drag it to the trash.

Copying iPod to iTunes

Regardless of which syncing option you use, updating an iPod is a one-way process – you copy from iTunes to iPod rather than the other way around. To import media from iPod to a Mac, you'll need some special software, such as:

iPodRip thelittleappfactory.com ($15)

Recording sound & making music

28

Though the two activities overlap, recording sound and making music on a Mac can be two very different things. One involves using audio recording software to get sound in from a hi-fi (for getting vinyl into iTunes, for example) or a microphone (for making podcasts, recording voice memos, and so on). The other usually involves "multitracking" layers of recorded and synthesized sounds with the aim of creating professional-sounding songs and other compositions. This chapter provides a whistlestop introduction to both areas.

Recording from mic or hi-fi

All Macs purchased in the last couple of years will have a line-in or mic socket, which will allow you to connect it to a microphone or hi-fi. However, some discontinued models, such as the iBook and first-generation Mac minis, lack this socket, so you'll need to purchase a simple external audio interface (see p.222) before you can get started. Once that's taken care of, follow these steps…

Macs & mics

All recent Macs except the Mac Mini and the Mac Pro have an internal microphone – fine for recording voice memos but not exactly hi-fidelity. An external mic will provide better quality; USB models are easily added to any Mac, while minijack mics can be plugged into Macs with audio line-in sockets or external audio adapters (see p.222). Some webcams and all VoIP phones also have built-in mics that can be set as the system-wide default audio input device within **System Preferences > Sound**.

record sound & make music

Recording software

Apple's own GarageBand can be used for basic audio recording. You probably already have it, so you may want to give it a go first. However, GarageBand is primarily a multitracking tool, so you might prefer the clean look and feel, and the extra tools, of a dedicated recording and editing tool. The obvious choice is the free Audacity, a great little program with loads of built-in effects. Grab it from:

audacity.sourceforge.net

Another option is CD Spin Doctor, ($39), which is designed for recording and "cleaning up" audio from vinyl, cassette and other analogue media. Find out more here:

roxio.com/enu/products/spindoctor

Perhaps the simplest option, however, is the completely idiot-proof Voice Candy ($13), available from:

potionfactory.com

For scores more audio editors, noise removers and other recording software, drop in to:

apple.com/downloads/macosx/audio

▶ **Stage 1: Hooking up** If you're recording from a microphone, attach it to your Mac or audio interface. If you're recording from a hi-fi, look on its back for a pair of RCA sockets labelled "Line Out" or "Tape Out" and run a cable from there to your Mac or audio interface (usually, the required cable will be an RCA-to-minijack, available inexpensively from any hi-fi shop). If your hi-fi doesn't feature a line-out or tape-out, you could connect it to your Mac via its headphone socket, though this isn't ideal. Finally, check that the correct device is selected as your Mac's sound input source.

▶ **Stage 2: Check your disk space** During the actual recording process, you'll need plenty of hard drive space: around 15MB per minute. (Once you've finished recording, you can convert the music that you've recorded into a space-efficient format such as MP3 or AAC, and delete the giant original.)

▶ **Stage 3: Choose some software** Recording from analogue sources requires an audio recording application. You may already have something suitable on your Mac, such as GarageBand, but there are scores of excellent programs available to download (see box, left).

▶ **Stage 4: Recording** The details from here on in vary according to which program you're running and the source you're recording from, but roughly speaking the procedure is the same. When you create a new file and press "record", you'll be asked to specify a few parameters about the sound quality. The defaults – usually 44.1kHz, 16-bit stereo – should be fine. Hit the red button, start recording and use the "stop" button when you're done.

▶ **Stage 5: Tidy up the sound** A graphic wave form will appear on the screen. Use the "cut" tool to tidy up any extraneous noise or blank space from the beginning and end of the file, and the fade tool to hide the "cuts". If your audio editor offers hiss and crackle filters, try them. However, don't go clean-up mad: removing hiss and crackle is good, but over-processed sound can seem sterile and cold to the ear.

▶ **Stage 6: Normalize** If there's a "normalize" function you could also use this to maximize the level without distorting it. This will ensure that, if you record tracks from various old vinyl discs, for example, they will all end up sounding roughly the same volume.

▶ **Stage 7: Save the file** Save the audio in either WAV or AIFF format and drag the resulting file into iTunes. To add it to your iPod (or simply to save space on your Mac), convert the file into AAC or MP3, via the **Advanced** menu, and consider backing up and deleting the original.

Multitracking

Multitracking means mixing and editing several separate audio recordings ("tracks") in one piece of music. The tracks might be the various members of a band, recorded simultaneously; they might be multiple takes of a single player or singer; or they might even be samples grabbed from CDs and vinyl, triggered from an electronic keyboard. But whatever they contain, each track can be individually chopped and changed, made louder and softer, and generally

> **Tip:** You should aim to get as high a level as possible without causing the little metre to "peak" (go into the red). Try to get this right using the recording-level slider *before* you start to play or speak.

> **Tip:** For a dedicated noise reduction application, try SoundSoap, available from bias-inc.com
>
> And for cleaning up recordings from shellac or vinyl, try ClickRepair: wwwmaths.anu.edu.au/~briand/sound

> **Tip:** If you find that your Mac struggles to play more than a few tracks at once, browse **System Preferences > Energy Saver** and from the Optimization dropdown menu, choose **Better Performance**.

played around with. Multitracking was pioneered back in the early 1950s by guitarist Les Paul and today almost every piece of popular music we hear is created in this manner – but on computers rather than reel-to-reel tape.

To start multitracking on your Mac, all you need is the right software and, if you want to record live sound from "real" instruments and singers, a microphone connected to your Mac (its built-in mic just won't cut the mustard). If you want to be able to record mul-

Tip: Some audio interfaces override the Mac's system volume control and recording level, instead providing a special mixer utility that allows you to make use of the multiple inputs and outputs.

Audio interfaces

You can add all kinds of sound connections to your Mac with an external audio interface. These plug in to your Mac via USB or FireWire, and carry a selection of input and output sockets; they take care of the conversion of analogue sound into digital data, and vice versa, in effect acting as an "external soundcard". This can not only result in improved sound quality, but it also relieves your Mac of some processing duties – which reduces the chances of glitches when recording and playing back lots of tracks simultaneously.

Audio interfaces range from simple devices such as Griffin's iMic ($39/£30), which provides basic line and mic sockets, to more professional units, such as M-Audio's FireWire 410 (pictured; $500/£300). These higher-end units typically feature studio-quality sockets, such as balanced phantom-powered XLR inputs for connecting professional microphones and MIDI ports (see opposite). Most also let you record multiple inputs simultaneously – essential for capturing a band session, for example – and come bundled with multitracking software.

iMic griffintechnology.com
FireWire 410 m-audio.com

For details and reviews of other models, visit:

PC Music Guru pc-music.com
SilentWay.com silentway.com/tips

tiple musicians or singers simultaneously, you'll need an appropriate audio interface (see opposite).

Finally, you might want to invest in a MIDI keyboard. You can get by without one and use your computer keyboard, or a clickable on-screen keyboard. But having a "real" keyboard is far preferable – especially if you already have a few basic piano skills.

Multitracking software

Among Mac owners, the most widely used multitracking application, or "sequencer", is Apple's own GarageBand. This is part of the iLife suite included with all new Macs, so you probably already have it; if not, iLife is available to buy for $79/£55. GarageBand is so fantastically easy to use that it makes an ideal choice for anyone just starting out with multitracking. Overleaf you'll find a brief tutorial on how to use it.

GarageBand isn't the only option, however. If you get seriously into music-making on your Mac, at some stage you'll want to check out a more serious sequencing package. Some of the industry standard applications – such as DigiDesign's Pro Tools – can only be purchased along with an expensive audio interface. However, others, such as Apple's Logic Pro and Steinberg's Cubase, are available as standalone applications. The full versions are expensive, but both are available in cut-down versions. Logic Express, for example, sells for roughly $200/£130, and Cubase SE costs around half that. To find out more, visit:

Logic apple.com/logic
Cubase steinberg.net
Pro Tools digidesign.com
PC Music Guru pc-music.com

MIDI instruments

MIDI (Musical Instrument Digital Interface) is a protocol that allows keyboards, drum machines and other electronic musical instruments to talk to one another – and to computers. Traditionally, MIDI instruments are connected to computers via MIDI cables (pictured below) but today some keyboards connect via USB. This is much more convenient, since you can't attach MIDI cables to your Mac without purchasing a suitable MIDI adapter (or an audio interface that features MIDI sockets).

For most home musicians, MIDI's primary use is to connect a keyboard, which you can then use to trigger (play) software instruments and samples stored on your Mac. However, MIDI works in both directions, and can also be used to give your Mac control over synths, drum machines or other MIDI instruments.

GarageBand

Recording podcasts

Fancy trying your hand at broadcasting? If so, why not use GarageBand to create a podcast? For more info, see p.189 or visit: apple.com/support/garageband/podcasts

Tip: To change the overall tempo, key and time signature of an existing song, double-click the Master Track; if you can't see it, hit ⌘B or look in the **Track** menu.

Like other competing packages, GarageBand allows you to record and edit layers of "real" sounds and "software instruments" (see box). What sets it apart is its foolproof user-friendly interface and its incorporation of "Apple Loops" – riffs, rhythms and sound effects that you can simply drag and drop into your songs. GarageBand takes care of the details such as making sure the loops you're using are all in the same key and playing at the same tempo, so absolutely no musical training is required to create something basic.

Following is a quick run through of how you might construct a song in GarageBand. It's certainly not comprehensive and neither is it prescriptive – if you're a musician, you may find Apple Loops appallingly limiting, and prefer to work from scratch.

Creating a backing track using loops

Launch GarageBand from **Applications** (or the Dock) and create a new song, or "project", when prompted. Pick a tempo, key and time signature if you like; otherwise go with the defaults. You can change them later if necessary using the Master Track settings (see Tip, left).

Your project will probably include a track for a grand piano. Ignore this for now and click on the eye button near the bottom-left (or hit ⌘L) to reveal the loop browser panel. Use the various category buttons and view options to browse what's on offer, clicking individual loops in the right-hand column to hear them. When you find something you like, drag it up into some empty grey space in the upper part of the window. A new track will appear, containing a coloured "region" of music. To extend it – for example to loop a rhythm throughout the duration of your song – hold your mouse pointer over its right-hand end and drag the region out to whatever length you need.

Keep adding more loops – drums, bass, guitar or whatever – until you've built-up a convincing backing track.

To quickly change the tempo of your song, select the "metronome" icon LCD mode and click the displayed tempo to reveal a slider control.

Real & software instruments

A key concept in GarageBand is the disinction between "real" and "software" instruments. Every chunk of sound falls into one of these two categories – including non-instrumental lines such as vocals. You can distinguish real and "soft" sections at a glance: real ones bear soundwaves, while soft ones look more like pianola rolls (see right). Each track deals exclusively with either software or real instruments.

Real instruments include anything you record via a microphone or a hi-fi and Apple Loops based on recorded snippets (a wah-wah-style guitar riff, for instance).

Software instruments, by contrast, are virtual pianos, drumkits, violins, and so on. You can play them using a MIDI or on-screen keyboard, or drag in loops based on software-instrument sounds. Either way, the "music" is essentially just a set of marks on a grid that instruct the computer to play particular notes at particular times. As such, you can change and delete individual notes, swap the instrument playing the passage, transpose the section between keys with no change in sound quality, and even view the passage in traditional musical notation.

When you're browsing for loops, the ones based on real instruments have a blue icon, and the ones based on software instruments have a green icon.

Real-instrument regions display the soundwave of the recording (top), while software-instrument regions display dots and dashes that repre-sent the individual notes (bottom).

Tip: To delete a track, select it and choose **Delete** from the **Track** menu (or press ⌘ ⌫).

Recording software instruments

You should have an empty **Grand Piano** track at the top of the
screen. If you'd rather pick a different instrument, either double-
click the piano's name or add a separate track using the "+" button
at the bottom-left of the window.

You can play your instrument of choice either with the on-screen
keyboard (⌘K), your computer keyboard (⌘⇧K shows you which
letter-keys are which notes), or a connected MIDI keyboard,
which you can set up in the **Audio/MIDI** pane of GarageBand's
Preferences (⌘,).

When you're ready to lay something down, make sure the relevant
track is enabled for recording by pressing the little red button below
its name. Then press the record button on the main GarageBand
control strip and start playing. When you're done, hit the ▶ button
– or your keyboard's spacebar – and a series of marks will appear
on the track, each representing a note that
you played.

To edit the notes you just recorded, double-click the relevant segment of music
– or select it and press the scissors button.
Play around with the notes in the grid view
and, if you like, hit the musical-note button
to see what your playing looks like in traditional musical notation. Play around with
the tools and buttons in both views to get a
sense of what's possible.

Recording "real" vocals or instruments

To get some homemade sounds into GarageBand, attach a mic or instrument to your Mac's line-in socket or audio interface. If you're recording an electric guitar, don't connect it directly to the Mac: plug it into a normal guitar amp and take a line out from there (or simply mic-up the amp).

Next, click the big "+" button (or use the shortcut ⌘⌥N) and choose to create a **New Real Instrument Track**. This also reveals the **Track Info** panel to the right where you can select the instrument you are going to record. If your instrument isn't there, choose **Basic Track**. The right-hand column offers various "styles", which add effects and EQs to the track. Note that the style isn't set in stone: you can switch off or change it at any time by double-clicking the track's title – or by selecting it and hitting the **Info** button (⌘I).

When you're ready to record, follow the same red-button procedure as before and hit the spacebar when you're done. A wave form will appear in the track to represent the sound you've recorded.

Double-click the newly recorded segment to open it in the wave editor. Here you can cut, copy and paste sections of wave (look in the Edit menu or use the standard shortcuts), tweak the tuning and tempo of a particular section, or change the overall pitch of the track. Have a tinker – if you make a mistake you can always go back a stage by pressing **Edit > Undo** (or hitting ⌘Z).

Tip: GarageBand's input/output settings work independently of OS X's. So set up devices and audio interfaces in the application's **Preferences**, not **System Preferences**.

Tip: When recording with a microphone, use headphones to "monitor" what's going on. Otherwise you might end up recording feedback, and the sound from the speakers will "leak" into the microphone.

Tip: Click **Details** in the Track Info panel to fine tune EQ settings and add additional effects. If you find the options overwhelming, plonk for the easy-to-use **Visual EQ** tool – to lauch it, check the tick box and then click the ⊘ button.

Tip: You can also import whole audio files (AIFF, WAV, AAC, Apple Lossless and MP3 formats) into your song by dragging them from Finder or iTunes directly into the GarageBand window.

Tip: You can temporarily silence a track, play it "solo" and lock it to avoid accidental changes using the row of buttons below its name.

iControl

If you get seriously into GarageBand, you may find that the humble mouse and keyboard are inadequate tools for music production. If so, check out M-Audio's iControl, which puts GarageBand controls – such as volume, pan, sends and effects – right under your fingers, and also features MIDI ports for connecting a keyboard or drum machine.

Mixing

Once you've assembled all the basic components of your track, it's time to get everything to work together. Obviously enough, you can cut, copy and paste segments of music, drag them around and delete them (by selecting them and pressing the backspace key). But mixing a song is not just about content – it's about fine-tuning volume levels and subtly "panning" tracks to the left or right side of the stereo spectrum – ie towards the left or right speakers.

You can change the overall level and pan for each track using its virtual knob and slider. But if you'd like to alter a track's volume over time, click the downward-facing arrow button to create a volume "envelope". Click points on the line and drag them about to plot the volume "shape" you'd like.

To create fade-ins and -outs for the whole song, open the master track (⌘B) and use the same technique.

Export your song

In the Share menu you'll find options for exporting your track to iTunes, iWeb, iDVD and for burning a CD. If you are sending the song to iTunes, next choose an artist name that you'd like to use, which iTunes playlist you'd like the song added to, and so on. You can also choose whether to create an MP3 or AAC file (see p.206) and the audio quality setting of the mix you are creating. If you want to save space or email it

Getting more loops and instruments

GarageBand comes with a good selection of loops and instruments, but before long you may be hungering for more. Apple sells a selection of so-called Jam Packs, ranging from "Remix Tools" to "Symphony Orchestra". Each one costs $99/£65 and contains more than 2000 royalty-free loops as well as numerous software instruments.

Jam Packs apple.com/jampacks

.Mac members (see p.34) can get hold of a bunch of free loops from the various Jam Packs. You'll find them in your iDisk under Software > Members Only.

But you don't have to get your loops from Apple – the Net is swimming in them and some are available for free. Start here:

Samples4 samples4.com
Mac Idol macidol.com
Mac Audio Guy macaudioguy.com
PowerFX powerfx.com

To import purchased or downloaded loops and instruments into GarageBand, simply drag them into the Loops Browser. If you're given a choice, add them to your Apple Loops Library to keep things tidy. Once the loops are installed there, you can delete or archive the original source files.

Creating loops

It's easy to turn a track that you've played or recorded into a loop. Simply select a "region" and choose **Add To Loop Library...** from the **Edit** menu.

to a friend, convert using the Good Quality setting, otherwise go with the default High Quality setting. You could even share your creation with other Mac music-makers online at:

Mac Idol macidol.com
iCompositions icompositions.com

Tip: If you're struggling to get GarageBand to do as you please, visit Apple's support site for tips and troubleshooting advice: apple.com/support/garageband

Kids' music software

Though you'll probably find that your kids take to a program such as GarageBand quicker than you do, there are also a number of packages available tailored especially for young Mozart wannabies. KidsSynth is just that, while Musicus cunningly disguises some basic note-duration theory within a Tetris-like game.

KidsSynth web.sfc.keio.ac.jp/ ~masuda/ks
Musicus ecsmedia.com

More music software

Besides the multitrack and recording applications already mentioned in this chapter, there are thousands of additional packages, plug-ins and software instruments out there. These range from analogue-modelling soft synths and Moog emulators (Minimonsta) to drum machines (Doggiebox) and notation applications (Sibelius).

Minimonsta arturia.com
Doggiebox doggiebox.com
Sibelius sibelius.com

Confused by BPMs? Download the Audio Calculator widget from: widgets.lensco.be/work/69

▼

And that's only the tip of the iceberg. For even more OS X audio software, drop in to:

HitSquad hitsquad.com/smm/mac
Pure-Mac pure-mac.com/music.html
OS X Downloads apple.com/downloads/macosx/audio

Pictures

Image basics

Whether you want to accrue a weighty digital photo library, "draw" pictures from scratch, or prepare an image for online use, it pays to spend a bit of time getting your head around the basics of digital images: pixels, file formats, compression and the various software packages. This chapter takes a look at all these things, as well as providing a brief run-through of the various options for downloading, creating and importing pictures. To learn about managing your pictures in iPhoto, turn to p.242.

Load up with pics

There are many ways to create an image on your Mac, and many ways to import pics from external sources such as webcams, websites, scanners – even mobile phones. Here's a quick look at how to get images from…

▶ **Digital cameras** It's easy to import pics from a digital camera – you probably won't even need to install the software that came with the camera. For more on downloading images from your digital camera, turn to our iPhoto chapter (see p.242),

▶ **The Web** If you see an image online that you want, perhaps to use as your desktop background or to email to a friend, simply click the image and drag it from the browser window onto either the desktop or an open Finder

A pixel primer

Most of the images that you'll come across on your computer, including anything you import from a camera or scanner, or grab from a webpage, are so-called "raster" images, which means they're made up of thousands of individual dots known as pixels. From a computer's perspective, such an image is essentially just a database that specifies the hue and shade of each pixel.

The "size" of a raster image is most commonly expressed in terms of its dimensions: for example, an image might be 1500 x 1000 (1500 dots wide and 1000 dots tall). However, when you're shopping for a digital camera, its maximum-quality setting is described in terms of the total number of pixels in the image. Expressed this way, our 1500 x 1000 image would be said to be 1.5 megapixels (because 1500 x 1000 = 1,500,000 pixels, and "mega" means one million).

It probably goes without saying that the more pixels an image contains, the better it can look. However, images of any size can be poor quality. It might have been taken on a low-quality camera, for example, or been ruined by being heavily compressed.

So how do pixels relate to "real" measurements such as inches and centimetres? On screen, when the image is viewed at 100 percent size, each of its pixels will take up one pixel on the screen, so the "real" size depends entirely on the resolution setting of your monitor. The higher the screen resolution, the smaller the image will appear. It's possible to zoom in and out on an image to make it take up more or less of the screen, but only at 100 percent will it look perfect.

When you're printing a picture, you're usually give the option of scaling the image up or down to make it fit as you want on the page. But the professional way to deal with print size it to specify the image resolution – the number of dots per inch (dpi) – using a program such as Photoshop. If we took our 1500 x 1000 pixel image and set the resolution to 100dpi, for example, the resulting print would be 15 x 10 inches. The higher the dpi, the better the quality, but the smaller the image. In the real world, images for Web and screen use are usually saved at 72dpi; images for printing are usually saved at 300dpi.

window. Easy. Alternatively, right-click the image and choose **Save Image As…** from the context menu to save the pic to a particular location. Note, however, that online images are usually relatively low quality, because they've been scaled down and compressed so they will download faster (see p.185 for more on this).

▶ **Flatbed scanners** You can import a copy of a photograph, magazine page or drawing – just about anything two-dimensional – into your computer with a scanner. These are inexpensive, and work a bit like photocopiers, except that instead of printing, they send a digital image directly to your computer, usually via a USB cable. The software that comes with scanners is generally pretty easy to use, though scanning can also be handled, somewhat cumbersomely, from OS X's Image Capture program. Open it from the Applications folder, browse for your scanner from the Device menu – it should be under the TWAIN device submenu. Check the Use TWAIN software box, and then click OK. Return to the Device menu, select your scanner, have a play with the options, and start scanning.

▶ **Bluetooth mobile phone** Most mobile phones these days take photographs, and they are easy enough to transfer wirelessly to your Mac – assuming both devices have Bluetooth capabilities. First, pair your Mac and phone (as described on p.54), trigger your image transfers from the mobile

Tip: Google Image Search offers an easy way to fish for images online; use the size options to filter out pics that may be too small for your needs and be sure to grab the full size version of the image, not the thumbnail preview offered on the search page.

Google images.google.com

Tip: Image Capture can also be used to automate image imports from other devices, such as digital cameras and Bluetooth phones.

and then wait for the Incoming File Transfer dialog box. If you are not sure where the image has been dumped, click the little magnifying glass icon to reveal the file in Finder.

▶ **Screen grabs** A screen grab is a snapshot of whatever is on your screen, or in a particular window, at a specific moment. They can be useful for everything from capturing a weird error, in order to send it to someone for troubleshooting advice, or to quickly capture the information displaying on one or more windows in a format that anyone will be able to open. They are especially useful if you want to capture a whole webpage rather than just a single image. The shortcut ⌘⇧3 will deposit a snap of your Mac's screen onto the desktop in the PNG or PDF format, but there's more to screen grabs than that (see box, left).

▶ **Photo Booth** OS X comes bundled with this little application that can be used to take snaps (and video clips) using either your Mac's built-in iSight camera (if it has one) or a compatible USB webcam. As well as regular shots, there are a bunch of mildly diverting special effects and options to send the images you create to iPhoto or attach them to an email.

▶ **iChat** You can also copy a still image from either an iSight or other webcam by pressing ⌘C when in iChat. This image can then be pasted (⌘V) into another application or location.

▶ **From scratch** Talent permitting, you could create images on your computer with drawing software (see opposite) or, at a push, using a photo editing program that features pencil and brush tools, such as Gimp or Photoshop (see p.249).

Drawing programs

Though it's possible to create pictures from scratch using an image-editing tool such as Photoshop (see p.249), it's certainly not ideal. Such programs are really designed for editing pixel-based images that already exist, so the tools they provide are essentially clever ways of tampering with one or more pixels simultaneously.

Instead, it's far easier to use a so-called "vector"-based drawing program that, instead of pixels, lets you work with editable lines and shapes. Once you're finished, you can export the image in a standard pixel-based format such as JPEG (see p.185) and treat it just like any other image – import it into iPhoto, email it, and so on. But you can also save the vector-based version so you can easily edit the shapes, lines, text and colours later.

The industry-standard drawing program is Adobe's Illustrator, which is part of the Creative Suite package. It's a great program, but costs big bucks and has more features than even professionals are likely to master in a lifetime. Just getting the basics right takes quite a while.

Illustrator adobe.com/illustrator ($600)

A more digestible and wallet-friendly alternative is iDraw, which features all the basic shape-drawing tools of Illustrator and lets you export your work in various different file formats.

iDraw macpoweruser.com ($40)

Also worth downloading is the open-source Inkscape application – it features loads of advanced features and, best of all, is completely free to download and use.

Inkscape inkscape.org (Free)

For something far more basic, try Tuxpaint, one of the many drawing applications aimed at kids. It's not particularly pretty, and deals in pixels rather than vectors, but it's extremely easy to use and gets the job done. If you've ever used Windows Paint, this is a bit like a Mac equivalent.

Tuxpaint newbreedsoftware.com/tuxpaint (Free)

Tip: If you want to try your hand at 3D architectural modelling, or just want to reconfigure your household furniture without the backache, download the brilliant, free, Google-owned SketchUp from sketchup.com.

Formats & compression

In the same way that there are various types of music file (MP3, AAC) and document file (DOC, TXT, etc), there is a wide range of image file formats, each of which has its own advantages and disadvantages.

Most of the images you'll come across will be in compressed formats. These use some very clever, behind-the-scenes mathematics to considerably reduce the size of the file (in terms of bytes, not dimensions) while only marginally reducing the quality. That said, over-compressed images look terrible, so when saving one, you need to strike a balance between quality and file size. Compressed formats include:

▶ **JPEG (Joint Photographic Experts Group)** *File extension: .jpg*
The most common picture format of all, JPEG is the default file type for most digital cameras, and for photographs used on the Web. When you save a JPEG, you can choose from a sliding scale of compression.

▶ **GIF (Graphics Interchange Format)** *File extension: .gif*
Also widely used on webpages, the GIF is best suited to images with large areas of flat colour (usually graphics rather than photographs). It also allows slide-show-style animations and transparent backgrounds – both widely used online.

▶ **PNG (Portable Network Graphics)** *File extension: .png*
PNG is a superior alternative to GIF, due to its fancy transparency abilities, and JPEG, though it's less widely used as less software supports it. Mac users are most likely to encounter PNGs when creating screen grabs (see p.236).

You may also come across some non-compressed formats, especially if you get seriously into digital photography or image editing. The most common are:

If you are unsure what format a file is, select its icon in Finder and hit ⌘I to call up the Info panel.

A word about colour

Macs have long been favoured in the print and publishing industries, partly because of their excellent ability to manage colours. OS X features the most advanced colour-managment systems of any operating system, which means that, on a day-to-day basis, the colours your camera or scanner capture should be very close to the colours you see on screen and in turn the colours that are churned out by your printer.

A digital image can contain millions of colours, but each of those various hues and shades is made up of a mixture of three primary colours. In painting, that's red, yellow and blue, but on computer screens it's Red, Green and Blue (RGB) – the so-called "additive" primaries. If you want to know the exact RGB value of any colour on screen, perhaps to recreate a nice shade you've seen on a website, open the DigitalColor Meter from **Applications > Utilities** or play with the colour picking tool (the little magnifying glass) under the **Calculator** tab of **ColorSync** (also in **Applications > Utilities**).

Occasionally, you might come across images saved in CMYK rather than RGB mode. CMYK images don't look any different, but they're processed differently by the computer. Here, each colour is defined as a combination of the so-called "subtractive" primaries: cyan, magenta and yellow (the opposites of RGB), with black (traditionally known as "key" in printing, hence the "K") added to provide extra clarity in darker colours. CMYK is used for professional printing, since cyan, magenta, yellow and black are the four inks used in a printing press.

Whichever colour mode is being used, OS X tries to ensure that all your devices and documents sing from the same songsheet: ie that they all have a common idea of the fundamental Red, Green and Blue ingredients. This is done using a system of so-called "colour profiles". It's too techie to go into in any depth here, but if you want to learn more, or if you have a colour-related problem in OS X, read:

ColorSync apple.com/macosx/features/colorsync

▶ **RAW (or Camera Raw)** *File extension: depends on camera*
Most digital cameras internally process their images into JPEGs to make them quicker to download and work with. This is convenient, but the resulting pictures are marginally less rich in terms of saturation, contrast, white balance and so on than the "raw" image data from the camera. So if you're serious about your photography, consider a camera that outputs RAW data instead of (or, ideally, as well as) JPEGs. Note, though, that different cameras have different RAW formats, so don't be surprised if iPhoto or any other image program fails to open them.

▶ **TIFF (Tagged Image File Format)** *File extension: .tif*
This flexible image format is most commonly used by publishing and graphics professionals, though many scanners and some cameras also generate TIFFs. It can be compressed, but very often it isn't.

There are numerous other image file formats, including BMPs, PICTs, TGAs, EPSs and more. Most are easily opened and resaved in an alternate format by OS X's Preview application…

Previewing, converting & resizing images

Tip: If you want to open an image in Preview, but double-clicking launches it in another application, then either open Preview and select **File > Open**; or drag the image in question to Preview's icon on the Dock or in the Applications folder. Also consider changing the default program for the image file type in question (see p.88).

With the right tools, it's easy to change an image from one format to another, to add compression, and to change its size in pixels. This is extremely useful if you want to shrink the file size of an image in order to make it quicker to email or post on a website or blog. It's also sometimes essential as not every program will recognize every file format, so you might need to convert the format simply to open a particular image in a particular application.

Convert & compress

In OS X, double clicking most image formats will, by default, open them into the built-in Preview application, which is a handy tool for viewing and resaving images and PDF documents. You can also open Preview from the Applications folder.

Once you have an image open in Preview, you can easily:

▶ **Resave in another format** Simply click **File > Export** and choose a format from the dropdown menu.

▶ **Resize** Choose **Tools > Adjust Size …** and you can change the print size or resolution. To adjust the size of the image in pixels, be sure that **Resample Image** is checked. To alter the print size without changing the size in pixels, leave this box unchecked.

▶ **Crop** To remove unwanted areas from an image, use the **Select** tool to define the new edges of the image, and then click **Tools > Crop**.

If you need to resize a whole bunch of images, you can do so with Automator (see p.122). You'll find the **Scale Image** Action under **Preview**.

Preview tips

▶ **Opening images en masse**
If you want to open lots of images in one single Preview window, select and drag all the files to the Preview icon. The "Drawer" will appear, which provides an easy way to switch between the images; to toggle the draw in and out of view, use ⌘⇧D.

▶ **Opening a folder of images**
To open a whole folder of images into Finder, hold down ⌘⌥ and drag the folder's icon to the Preview icon.

▶ **Opening images from Preview**
The thumbnails displayed in the "Drawer" are live icons, meaning you can drag an individual image directly from there into a folder (to copy it) or onto the icon of another application (to open it into that application).

▶ See p.149 for more on PDFs and Preview.

Tip: Another way to batch convert images is using Folder Actions (see p.124).

30 iPhoto

iPhoto is Apple's flagship photo management application. It's a tool for importing pics from digital cameras and elsewhere, keeping them organized, removing red-eye, making other tweaks, and sending them on to friends, printers or print shops. You may have got a similar package on CD with your digital camera, though in almost all cases you'll be far better off with iPhoto, perhaps supplemented by a more powerful image editor and some choice plug-ins.

If your Mac shipped with OS X Leopard, you should already have iPhoto '08, the most up-to-date version at the time of writing. You'll find its icon in the Applications folder and perhaps already on your Dock too.

If you have an earlier edition of OS X or you purchased Leopard as an upgrade, you probably have an older version of iPhoto, since the new one is only available as part of the iLife '08 suite, which ships with new Macs but otherwise has to be paid for ($79/£55). Earlier versions are OK, though the upgrade is worth considering, since iPhoto '08 boasts a number of excellent new features.

Importing pics into iPhoto

From a camera…

The first time you connect a digital camera to your Mac, a dialog box should appear asking if you want to use iPhoto as the program for importing and organizing pics from that camera. If you say yes, from that point on, connecting the camera will cause iPhoto to launch automatically so that you can import your pics.

Importing with iPhoto is easy. When your camera is connected, it will appear on the left with its contents displayed in the main part of the window.

First, add an **Event** name for the imported pictures – "Trip to France", say, or "Ruth, Tracy and Joe". You can always change this later if you like. You may also want to add a description, though don't feel you have to.

Once that's done, click **Import All…** or, if you prefer, select one or more images and press **Import Selected**. To select and deselect multiple images, click individual images or drag over groups of images while holding down the ⌘ key.

…from elsewhere

You can also get images into iPhoto from other locations on your Mac or network. Simply drag them into the iPhoto window. Alternatively, choose **Add to Library…** from the **File** menu, or use the shortcut ⌘O, and browse for the files you want.

Tip: Most digital cameras need to be set to "Play" mode to be recognized by a Mac. If yours still isn't recognized, you may need to install the software that came with the camera. Or the camera may simply be incompatible with OS X, in which case investigate the possibility of getting a media card reader to download the pics from the memory card rather than the camera.

Tip: Check that the time and date on your digital camera are right, as this information is imported into iPhoto along with the images and becomes a useful means of searching for shots using the iPhoto Calendar.

Tip: Importing an image into iPhoto from anywhere creates a copy of the file in your iPhoto Library folder. So if space is at a premium on either your hard drive or camera, delete the original after you import.

Organizing photos

iPhoto works with pictures in just the same way as iTunes works with songs. Everything you import is added to your Library, which is easily accessible at the top of the Sources area on the left and can be organized and viewed in various different ways.

You can view your Library either by **Photos** (a total list of every picture you ever imported) or by **Events**…

Events

When you import photos from a camera (or elsewhere), iPhoto bundles them together as an "Event". Think of it like a roll of film. To view the contents of an Event, double-click it. Or, to see the images it contains as a slideslow, click the ▶ button.

Each Event is represented within your Library by one of the images it contains. You can quickly select an image by hovering your mouse pointer over the Event and moving left to right. When you find the image you'd like to use, simply press the spacebar.

To combine two Events, simply drag one onto the other. It's also possible to drag individual photos between Events; this is best done by choosing the **Photos** view under **Library** and opening and closing Events using the little triangles next to their names.

Finally, to split an Event in two, open it, select the images you'd like to separate off, and choose **Event > Split Event**.

Albums

Each image can be added to one or more albums – rather like playlists in iTunes. There are two main reasons for creating albums, rather than just organizing them as Events. First, they allow you to gather together images from different times – you might, for example, have an album of photos of a particular person that draws on many different Events. Second, you can browse by album when looking at your photos on an iPod or iPhone.

To create a new album, press the "+" button at the bottom-left of the window, or hit ⌘N. Then you can simply select one or more images in your Library and drag them into the album.

If you want to combine a number of related albums, create a folder to drop them into. This is easily done using the **New Folder** option in the File menu. Folders can also hold Smart Albums and Slideshows.

Adding info

It's worth taking a little time to "tag" images with titles, ratings and keywords. This makes it easier to quickly find photos later and also to stay organized using Smart Albums (see overleaf).

To add info to a single image, make sure the **Title**, **Ratings** and **Keywords** options are checked in the **View** menu and then hover below individual photos to see the various options. Or, if you want to add more extensive information to a particular photo (what was happening when you took it, for example), click the "i" button and enter your text as description.

It's also possible to edit multiple images simultaneously. Simply select the images in question and:

▶ To add a rating, right-click or hit ⌘0 through to ⌘5.

▶ Click **Photos > Batch Change** for title or description.

▶ Click **Window > Keywords** to apply or remove one or more keywords.

Smart Albums

A Smart Album is a special kind of iPhoto album that uses a set of parameters, determined by you, to decide which images it is to include. It's exactly the same principle as Smart Playlists in iTunes, and just as much fun. However, Smart Albums only work well if the images in your Library are liberally tagged with comments, titles, ratings and keywords.

Tip: You can also add keywords to images using the Preview application. Choose **Get Info** from the **Tools** menu and make additions under the **Keywords** tab.

Tip: When creating Smart Albums, be careful how you use the "All" tag – it is often the reason an Album comes out empty when you expected it to be full.

To create a new Smart Album look in the **File** menu, or hold down ⌥ (**Alt**) and click the "cog" button that appears in the bottom-left. Experiment with the various options, pressing the "+" and "–" buttons to add or remove extra criteria. Once you're done, press **OK**. If you don't like the results, select the relevant icon in the Source List and click **Edit Smart Album** in the **File** menu.

Rotating images

Like babies, digital photographs don't always arrive the right way round, so it's worth taking a few minutes to make sure that each newly imported pic is orientated correctly. To do this, make selections in the main window and then hit the **Rotate** button at the bottom of the iPhoto frame; holding ⌥ as you click changes the direction of rotation. Rotations can also be handled from the keyboard:

▶ To rotate clockwise use ⌘R
▶ To rotate anti-clockwise use ⌘⌥R

Deleting images

Deleting images is simple: select one or more pics and then either hit the **Backspace** key on your keyboard; choose **Move to Trash** from the **Photo** menu; or simply drag them onto the Trash icon at the bottom of the Source List.

Note, however, that deleting an image from a playlist or slideshow won't actually remove the offending photo from your Library. To do this, first click **iPhoto Library**, and then delete the image, as described above.

Deleted images go to the iPhoto Trash, where they'll remain until you either drag them out or choose **Empty Trash** from the **iPhoto** menu (also achieved with the shortcut ⌘⇧⌫).

Hiding images

If you'd like to render one or more photos invisible, but not actually delete them from iPhoto, simply select the photos in question and press Hide. To bring them back into view later simply click **View > Hidden Photos**.

Tip: The default direction of rotation can be set in **iPhoto Preferences**, under **General**. Play with the other options under **Appearance** and also in the program's **View** menu to get things looking just the way you want them to.

Tip: Deleted something by mistake? You can always undo your last action with the shortcut ⌘Z. Deleted it from your camera? Try the data recovery software listed on p.298.

Tip: In iPhoto **Preferences**, under **General**, you can choose to have an image open into a separate editing window when it is double clicked. Here you can also choose to have the image open into another application for editing (see box overleaf).

Editing photos

In the bad old days, photos came back from the lab as glossy testimony to our amateur photographer status. Though iPhoto isn't going to turn you into a world-class snapper, it does give you a second chance at getting things right, whether that means adjusting the frame of your shot, improving the colours and light or removing the scourge of red-eye. To start editing, select an image with a single click and hit the **Edit** button at the bottom of the window.

iPhoto's editing tools are pretty straightforward, so they shouldn't take too long to get used to. And, in the event that everything goes pear-shaped, you can always choose **Revert to Original** from the **Photos** menu. Here are a few pointers to get you going:

▶ **Crop** Drag the corners of the "crop" area to re-frame your shot within any rectangle of your choosing. Check the **Constrain** box before doing so to maintain the original proportions.

▶ **Adjust** Experiment with the Adjust palette settings, and also the order in which you make adjustments. For example, the **Sharpness** tool produces its best results when used last.

▶ **Red-Eye** This is that rare thing: a tool that does exactly what you want it to, nearly all the time. Simply click the button and then click on the affected eye to remove the red.

▶ **Retouch** Designed to remove blemishes from faces, clothes or elsewhere, the **Retouch** tool can be useful, but employ it sparingly, as the results are rarely perfect. And, when using it, always zoom right in to the image so you can see exactly what you're doing.

Image-editing software

iPhoto is essentially a photo management application. And though it offers a decent suite of tools for tweaking digital photos, they barely scratch the surface of what's possible with dedicated image-editing packages. These allow you to do everything from completely reworking colour and brightness levels, or filtering something flat to make it look three-dimensional, to merging images together to create an apparently realistic snap of some real-world impossibility (if you want a shot of yourself taking a keyboard lesson with J.S. Bach, say, this is the route you would need to take).

The professional's image editor of choice is Adobe Photoshop, which is fantastic, but has a price tag that reflects its quality. Download the trial version from:

Photoshop adobe.com

The best of the free options is the open-source powerhouse known as GIMP. It's superb, though installing it can be a bit challenging as it only runs on OS X using the so-called X11 system. Read more at:

GIMP gimp.org/macintosh • macgimp.org

For help using these serious image editors, scour their respective websites, or try:

CreativeMac.com creativemac.com
Gimp Guru gimpguru.org

Or to find and download some smaller-scale freeware or shareware image editors, browse the "Imaging" section of:

OS X Software apple.com/downloads/macosx

Apple's professional alternative to iPhoto is called Aperture and is marketed as "the first all-in-one post-production tool for photographers". Its features are very impressive and go way beyond regular domestic needs. There's a 30-day free trial available if you fancy giving it a go, though it will cost you $299/£219 if you want the application for keeps. Find out more at apple.com/aperture.

Slideshows

To view a set of images as a full-screen virtual slideshow, simply select either a number of individual images, an entire album from the sidebar or an Event in the main iPhoto window, and click the ▶ button. Hold down ⌥ when clicking to avoid being presented with options relating to music, transitions, etc.

For a more elaborate slideshow, complete with carefully crafted transitions between pics, click the "+" below the iPhoto sidebar, choose slideshow, and then play around with the settings. Once played, this slideshow will appear in the sidebar so that you can replay it and edit it as many times as you like.

Release your photos

Having a Library of edited, organized images is all very well, but before long you'll be itching to get your images out of iPhoto and into the wider world – on paper or online. Here's a brief run-down of your options…

▶ **Print** iPhoto provides a good set of home printing options and presets for turning your snaps into greeting cards, cramming multiple images onto a single sheet, and so on. Select one or more images, hit **Print** in the **File** menu or on the toolbar (or press ⌘P) and explore the options. Alternatively, if your printer's not up to the job, order a hard copy via the Web (see overleaf).

▶ **Email** This toolbar option (also found in the **Share** menu) slots selected images into the body of an email ready for you to address and send. If you (or the recipient) have a slow Internet connection, select the smaller image size options.

▶ **Burn a CD** This is useful for taking pics to be developed at a store or for sending snaps by snail mail. You could choose **Burn** from iPhoto's **Share** menu but this will generate a CD with an array of folders, pic files and thumbnails guaranteed to confuse print shops and relatives alike. A better solution is to select the pics or albums you want to burn, drag them out of iPhoto and burn them to CD with Finder (see p.85).

▶ **As a movie** Click **Export** in the **File** menu, and you can save selected images or albums as a QuickTime movie – just like a Slideshow, complete with music and transitions. If your Mac has a SuperDrive, you could also send images straight to be burned to a DVD (complete with menu screen and effects) to view on a TV through a regular DVD player. To do this choose **Share > Send to iDVD**. For more on iDVD, see p.261.

▶ **File Export** You can drag images out of iPhoto onto the desktop or any Finder window to export a copy, but for more options choose **File > Export** (or use ⌘⇧E) and browse for a destination to save the new file to. This can be done for single and multiple files.

▶ **Sharing over a network** Just as you can share music across networks in iTunes, iPhoto lets you share your Library with other iPhoto users on a network, wirelessly or otherwise. To share your pics, open **iPhoto > Preferences > Sharing** and check **Share My Photos**. To see other users' pics, check **Look for Shared Photos** – if any other iPhoto users are on the same network, their Library will pop up on your iPhoto sidebar.

▶ **A desktop background** To set any Library image as your OS X desktop "wallpaper", select its thumbnail and click **Share > Set Desktop**. If you don't like the way your Mac displays the image, use the Crop tool to crop and re-frame the shot, and then try again.

Tip: Another way to email images is as a PDF document – press **Print**, and then choose **Mail PDF** from the **PDF** button at the bottom of the Print dialog box.

Tip: Before sending images to iDVD, crop them to a 4x3 aspect ratio (TV resolution) using the Constrain/Crop tool. Many basic digital cameras use 4x3 anyway, but if you have a digital SLR you may well find that your snaps have a different aspect ratio.

Sharing your photos online

If you want to put your pictures on the Web, where everyone can see them, you have a few more options still:

▶ **.Mac Web Gallery** If you have a .Mac account (see p.34) choose **Share > Web Gallery** to swiftly and painlessly publish snaps online.

▶ **Your own site or blog** If you already have your own website, you could either manually create a page with your pictures on or select an album or group of images in iPhoto, click **Export** in the **File** menu (or hit ⌘⇧E) and choose the **Web page** tab. With or without a .Mac (see below), you can also send pics to iWeb (see p.182) via the **Share** menu.

▶ **Photo sharing sites** There are loads of websites and online communities that allow you to post images online for free for either the world, or close friends, to see. iPhoto plug-ins are available for many of the more popular sites (such as Flickr and Facebook), which make it easy to upload fresh images each day.

Facebook facebook.com
Flickr flickr.com

▶ **Online gallery** There are also many services that, for a small fee, will provide you with a ready-made photo gallery online. For example:

Fotki fotki.com
Phanfare phanfare.com

▶ **.Mac Slides** The **Share > .Mac Slides** option in iPhoto lets .Mac account holders publish selected images to the Web as screen savers. Other OS X users can subscribe to these slides via their **Screen Savers** panel in **System Preferences** by selecting **.Mac & RSS**, clicking the **Options** button and then using the "+" button to enter the account name of the .Mac member who is hosting the slides.

Video

DVDs & TV

All recently bought Macs have the capability to play back DVDs and, with the right software, it's also possible to "rip" the contents of a DVD onto your hard drive. If your Mac features a SuperDrive you'll also be able to burn DVDs – either to backup data files (see p.287) or create your own movie discs that can be played back on any DVD player. Less well known is the fact that, with the right hardware, it's possible to use your Mac as a TV. This chapter reveals all.

Watching DVDs

Bundled within OS X is a little application called DVD Player – slot a disc into your machine and the program will automatically launch. It's very easy to use and will either fill your screen instantly or present the DVD's menu screen in a smaller window. When viewing DVDs in full-screen mode, the controls appear as a pop-up panel at the bottom of the screen, much like the Dock with Hiding turned on (see p.80). At other times these controls appear as a floating panel (pictured). Explore what's on offer – you'll find buttons for slow motion, subtitles and special DVD features such as alternate view-angles. Here are a few more features and shortcuts worth mentioning before we move on:

Tip: To create a catalogue of your DVD collection on your Mac, use the free Fennel DVDManager program, downloadable from dvdmanager.free.fr

Tip: If DVD Player doesn't open (or you want to use an alternate player as your default) alter the setting in **System Preferences > CDs & DVDs**.

Tip: All recent Macs feature a video output port that, with an optional adapter, will output the screen in S-video or Composite video – useful if you have a widescreen TV and want to use your Mac as a DVD player. If you have a laptop, you could also consider hooking up to a bigger computer screen. iBook owners may first want to consider running Screen Spanning Doctor (macparts.de) to allow better resolutions.

▶ Open the **Audio Equalizer** and **Video Color** (pictured) panels from the **Window** menu to make fine adjustments to sound and picture quality, respectively. Only one can be open at a time, the other then being available from the dropdown menu at the top of the panel.

▶ The same dropdown also offers the **Video Zoom** control, which lets you magnify and reframe the action in the viewer window. This option is also accessed from the **Window** menu.

▶ By selecting either **Bookmarks** or **Video Clips** from the **Window** menu you can open a panel that stores shortcuts to your favourite moments (Bookmarks) and segments (Video Clips) on a DVD, making them easy to find next time you play the DVD.

Tip: If you minimize the DVD Player it keeps playing in miniature on the Dock, so you can keep an eye on the movie while getting on with something else.

Tip: Want to know what to watch? There are loads of movie trailers available to stream from the iTunes Store and also via the Dashboard Movies widget.

DVD Player shortcuts

Play or pause	**Space bar**
Stop	⌘.
Skip to next chapter	→
Skip to previous chapter	←
Scan forward	⌘→
Scan backward	⌘←
Go to beginning of disc	⌘⇧D
Go to menu screen	⌘`
Toggle closed captioning on and off	⌘⌥T
Add bookmark	⌘=
Volume up or down	⌘↑ or ⌘↓
Toggle Mute on and off	⌘⌥↓
Show or hide the Controller	**Escape**
Toggle full-screen mode on and off	⌘0
Switch to Finder	⌘⌥F

Other players

Apple's DVD Player is not the only player available for use in OS X. Of the alternatives, VLC Media Player is the best, largely because of its ability to handle DVDs with any region code. XinePlayer is also worth a try:

VLC videolan.org/vlc
XinePlayer xineplayer.berlios.de

Tip: DVDs can also be played using an Apple Remote and OS X's Front Row full-screen media player. For full details, see p.212.

The "region" issue

Most purchased DVDs contain a region code (indicated by a number on the back of the packaging), which in theory determines where in the world the disc is to be distributed and viewed. In turn, most DVD players and drives contain a piece of software that locks them to the specific region of their owner (though "Region 0" players that can play any DVD are available, as are "Region 0" DVDs that should play in any machine).

In the case of the DVD drive in your Mac, you are given five opportunities to change the region setting before it becomes hardwired. If you only ever watch movies from your own region (in the US and Canada it's Region 1, and in Western Europe it's Region 2) then you don't have a problem – you will never see any dialog boxes asking you to choose. But if you are one of the growing number of film-lovers who buy titles from around the globe, you certainly don't want to find yourself locked into playback of a single region code.

One way around this problem is to try using the free VLC Media Player (see overleaf), which you may find allows you to completely bypass the regions issue. Alternatively you could try an application such as Region X (xvi.rpc1.org/region), which lets you reset your region code as many times as you like (assuming your drive is not locked already). But be aware that this kind of tinkering could void your Mac's warranty.

Still no joy? Try ripping the DVDs (see p.258) instead.

Watching downloaded video

If you downloaded a movie file from the Internet, you may need a special application to play it back – even if it seems to be a "regular" file type such as AVI or MPEG. The reason is that both these formats can hold video encoded in various different ways (using different *codecs*).

The extra video players you're most likely to need are:

DivX divx.com/divx/mac
Windows Media Player windowsmedia.com

There are also now video equivalents of MP3 CD players – DVD players that can read DivX and the like. See:

Kiss-Technology kiss-technology.com

Importing & copying DVDs

In most cases, it's perfectly possible to import DVDs onto your Mac. In some countries this may not be strictly legal when it comes to copyrighted movies, but as long as you're only importing your own DVDs for your own use, no one is likely to mind. You can store your imported files in iTunes just as you do with songs from CDs, though iTunes cannot handle the import process. For that you will need a third party application such as HandBrake (see below). The main problem is that it's a bit of a hassle. A DVD contains so much data that it can take more than an hour to import each movie in a format that'll work with iTunes and, if you so desire, an iPod or Apple TV (see p.258).

Using HandBrake

Of the various free tools available for getting DVDs onto a Mac, probably the best is HandBrake; you can download the most up-to-date version for free from handbrake.com. Once the application is installed (see p.106), the process works something like this:

▶ **Insert the DVD** and, if it starts to play automatically, quit your DVD player program.

▶ **Launch HandBrake** and it should detect the DVD (it may call it something unfriendly like "/dev/rdisk1"). Press **Open**, and wait until the application has scanned the DVD.

▶ **Choose your settings** Choose a preset option from the Presets drawer that pops out to the right when you click the **Toggle Presets** button. Some presets are pretty self-explanatory (eg, Apple TV, iPod Hi-Rez, etc), but others might require more elaboration – allow your cursor to hover over each option to reveal tooltips that explain exactly what the preset should be used for.

Tip: To make sure you have all the most up-to-date presets, Update Built-in Presets from the Presets menu.

Tip: If you check the "2-pass encoding" box, this will double the time it takes to process your movie, but the quality will be better, and with no increase in the size of the final file.

▶ **Check the source** It's also worth taking a quick look at the "Title" dropdown menu within the Source section of HandBrake. If the list offers several options, choose the one that represents the largest amount of time (for example 01h22m46s) as this should be the main feature. If nothing of an appropriate length appears, then your DVD is copy protected, and you may find that you have more luck with another application, such as Mac The Ripper (mactheripper.org) or ffmpegX (homepage.mac.com/major4).

▶ **Subtitles** If it's a foreign-language film, set **Dialogue and Subtitles** options from the dropdown menus behind the **Audio & Subtitles** tab.

▶ **Rip** Hit the **Start** button at the top of the window and the encoding will begin. Don't hold your breath.

▶ **Drop the file into iTunes** Unless you choose to save it somewhere else, the file will eventually appear on the Desktop. It will probably be in the region of a few hundred megabytes, depending on the length of the DVD. Drag the file into the main iTunes window. This should create a copy of the new file in your iTunes library (there's a check box in **iTunes Preferences** > **Advanced** > **General** that makes sure this happens) allowing you to then delete the original file from your Desktop.

Video formats

Video files are more confusing than most, as you have to worry not only about the file format (which you can usually tell by the file extension: eg .mov and .avi) but also the "codec" (compression technique) used to create the file.

In short, iPods, iPhones and Apple TVs support files in the .m4v, .mp4 and .mov formats created using H.264 and MPEG-4 codecs. For full details, see the apple.com product page of the device you want to play video on.

You will find that you can also add some movie files to your iTunes library that won't work with an iPod or Apple TV, but can be converted to do so using the options in the Advanced menu.

To convert other common video formats (such as .avi files) to an iTunes-friendly format, download either QuickTime Pro or VisualHub

QuickTime Pro
apple.com/quicktime
VisualHub
techspansion.com/visualhub

Copying DVDs

Duplicating a copyrighted DVD may be illegal, depending which country you live in and what you intend to do with the copy. In general, it's fine to make a back up for your own use, but not to distribute it to anyone else. Obviously, there are no limitations on duplicating home-made DVDs.

The procedure for duplicating a DVD depends on whether or not the disc includes any copy-protection. If not, you can create a disk image of the DVD using OS X's Disk Utility and then burn that to DVD using Finder (see p.47). If there is copy protection of some sort, however, you'll need to employ some extra software, such as Mac the Ripper (see p.258).

Of the commercially available DVD copying programs, the best-known is Popcorn, which allows you to do clever things such as compress a double-layer DVD so that it fits on a standard DVD-R, and also remove unnecessary baggage such as additional language tracks. However, you may have to combine it with other programs to get around copy protection (see p.258).

Popcorn roxio.com/popcorn

Creating your own DVDs

With a SuperDrive, you can burn any type of files onto a recordable DVD either by using Burn Folders (see p.85) or by inserting a blank disc, dragging files onto its icon and clicking **File > Burn Disc...** in Finder. But if you want to burn movie, music or photo DVDs for playback in standard household DVD players, you'll need to use a special application such as iDVD.

iDVD

iDVD is Apple's own DVD authoring program (if it's not in the Dock, look in your Applications folder) and ships with all new Macs as part of the iLife suite, so you probably already have it. For the home user, it's an excellent program that makes the whole process of creating a DVD – complete with fancy menu screens – extremely easy. Follow these steps:

▶ **Pick a theme** First, click **Create a New Project** , choose between standard and widescreen formats, and then pick from a selection of bundled "themes" (many of which are widescreen-only) for your menus.

▶ **Add some content** Click the **Media** button to pull in audio, pics and video files. You can also drag files from Finder, or click **File > Import**.

▶ **Customize** Most of the themes are relatively tasteful, but you can select and delete elements you don't like. Also, click **Buttons** and experiment with the alternatives on offer.

Tip: If you don't have a SuperDrive, but you know someone who does, you could create DVD projects on your own Mac using iDVD, save them as a disk image file when you're done, and move that file to your friend's Mac later for burning to DVD.

Tip: You can also buy more themes in the form of the third-party DVDPak (available from dvdthemepak.com) but expect "fun" rather than anything very stylish.

Tip: If you burn to rewritable DVDs, they need to be blanked before each new use. This can be done using OS X's Disk Utility (in **Applications > Utilities**).

Tip: Choose **View > Show TV Safe Area** (or hit ⌘T) to make sure that your page elements won't be cropped out when your DVD menus are viewed on smaller TV sets.

▶ **Add extra menus** You can only have six items on your main menu. If you want more items than this, you'll have to create submenus. To do this, click the + button and choose **Add Submenu**. Each submenu, when clicked, will lead to another customizable menu, complete with a back arrow for returning to the main menu screen.

▶ **Map things out** Click the **Map** button to see a tree diagram of the whole disc, and delete any unwanted bits (select the media in question and hit **Backspace**).

▶ **Add some files** You can add regular files to your DVD, which will be accessible if someone puts the disc in a computer. Choose **Advanced > Edit DVD-ROM Contents…**.

▶ **Get burning…** Hit the **Burn** button and insert a blank disc when instructed. Or, to burn it later, or on another machine, choose **File > Save As Disc Image…**.

▶ **Save** Save your project so you can open and edit it later.

DVD Studio Pro

iDVD is great at doing what it does, but if you have Hollywood ambitions, you might want to investigate something more powerful. The obvious choice for Mac users is DVD Studio Pro, part of Apple's Final Cut family (see p.268). It features an almost bottomless barrel of professional encoding variables and handles all the latest high-definition formats. Unfortunately, it has a price tag to match. For more information, see apple.com/dvdstudiopro.

Connecting to a TV

Depending on its screen and its location in the home, your computer may already be perfectly situated for watching your downloading or imported movies and TV shows. In many cases, however, it's preferable to play them through a regular TV.

To connect recent Macs directly you'll need the appropriate Mini-DVI adapter – one end plugs into the DVI port of your Mac, and the other end connects to the appropriate cable for the ports on your TV (S-video, composite video or VGA). To see which video adapter you require and which video output methods your Mac supports, check the Tech Spec page of your model at apple.com/mac.

If you have a wireless network, the neater solution is the Apple TV – also known as tv. The device connects to your TV via a cable and to your Mac via your wireless network. It can import files from iTunes to its own hard drive for playback, or stream them directly from your Mac in real time. It can also be granted access to the Internet, allowing you to watch free movie trailers and browse YouTube (though not the rest of the Web) on your TV. Playback is controlled with an Apple Remote and an on-screen menu system similar to that of Front Row.

All video from the iTunes Store will work with an Apple TV – and they can look surprisingly good, despite their relatively low resolutions. Video from other sources will need to be prepared using the "Convert Selection for Apple TV" option in the iTunes Advanced menu. For ripping DVDs, use the Apple TV preset in HandBrake (see p.258).

You'll also need the right cables (not supplied) and the right sockets to connect them to. The basic option is a component video cable (three phono-like connectors coloured red, green and blue) plus a phono or optical cable for the audio. If you have the right port on your TV, you could use an HDMI cable instead. These offer excellent video and audio quality all-in-one, but they're very expensive.

For more details about Apple TV connection requirements, go to: apple.com/appletv/connect.html.

▲

Once setup, the Apple TV appears in iTunes with a series of tabs allowing you to choose which videos you want to copy across to the device. You can also browse your entire iTunes Library direct from Apple TV and stream the files in real time. This is fine for music, but depending on the speed of your network, not ideal for video.

Tip: Note that video files converted for Apple TV *won't* play back on iPods, but Files prepared for iPods *will* play back on an Apple TV.

Browsing through channels using the EyeTV software. Naturally, it's also possible to view in full-screen mode (as shown below).

Mac as TV

The distinction between computers and televisions has been slowly eroding for some time, and doubtless within a decade or two there'll be no line at all between the two. Though relatively few people yet know about it, it's already possible to use your Mac as a fully functional TV. Doing so may not only save you money and space (why have two screens in your house when you only need one?), but will also give you a whole raft of features such as the ability to pause and rewind "live" TV and record shows directly to your hard drive. The picture tends to look a bit "digital", but is clearer than you get from most regular televisions.

To use your Mac as a television, you need a TV receiver that will connect to your computer via a USB or FireWire cable. A handful of companies produce Mac TV receivers, but few are as good as Elgato's "EyeTV" series, which includes analogue and digital receivers on both sides of the Atlantic. Some models – such as the EyeTV Diversity (pictured) – are not much bigger than a matchbox.

Setting up an EyeTV system takes seconds: simply connect the device to your television antenna cable or the supplied antenna and your Mac (no need for a separate power plug), and drag the software off the included CD. The EyeTV automatically finds, saves and names channels, and you can flick between stations using either the on-screen controller or the included remote. Some models even feature their own mini-ariel for use in areas with good signal strength, making it totally mobile – great for Macbook owners.

Prices start at around $75/£50. For more information, see:

Elgato elgato.com

Making movies 32

If you want to make your own movies, then the Mac is the computer for you. Apple have created some of the most intuitive and user-friendly video tools available. Even many film students and professionals at times turn around iMovie and iDVD, both members of the iLife suite, for their combination of powerful features and an unfussy interface.

But the iLife software is not the only option available, so the following pages point you towards some of the alternatives in addition to showing you how to get the most from iMovie. But before you start worrying about editing your masterpiece, you first need some footage. This could come from several sources…

DV cameras

Most camcorders on the market today fall into the DV (digital video) category. Compared with earlier analogue models, these mark a huge improvement both in picture quality and the ease with which you can transfer the footage to a computer – something typically done using a FireWire cable and a video-editing application such as iMovie (see p.268). Despite the availability of cameras that can record straight to DVD or hard drives, most consumer and semi-professional cameras store their footage on MiniDV tape.

> **Tip:** You can get video footage into a video-editing program in two distinct ways: either by **importing** files that already exist on the machine (or a connected drive) or by **capturing** footage from a connected camera.

Recording VHS

If you want to import footage from VHS cassettes, you have two options. One is to connect your VHS player to your Mac via a Mac TV receiver (see p.264). Run a regular aerial cable between the two, "tune" the TV software on the Mac to find the VHS signal, and then start recording. The other technique is to run a cable from your VHS player to a DV camera, enabling you to capture the footage directly into iMovie.

Tip: Some video software won't accept webcams as an input source, as they only recognize DV as a capturable format. iMovie, however, will import footage from your Mac's built-in iSight.

Tip: If you have a mobile phone that can record video clips, you may well be able to move the results onto your Mac via Bluetooth, just as you would images (see p.235), and then import them into iMovie.

TV

With a television receiver such as an Elgato EyeTV (see p.264) you can record shows directly onto your Mac, ready to export as QuickTime and open into iMovie.

Ripped DVDs

Another way to get video footage onto your Mac is to rip it from a DVD. With a program such as HandBrake (see p.258) you can convert DVD video into MPEG-4 files that can then be imported into iMovie.

Video grabs

A video grab is a moving-image version of a regular screen grab (see p.236), recording whatever is happening on your screen to a video file. Using a video-grab application such as Snapz Pro X or Display Eater, you can grab any video playing on your screen – even if it's streaming from the Web.

Display Eater reversecode.com
Snapz Pro X ambrosiasw.com

Photographs

iMovie lets you transform still images into video clips, but there are other applications that do a better job. CameraMover is a good example – you drag and zoom a frame across an image in real time and end up with either a high-quality video clip or a bunch of individual JPEGs if you want to edit frame by frame.

CameraMover info-services.net/cameramover

Buying a camcorder

If you want to buy a camcorder for use with iMovie, the best place to start is the **Apple Store** – even if you don't get as far as opening your wallet. You can guarantee all the models that Apple stock will seamlessly integrate with Mac software and hardware, so it's a good place to do some research.

Apple Store store.apple.com

When choosing a specific model, consider what you actually want the camcorder for: indoor or outdoor use (cheaper cameras tend to perform poorly in weaker light); general holiday fun or serious amateur filmmaking (for the latter, you'll need a decent optical zoom and a good-quality mic). There's also the question of whether you want to make use of iMovie's widescreen, high-definition functionality. If so, go for a HD camcorder.

Also consider connectivity. FireWire or USB2 is a must. And, if possible, get a model with DV-in as well as DV-out, so you have the option of recording your edited work back onto the camera. A regular video-in is also handy for copying footage from older video formats to stick into the Mac from your MiniDV camera.

You'll have to choose which media to use for recording, too. At the time of writing, MiniDV camcorders offer better value than newer alternatives such as those that record to DVD, Flash memory or an internal hard drive. But each has its own advantages. Furthermore, things change, so read reviews – and certainly don't be convinced by some Muppet in a chain store who claims to know his or her stuff. Visit:

CamcorderInfo.com camcorderinfo.com
SimplyDV simplydv.co.uk

Once you've decided on a model, head for a price-comparison website to track down the best deal. As for actually using your new toy, don't expect to become the next Stanley Kubrick overnight. For a few pointers on composing shots, lighting and other such issues, see:

Exposure exposure.co.uk

Tip: DV camera footage is generally in one of two standard modes – PAL or NTSC – depending where you are in the world. If your capture software gives you a choice when you connect to your camera, choose NTSC if you live in North America and PAL in Europe.

Tip: For a host of other Mac video apps and widgets, visit: apple.com/downloads/macosx/video

Hardware

If you do get serious with DV editing there are also several application-specific keyboards on the market, with scrubbing wheels and colour-coded shortcut keys. To find out more visit Bella:

Bella bella-usa.com

Tip: Video-editing programs such as iMovie and the others listed on this page are described as "non-linear editing systems" as they can access the footage on your hard drive in any order – as opposed to the tape-based, linear editing system that emerged in the early days of video. Of course, old-style splicers-and-sticky-tape film editing is also non-linear.

Choosing your software

There are many video-editing programs on the market. Apple's own professional alternatives to iMovie come under the umbrella of Final Cut. Another package widely used by professionals is Avid.

Final Cut apple.com/finalcutstudio
Avid Express Pro avid.com/xpresspro

The fundamental process in these packages is the same – you capture footage, organize clips in a timeline, add effects and transitions, and then export your movie. iMovie also adheres to these protocols, so even if you intend to get seriously into video editing, it's a good place to get your bearings. You probably already have iMovie on your Mac, so read the rest of this chapter and have a play...

Using iMovie

In a nutshell, iMovie (part of the iLife suite) is an application for importing and editing video footage. It allows you to capture raw footage from a digital video camera; import footage, audio and stills from pre-existing files; and to edit everything you have captured and imported into a professional-looking film, complete with effects and transitions. And once you have create your blockbuster, the application makes it very easy to publish to a website, or even directly to YouTube. What's more you can easily export versions of your movie to use with iPods, iPhones, and Apple TVs (see p.263).

The low down on high def

High definition video – aka HD or HDV – is the latest standard to have filtered through to the camcorder market. HDV can be recorded onto the most common existing media – MiniDV cassettes.

As is so often the case with such technology, we are talking about bigger being better, and in this case widescreen. Cameras that support HDV can capture an image with an aspect ratio of 16:9 (compared with standard 4:3) and at a frame size of 1280 x 720 pixels.

This format looks set to become the norm over the coming years, especially considering the popularity of widescreen TVs.

As an interesting footnote to all this, the widescreen aspect ratio was originally developed in the movie industry in reaction to the popularity of television, which had pinched the 4:3 ratio from the traditional cinema "Academy format". To get bums on seats, the cinema movers and shakers reinvented the cinema experience to differentiate it from TV, and simultaneously to ensure that movies shot in 16:9 would have to be either cropped or "letterboxed" on a standard 4:3 TV.

Capturing footage from your camera

When you connect your camera to your Mac using a FireWire cable to capture footage from MiniDV tapes, make sure that, first, your camera is in its "Player" mode (sometimes labelled "VTR"), and then click the iMovie "camera" button (pictured) to open the **Camera Import** window. With any luck you will have established communication with the camera, and the window will now be displaying the contents of the DV tape, and the on-screen

Tip: If you don't get on with the video capture software built into iMovie or whichever video editing package you use, you could consider using the Pro version of Apple's QuickTime player as a video capture tool. It'll cost you a few bucks, but's easy to use. Download it from: quicktime.com

Tip: If you're feeling really lazy, use the **OneStep DVD…** feature in iDVD, found in the **File** menu: just plug in your camcorder, and iDVD captures all the footage, arranges the clips, and a few minutes later spits out a DVD.

Tip: Make sure the time and date are set on your camera, as this can sometimes be the cause of camera-to-Mac communication problems.

Tip: To open older iMovie HD projects into the iLife '08 version of iMovie use the option in the File menu. Irritatingly, titles, transitions and music are not carried over from iMovie HD, so you will have to reinstate these elements once the import has completed.

Tip: Use the **Spacebar** to stop and start video capture; also to play and stop when editing and previewing.

controls can be used to play, pause, rewind and fast-forward the tape in the camera. If the connection doesn't work, it may be because your camera has gone to sleep; turn the camera off and then on again (this is known as "cycling the power"). If you see yourself rather than the contents of your DV tape on the screen, you more than likely have your Mac's iSight camera selected as the input device. Use the dropdown menu at the bottom of the **Camera Import** window to select your DV camera instead.

It's worth bearing in mind, while capturing, that digital video will rapidly consume the space on your hard drive. For this reason, it's worth logging your MiniDV cassettes. Go through your footage before you start capturing and make a note of the time-codes where you want to start and stop capturing; this will save you both time and disk space.

Working with Events

Before you know it, you should have a bunch of clips in your iMovie **Event Library** (pictured opposite), arranged into Events and ready to be added to specific Projects. Each time you either capture or import footage it can either be added to an existing Event or named as a new Event. Here are a few tips for using the Event Library:

▶ Hold ⇧ while you click to select and view the contents multiple Events.

▶ To merge Events, simple drag one onto another and rename the new merged Event when prompted.

▶ Use the Show dropdown at the bottom of iMovie to determine which clips are displayed in the Event Library.

▶ Use the slider in the bottom-right corner of iMovie to expand and contract clips within the Event Library.

Working with Projects

Once you've assembled your Events Library, its time to arrange your clips in the Project timeline, and add audio, effects and transitions from their respective panes, as and when you need them. The best way to learn is to experiment. Here are a few pointers to help you find your way around:

 Use this button to toggle the Project and Event areas between the upper and lower iMovie frames

Project timeline

Viewer window...
Small ⌘5
Medium ⌘6
Large ⌘7

 Use these buttons, and the panel below them, to import music and photos, add titles, and add video transitions between clips

Projects

Events

 Click the microphone button and then tap a clip to record an audio overdub using your Mac's built-in mic

Select a clip in the timeline area and use the crop/rotate tool to zoom, rotate and reframe the footage

 Adjust audio settings – ducking, volume and fades – to tweak the sound of selected clip

 Adjust video settings and white balance for a selected clip

Editing shortcuts

iMovie features loads of hotkeys that should drastically speed up your editing and generally turn you into a cutting-room guru:

Move playhead/selection back	→
Expand selection forward	⇧→
Move playhead/selection forward	←
Expand selection back	⇧←
Move playhead at speed	Hold down ← or →
Reject selection (in Events)	R or ⌫
Mark as Favourite (in Events)	F
Unmark as Favourite (in Events)	U
Trim clip (in Projects)	⌘R
Trim to selection (in Projects)	⌘B
Play selection	/
Play around current frame (1 sec)	[
Play around current frame (3 sec)	]
Play in full screen mode	⌘G
Export movie to file	⌘E

Extra effects

There are hundreds of third-party iMovie plug-ins and standalone applications available online – for everything from cleaning grainy footage (Discreet's Cleaner) to removing unwanted wobble (iStabilize). Some cost a few dollars or pounds (depending on where the developer is based), but others are free. Start here:

PluginsWorld imovie.pluginsworld.com
Stupendous Software stupendous-software.com
Apple apple.com/downloads/macosx/video

Many plug-ins are installed by a downloadable installer, while a few may need to be dragged into the **iMovie > Plug-ins** folder within your user or computer **Library** folder, depending on whether you want to install them for just you or for all user accounts on the Mac.

There are even more plug-ins available for some of the other video-editing packages, one of our favourites being the Russian Lomo Kompakt Automat for Final Cut Pro, which allows you to achieve that retro Soviet look in order to "exceed the limits of that which was formerly known as maximum hipness":

RussianKamera riverrockstudios.com/riverrock/
pages/russianKamera.html

Find an audience

There are various options for getting your new flick out of iMovie and into the wider world, all of which are found via the **Share** menu. The export options that you are presented with are pretty much idiot-proof. Check the boxes that relate to your intended use of the file (if you need a little help deciding, hover your mouse over the "i"s to the right to view the parameters and size of the file each option will generate).

When you are ready, hit the **Export** or **Publish** button and the job is done. In brief, your export alternatives are:

▶ **iTunes...** This dumps your movie straight into iTunes ready to be synced with an iPod, iPhone or Apple TV, or simply stored for posterity.

▶ **Media Browser** This makes your movie file available for quick access from other Apple applications such as iDVD, iWeb and Mail.

▶ **YouTube** With a YouTube account use this option to upload your flicks straight from iMovie. To set up iMovie with either a new or existing YouTube account, select this option and click the **Add...** button.

▶ **.Mac Web Gallery** If you're signed up with .Mac (see p.34), choose this option to export your movie directly onto your Web Gallery (see p.252). From there it can be viewed online or downloaded from anywhere with Web access. If you don't have .Mac, you could always publish the movie to a self-built website by instead choosing **Export Movie...** and uploading the resulting file manually.

> **Tip:** Once you have captured and edited all your footage, you can strip out the dead wood by choosing **File > Space Saver....** This sends any unused clips to the trash, allowing you to reclaim space on your hard drive. By default, clips that you have marked as **Favourites** using the ★ button are not banished.

making movies

Tip: If you only want friends to see your Web Gallery movies, you can protect the page with a password.

▶ **Export Movie** This menu item releases your movie as a file that can be saved anywhere on your system.

▶ **Export Final Cut XML** This option exports your movie as a project file that can be opened by applications from the Final Cut Pro family, though don't expect all the transitions to translate perfectly.

▶ **QuickTime** Of all the alternatives, this one gives you the most flexibility, offering everything from AVI export options to AIFF and WAV audio options. Useful if you have specific file-format requirements.

Find out more

This chapter has only really scratched the surface of what it is possible to do with iMovie. If you want to take it to the next level, get online and search for tips, tricks and tutorials. A good place to start is Apple's iLife Tutorials page:

iLife Tutorials apple.com/ilife/tutorials

Security & maintenance

Privacy & passwords

From emails and Web histories to saved passwords and work documents, computers store all sorts of data about their owners and the people they know. Choosing a Mac, as opposed to a PC, makes you significantly less vulnerable to Internet-based privacy invasions (for more on online security, see p.160). But anyone with a little bit of know-how and physical access to your computer – a thief, an unpleasant colleague, or whoever – could probably access all your data. The following pages explain what you can do about it, and also takes a look at Keychains, which OS X uses to store all your passwords.

First, the obvious stuff. If you're worried by the prospect of someone else being able to access your data, make sure you have a password set up for your account (see p.53), and make sure you've disabled **Automatic Login** so that no one can access your account just by switching on the Mac. To do this, open **System Preferences** > **Accounts** and click **Login Options**. You may first have to click the lock icon at the bottom.

Next, get your Mac to request your password when it is awoken from sleep (standby) or from a screen saver. You'll find this option in the **Security** panel of System Preferences.

Forgotten password?

If you're locked out of your account, see p.53 for instruction on getting back in.

Tip: Unless you're in the habit of saving or moving files to random places on the hard drive, all your private data lives in your home folder. That includes not just your documents, movies, etc, but all your emails, Web cache, saved passwords (all of which live in your **Library**) and everything on your desktop.

These tricks will make sure that no random outsider can get immediate access to your files. But that doesn't means they're safe. As we've seen (see p.52), anyone set up as an administrator on the computer can easily reset your password and log in as you. And even if you're the only administrator, someone with a Mac OS X install CD can reset your password; it's also possible to pilfer data by booting a Mac as a hard drive (see p.296). For more comprehensive security, investigate the following.

#1. FileVault

FileVault, introduced with Mac OS X v10.3, brings military-grade file encryption to your home folder. It scrambles the folder so that even if someone can access your system by booting from CD – or even removes the hard drive – they won't be able to access your files without your password.

One problem with FileVault is that, since it encrypts and decrypts your data in real time, it can marginally slow down your computer. Today, the effect shouldn't be all that noticeable (unlike with the first version of FileVault that was released) but it still might bother you. Also note that some users have also reported strange problems that have been solved simply by turning off FileVault.

To switch on FileVault, look in the **Security** panel of **System Preferences**. Before doing so, though, consider setting up a master password for the computer – if you haven't done so already. This is basically just a backup in case you ever forget your account login password. Make a note of this one somewhere – if you forget both, you can kiss goodbye to all your files forever.

Tip: If you share your Mac with friends or family members, but you find it more convenient to have only one user account set up, consider locking the various **System Preferences** panels by opening them and clicking the padlock icon. That way, if anyone accidentally (or deliberately) tries to change any settings, they'll need to enter your password.

Tip: If you have problems with FileVault, but you want to encrypt your data, look into PGP desktop, a third-party application that offers a similar level of protection.

PGP desktop pgp.com

#2. Encrypting files & folders

If you just want to restrict access to certain files and folders, rather than your whole account, the easiest option is to put them into an encrypted disk image file (see p.107 for more on what that means). It's a bit like making a password-protected folder.

First, assemble the files you want to protect in a folder. Then open **Disk Utility** from **Applications > Utilities**. Next click **File > New > Disk Image from Folder...**, pick a name and location, choose either **128-bit AES** or **256-bit AES** from the **Encryption** menu (the latter is more secure but takes longer to encrypt) and hit **Create**. When prompted, enter a password and deselect **Remember password** for extra security.

Alternatively, click the **New Image** button to create a disk image of any particular size, which leaves room to drag in extra files later.

Your new disk image file will appear and be "mounted" as if it were a hard drive. Once all your private files are in the DMG file, you can delete (maybe "secure" delete: see p.47) the originals. Next time you want to access the files, or add extra files to your protected area, double-click on the disk image file and enter your password. Don't forget the password or, as with FileVault, your files will be lost forever.

DES & AES

FileVault and encrypted disk images are based on the Advanced Encryption Standard (AES), a very sophisticated system that marks a vast improvement over the earlier Digital Encryption Standard (DES). AES is, at the moment, essentially impossible to crack. According to Apple's calculations, a computer capable of "cracking" DES in a single second would take nearly 150 trillion years (longer than the life of the Universe) to work out your FileVault or disk image password.

Top Secret Folder.dmg

Top Secret Folder

Double-click the DMG file to reveal the password-protected virtual drive. Don't forget to "eject" the drive when you've finished.

#3. Open Firmware Password

If you don't want to use FileVault but you want to protect your files – or if you're keen to protect the entire computer rather that just your home folder – then employ the Open Firmware Password utility (found on your OS X software installation CD under **Applications > Utilities**). Once installed, the system won't allow any of the special start-up routines that can compromise security – such as booting from CD or starting up as a target drive.

If for some reason you *do* need to boot from CD, or use any other special start-up routine, hold down ⌘⌥OF and power up your Mac. When the Open Firmware prompt appears, type reset-nvram and hit **Enter**. Key in the password you created when installing the application, and hit **OK**. When the **Open Firmware** prompt appears, type reset-all and hit **Enter**.

Password Keychains

Computer users quickly accumulate lots of passwords: for Internet connections, email accounts, websites, routers, network folders, online banks, disk images… the list goes on. When you enter a password on your Mac, OS X will usually offer to remember it. If you accept, you shouldn't need to enter that password again, as it will be stored in your virtual "Keychain", and OS X will insert it when required.

Keychains are very handy, but if you're worried about someone being able to access all your passwords when you leave the room for a few minutes, you could ramp up the security by asking OS X to "lock" the Keychain, either permanently or after a period of

Tip: If you ever forget a password that has been stored on your Keychain, open Keychain Access and locate the relevant item in the list. Double-click it and select **Show Password**. You'll need to enter your Keychain password (the same as your account password unless you've changed it) and then the missing password will be revealed.

inactivity. When locked, the Keychain will request your overall Keychain password before dishing out any information.

By default, this Keychain password is the same as your account password – which is handy, but it means that if someone can access your account, they can also access your passwords. For even more security, you could change your Keychain password, or even add a second Keychain with a separate password.

All these changes can be made within the Keychain Access utility, accessible from the **Applications > Utilities** folder. Click the padlock icon to toggle the lock on or off; or select **Change Settings for "Keychain Login"** or **Change Password for "Keychain Login"** (your default Keychain) from the **Edit** menu.

> **Tip:** If you just want to password protect some text information – numbers and the like – create a Secure Note using Keychain Access.

Other privacy issues

▶ **Deleting files** When you delete a file, it goes to your Trash, so anyone with access to the account can recover it. Emptying the Trash stops this happening, though in theory the deleted files could still be resuscitated using special recovery software. To avoid this possibility, select **Secure Empty Trash** from the **Finder** menu, and the files will not only be deleted but completely blanked from the hard drive.

> **Tip:** Also consider privacy threats on the Internet (these are covered overleaf) and over your wireless network (see p.69).

▶ **Private browsing** Your browser records all the websites you've been to in your History, cookies, searches and more. To stop this happening, enable **Private Browsing** from the **File** menu in Safari. Or choose **Reset Safari** to delete all the saved info.

▶ **Recent Items** If you don't want all your recently accessed files and programs – as well as any servers you've connected to – listed for all to see, go to > **Recent Items** and click **Clear Menu** right at the bottom. Individual applications usually have a similar list in the **File** menu.

34 Hackers, viruses & scams

As we've already mentioned, one of the best things about Macs, when compared with PCs, is that they're so much less prone to online security threats. It's not that OS X is the computer equivalent of Fort Knox – though undoubtedly the solid UNIX foundation helps. Much more important is that "hackers" and the mischievous programmers who dream up viruses and "malware" tend to focus on Windows, since that's what most of the computing world is stuck with.

This is all cause for celebration for Mac users, but it shouldn't be cause for complacency – not least because Mac users are just as prone to scams as anyone else. Here's a quick breakdown of what you need to know about hackers, viruses and scammers.

Hackers

The term "hacker" is somewhat fuzzy, as its original meaning – still in use among the computerati – is a legitimate computer programmer (see en.wikipedia.org/wiki/Hacker). But it's the popular definition that concerns us here: someone who wants to break into, or meddle

A karma thang?

Some commentators think that the comparative lack of Mac security threats isn't just down to Apple's small market share, but also relates to the fact that OS X is so pleasing and elegant to use. As Kelly Martin from Security Focus has written: "if a Windows programmer or security researcher can try a new operating system and enjoy it just enough to not want to destroy it, then there's hope for us all."

with, your computer. They may be a professional out to steal your secrets or a "script kiddy" playing with a prefab Trojan. They might be a vandal, a spy, a thief or simply just exploring. As far as you're concerned, it doesn't matter. You don't want them, or their handiwork, inside your computer. The best way to avoid hackers is to activate a firewall.

Firewalls

A firewall, which can be either a hardware device or a piece of software, prevents people from being able to detect and invade your computer via the Internet. Mac OS X comes with a pretty decent firewall installed, but you may need to turn it on. To do this, open **System Preferences > Security**, click the **Firewall** tab and select **Block all incoming connections**. For most users, that's all you need to know. But if any Internet-related applications stop working after you switch on the Firewall, it probably isn't a coincidence. Try turning the Firewall off again and, if that solves the problem, choose the **Limit incoming connections...** option and the + button to add specific applications to the allow list (this will open the relevant "ports" for the application in question).

The firewall built in to OS X is perfectly good enough for most home users, but if you're really worried about intrusions, or you want to be able to monitor all the "network traffic" coming in and out of your machine, grab a third-party application such as:

Little Snitch obdev.at/products/littlesnitch ($25)
Norton Personal Firewall symantec.com ($50)

Tip: You're much less prone to all kinds of online privacy threats if you regularly install the latest patches and updates. Run > **Software Update** every week or so and always accept any security fixes or OS X upgrades that you are offered.

When you activate any of the sharing options under the **System Preferences > Sharing**, the relevant type of network traffic is automatically added to OS X's Firewall "allow" list.

Viruses

Are Mac users at risk from viruses, worms, Trojans and other such malware? Companies with scanning software to sell might say "yes", and it's true there's no reason why a killer OS X virus shouldn't emerge next week. In truth, though, the risks are very small. After all, there are nearly 150,000 PC viruses in circulation, and the majority of PC users have suffered little or no inconvenience at the hand of viruses. For OS X, by comparison, there has never been a single virus circulated. If, despite this, you still want the extra protection of virus software, the most popular choices are:

Norton AntiVirus symantec.com/nav/nav_mac ($50)
McAfee Virex mcafee.com ($36)

One point to note. Most of the viruses that have affected pre-OS X Macs were macro viruses, spread via Microsoft Word and Excel docs. If you ever receive a doc with embedded macros, choose the **Disable Macros** option when asked.

What about spyware?

Spyware is software designed to snoop on your computing activity. Most commonly it's planted by some kind of marketeer, who wants to find out about your online surfing and spending habits. But it might be more sinister: a keystroke-logger that records whatever you type when, say, logging in to an Internet banking site.

Recent reports suggest that the majority of PCs are infected with some kind of spyware (mostly the non-dangerous types), but, once again, Macs users are relatively safe. No widely employed Mac spyware applications are known. So unless you have a particular reason to believe there's a snitch in your system, you shouldn't need this Spyware scanning package:

MacScan macscan.securemac.com

Scams

Mac users, understandably, get a little bit smug over their lack of virus woes, but they're no less susceptible to online scams, and these are often more threatening than hackers and viruses…

▶ **Beware the phishermen** "Phishing" is a cunning form of online scam in which someone pretends to be from your bank, ISP, online payment system or any other such body, and asks you to hand over your personal information either directly or via a webpage. The classic example is a scammer sending out a mass email claiming to be from a bank, with a link pointing to a webpage purportedly on a real bank's website. In fact, all the details are slightly incorrect (for example, the page might be at www.hsbc-banking.com instead of www.hsbc.com) but the recipient doesn't notice, assumes the email is legitimate and follows the instructions to "confirm" their online banking details on the fake site – in the process giving them to

A classic phishing attack, received on a Mac by one of this book's authors. The payment never took place, but the sender was hoping to scare recipients into logging in to a fake PayPal site, thereby handing over their usernames and passwords.

hackers, viruses & scams

Tip: If you get one of the notorious messages inviting you to make millions from taking part in African money-laundering, beat the scammers at their own game using this site: flooble.com/fun/reply.php

a criminal, who can then empty their account. The moral of the story: never respond to emails – or instant messages – requesting private information, however legitimate they seem.

▶ **Don't respond to spam** Those "get paid to surf", "stock tips", "work from home", "recruit new members", "clear your credit rating" and various network-marketing schemes *are* too good to be true. It should go without saying that ringing a number to claim a prize will only cost you money.

▶ **Paying by credit cards** online is actually usually safer than sending a cheque in the post, since most cards offer some degree of protection against fraud, businesses going bankrupt before you receive your goods, and so on. Read the fine print on your agreement for specifics, but normally you're only liable for a set amount. You also might be able to pay a yearly surcharge to fully protect your card against fraud, though this is usually bad value unless you think you're more at risk than others. If you suspect you've been wrongly charged, ask your bank what to do, but also contact the site in question – eBay even picks up the bill if you've been conned.

▶ **Only enter card details on secure webpages** When a webpage is secure, the beginning of the address is https:// and a little lock symbol appears on your browser window. If you're concerned about a site's security, shop elsewhere or phone through your order, but never send your credit card details by email.

▶ **Don't give extra information** To make an online purchase you should only need to provide your name, billing address, delivery address, credit card number, account name, expiry date and, sometimes, the three-digit security code on the signature strip. You should never need any other form of identification such as your social security number, health insurance details, driving licence or passport number.

Backing up

35

Any computer file, whether it resides in a scruffy old grey PC or an elegant iMac, can be deleted or become corrupted. Though it's often possible to "recover" files that seem to have been erased or overwritten, this is of no use if your computer gets stolen or destroyed. So if your Mac contains valuable documents, a library of music or a collection of irreplaceable digital photographs, it's unquestionably worth regularly backing up your files to some kind of external media. Leopard's Time Machine feature makes both backing up and recovering data very straightforward. Let's take a look at how it works and also outline a few alternative backing up strategies.

Time Machine

There are several different ways to back up, but the most conven-ient method by far is to use OS X's built-in Time Machine applica-tion in conjunction with an external hard drive. Such drives are fast, capacious and connect to your Mac via either a FireWire or USB2 cable (see box overleaf). Time Machine, meanwhile, can be set up in a couple of minutes and then be forgotten about; it even makes the process of recovering lost data enjoyable.

Buying a hard drive

External drives start at around $75/£50, with prices varying according to capacity, quality and any special features. If you intend to use your drive with Time Machine (or any other application that accumulates incremental backups) aim to purchase a drive with a capacity roughly double that of the amount of data you intend to back up. To see how much data is currently stored on your Mac, select Macintosh HD on the Desktop and choose **File > Info** (or hit ⌘I). When making your calculations, take into account how much media (music, video, photos, etc) you are likely to accumulate over the next year or two. If you intend to use Time Machine, also consider that the larger your drive, the further back in time you will be able to go to restore files.

Tip: You can use Time Machine to back up multiple Macs to the same drive – as long as the drive has enough space.

Setting up Time Machine

When you connect a hard drive to your Mac, Time Machine should spring into life automatically and ask if you'd like to make a backup. If this doesn't happen, open Time Machine from the Dock or Applications, or go to System Preferences and choose **Time Machine**. Next, hit **Choose Backup Disk…** and select your connected drive from the list.

By default, Time Machine will back up all the data on your machine the first time you use it and then, over time, append accumulative updates of all the files that change. That means the amount of backed-up data will grow over time, so if possible use a backup drive with enough capacity to keep you going for a while (see box). When Time Machine runs out of space it automatically starts deleting the oldest backed up files to make room for newer ones.

If you think space will be an issue, or simply don't want to back up all of your data, selected files and folders can be excluded from by hitting the **Options** button within **System Preferences > Time Machine** and then using the "+" button to add items to the **Do not back up** list. If you choose to exclude any folder that contains system files you will be offered the option to **Exclude All System Files** – the logic being that these files can be restored from the System Restore disk that came with your Mac.

Restoring from Time Machine

This is where the fun starts. When you want to recover a deleted file or folder, or restore a file or folder to an earlier state, select the item in question in Finder and then launch Time Machine from the Dock or Applications.

Similarly, to restore iTunes, iPhoto, Address Book and iCal to an earlier state, click into the window of the application in question and launch Time Machine.

Your Mac is then whisked off to what appears to be the edge of a black hole. Here you can skip through your Mac's backups by either clicking through the stack of windows, tapping on the arrows (lower-right) or scrolling up and down the "time line" on the screen's right-hand edge. When you find the item in its desired state, hit **Restore**.

Tip: Time Machine can be used to back up to a network server or drive – even via wireless, though this can take a while.

Tip: If you don't want to give up your entire hard drive to Time Machine, first split the drive into two partitions using Disk Utility (see p.279) and then select one of the partitions as your backup drive in Time Machine.

Tip: By default, Time Machine will carry out regular backups according to the schedule specified in **System Preferences > Time Machine**. But if your Mac is not permanently connected to your backup drive (say if you have a laptop) then backups will take place whenever you plug the drive in.

What to back up

When backing up your Mac, you ideally want to cover everything that could be a pain to lose – including emails, photos, music, movie footage, documents, bookmarks, preferences, contacts and calendars. The obvious way to make sure you don't forget anything is to back up the entire contents of your hard drive (the Time Machine default option).

A slightly more efficient alternative is to back up just your home folder. This way you should get all your personal files and data but you won't waste space backing up applications or OS X system files that could be easily reinstated from the original discs or downloads (see box, left).

If there's more than one user account set up on your Mac, there will be more than one home folder. If you have administrative powers, you could deal with them all at once by backing up the entire **Users** folder, found in the top-level of **Macintosh HD**.

If you don't have room for your entire home folder, you'll need to be more selective. A few pointers:

▶ **Music** The music files that make up your iTunes Library live within your home folder under **Music > iTunes > iTunes Music**. You can back up individual artists or albums from there, but if you want to retain playlists, album artwork and other such extras, you'll need to back up the entire **iTunes** folder.

Tip: If you're only backing up your home folder, have a think about whether you've ever saved anything elsewhere – such as shared widgets, screen savers or fonts in **Macintosh HD > Library**.

▶ **Photos** Again, you can back up individual pics, but to safeguard your albums, Events and other such data, simply back up the **Pictures > iPhoto Library**, which contains the whole kit and caboodle.

▶ **Library** If possible, back up the entire **Library** folder within your home folder, as this contains things such as emails, contacts and calendars. If you don't have space for it all, at least grab the following…

▶ **Email** If you use Mail, you'll find your email files within **Library > Mail**. For other email clients, look for a folder named after the application in either your home folder's **Documents** or **Library** folders.

▶ **Bookmarks** For Safari bookmarks, back up the **Bookmarks.plist** file (found within **Library > Safari**). If you use Firefox, back up the **Library > Application Support > Firefox**.

▶ **Contacts & Calendars** Address Book contacts and iCal calendars are found under **Library > Application Support > AddressBook** and **Library > iCal** respectively.

▶ **Fonts** Don't worry about fonts that came with OS X, but any that you've added can be backed up via the various **Fonts** folders (see p.135).

Backing-up without using Time Machine

If you have an external hard drive, a flash drive or even an iPod (see overleaf) you can easily back up individual files or folders by simply dragging and dropping them onto the device in question. To keep things tidy, however, first create a folder on the drive and name it with a date (eg backup 04.02.06). Each time you overwrite its contents, rename the folder with the new date. This way you can see at a glance when you last backed up. Other backup options include:

> **Tip:** The items on your desktop are covered if you back up your home folder, but if you are backing up selectively, don't forget anything important that you keep there.

▲

USB flash drives such as this one from Samsung, are inexpensive and eminently portable – great for backing up essential documents.

Tip: Another option is to set up an email account with an online provider such as Yahoo! or Gmail and back up key files by emailing them to that account. However, with most accounts you'll be limited to sending around 10MB per email.

▶ **CDs & DVDs** If you don't want to buy an external drive, you could back up files onto writeable CDs or (if your Mac has a SuperDrive) DVDs. CDs are not ideal because of their relatively small capacity (around 700MB per disc); DVDs are better, but the whole process is still slower and more cumbersome than using an external drive. For more on burning CDs and DVDs, see p.85.

▶ **Online backups** In a sense, backing up data online is ideal, insofar as your precious files are duplicated to a remote location. However, uploading lots of data can take an age, so in reality this is only an option if you want to back up certain key files rather than your whole system. A .Mac account (see p.34) features tools for backing up online, though you'll get more webspace for your money with a dedicated online storage service such as that provided by xdrive.com.

iPod as back-up drive

iPods are basically just external hard drives or flash drive storage drives in pretty cases. Though they don't work with Time Machine, you can use iPods to manually back up and transfer all kinds of files – without even affecting their ability to play music. First, attach your iPod to your Mac, open iTunes and under the **Summary** tab check **Enable disk use**. The Pod will now function exactly like any other hard drive – when you attach it, its icon will appear on the desktop and Finder Sidebars, ready to receive files. Note that, as with any other drive, you'll now have to eject the Pod (see p.47) before physically disconnecting it – even if you're just using iTunes.

If there's room on the iPod, you could back up your entire system. But if you're short of space you may want to drag files on selectively – perhaps avoiding music and/or photos that are already stored on the Pod. That said, bear in mind that you'll need to use special software if you ever want to move your iPod's music archive back onto your Mac (see p.218). And if you're relying on your iPod's photo archive as a backup, make sure you have it set up to grab the full-resolution versions each time you connect the Pod to the Mac: connect your iPod and look for the option under the **Photos** tab in iTunes.

Help!

In terms of reliability and ease of use, Macs have come a long way since the dark days of OS 9. Still, no personal computer functions flawlessly, and your Mac may occasionally refuse to co-operate. There are whole books dedicated to OS X troubleshooting and it's obviously beyond the scope of a guide such as this to tackle every problem that you may encounter. Still, this chapter covers the most common headaches.

My Mac has frozen

When your Mac is busy processing something, or it's frozen ("crashed"), your mouse cursor will turn into a colourful spinning disc. Affectionately known as the spinning beachball of death, the colourful disc will sometimes disrupt only one application, but at other times everything will grind to a standstill. Either way, give the Mac a few minutes to sort itself out, and then try to quit the application, either from its application menu or with the shortcut ⌘Q.

If that doesn't work, choose > **Force Quit Applications** or roll out the three-fingered salute: hold down ⌘ and ⌥ and press **Esc**. A box will appear listing the applications that you currently have running. If one of them says "Not Responding", select it and then press the **Force Quit** button;

Tip: When you Force Quit an application you'll lose any unsaved work in that application. So if you're working on something important and you haven't saved for a while, give the machine five minutes or so to find its feet before trying to Force Quit.

help!

Another way to Force Quit an application is to click and hold its dock icon and then press the ⌥ *key to reveal the* **Force Quit** *option.*

▼

Startup modes

When troubleshooting your Mac, there are various key combinations that do useful things during startup – some of which are referred to in this chapter. In each case, you have to make sure the Mac is switched off (hold down the power button for five seconds if you're not sure). Then switch on and as soon as you hear the startup "chime" hold down one of the following until something appears on the screen:

⇧	**Safe Mode**
⌘S	**Single User Mode**
C	**Boot from CD**

if "Not Responding" doesn't appear, pick the application you suspect has caused the problem and Force Quit that. If the application isn't in the list, see whether it shows up in the Activity Monitor list (see opposite) – if it does, select it there and press **Quit Process**.

If this doesn't work, try selecting Finder in the Force Quit box and pressing the **Relaunch** button. Still no joy? Hold down ⌘^⏏ to quit all applications and restart. If there is no response to this command, you may have to force your Mac to shut down: hold down the power button for around five seconds. Then wait for ten seconds or so and restart. Hopefully, everything will now be fine. If not, try repairing permissions (p.296). Or if the machine won't start up again…

My Mac won't switch on

If your Mac won't even begin to start up, check the obvious stuff. Is it definitely plugged in? Is the wall-socket working and switched on? All fine? Could it be that the Mac is already turned on and has frozen up with a dark screen? If so, hold down the power button for five seconds. After ten seconds or so, try again.

Still no joy? Try unplugging all external devices (scanners, printers, iPods, etc) except your mouse and keyboard. If you recently installed any internal parts, such as extra RAM, remove those too. Finally, if you have a Mac laptop, try a System Management Controller (SMC) reset by pressing ^⌘ (**Ctrl** and **Command**) at the same time as the power button.

My Mac freezes-up during startup

First, force your Mac to shut down by holding the power button for five seconds. After ten seconds or so, start up again. Still freezing? Force shut-down again and, if you have an Ethernet cable attached

Activity Monitor

Activity Monitor, which you'll find in **Applications** > **Utilities**, is a useful tool for seeing what your Mac is up to behind the scenes. One thing it lets you do is select and Force Quit individual "tasks" – such as utilities and Finder plug-ins that have frozen. But Activity Monitor also allows you to keep an eye on your system's CPU, RAM and disk activity – which can often be useful when troubleshooting. If a small inactive application is consistently using up 50 percent of your processing power, say, that's a good signal that all is not well with that application.

To keep an eye on CPU, RAM or disk activity while you work, click and explore the options in the **View** menu. If you like, it will even display a real-time graph of your CPU usage on the utility's Dock icon.

to your Mac, disconnect it. Switch back on. No joy? Try Emptying your PRAM (which stands for Parameter RAM, and is pronounced p-ram). Don't worry about what this means, just restart your Mac and as soon as you hear the "chime", hold down these four keys: ⌘⌥PR. Keep them held down until you hear the chime again. Then release the keys to let the Mac start up.

If the problem persists, reboot in Safe Mode (see box opposite) and delete any non-Apple items found within these two folders: **Macintosh HD** > **Library** > **StartupItems** and **Macintosh HD** > **System** > **Library** > **StartupItems**. It that doesn't fix it, boot in Safe Mode again, open **System Preferences** > **Accounts** > **Login Items**, and select each entry in turn and remove it by clicking the "–" button. Restart.

Still won't work? Try booting in Single User Mode (see box opposite). When the scary-looking white text appears, carefully type the following lines, hitting the **Enter** key after each line…

Startup beeps

If your Mac makes one or more beeps when you switch on, there may be something wrong with its memory (RAM). Assuming you can get to the internal slots, make sure the chips are firmly pushed into place. If you recently upgraded the RAM, remove the new chips and try using only the originals.

```
mount -uw /
mv /Library/Preferences/com.apple.loginwindow.plist preferences2.old
mv /Library/Preferences/com.apple.windowserver.plist preferences3.old
reboot
```

Repair permissions

OS X's permissions settings sometimes go pear-shaped, leading to all manner of problems. To repair permissions, open Disk Utility from **Applications > Utilities**. Select your Mac's hard disk in the list and click **First Aid** then **Repair Disk Permissions**.

If you can't access Disk Utility, insert the Software Install disc that came with your Mac and reboot while holding down **C**. You'll find Disk Utility in the **Installer** menu.

Mac as hard drive

Target Mode allows you to boot your Mac as an external hard drive to another Mac. Turn off the Mac you want to use as a hard drive and connect it to the other Mac with a standard FireWire cable. Then hold down the **T** key on the first Mac and restart. Its hard drive should appear on the desktop of the other Mac. This can be a lifesaver if you can't start up your Mac and you want to access its files; or if you've forgotten your password and don't have your OS X startup disc to hand.

Finally, if you can't even access either of these modes, try running repairing permissions (see box) via Disk Utility from the Software Install CD that came with your Mac.

Other Mac misbehaviour

When your Mac does anything strange – such as messing up your icons, continually freezing up or running slowly – and you don't know what the problem is, follow these three steps, in this order, before trying anything else:

▶ **Restart the Mac** This will fix the majority of problems.

▶ **Check your hard drive space** A full hard drive can cause slowness and other problems. Select your hard drive's icon on the desktop and click **Get Info** in the **File Menu**. If the figure next to **Available** is in megabytes (MB) rather than gigabytes (GB), then delete or back up some unwanted files and empty the trash.

▶ **Repair permissions** See box, left.

OS X won't let me access a file or folder

If you can't open, delete or move a file or folder, make sure it isn't locked (see p.89) and that you have "Read & Write" permissions (see p.59). Still no access? Repair permissions (see box, left).

The Trash won't empty

If you get an error message when you try to empty the Trash, quit all applications and try again. Still no luck? Open the Trash from the Dock and check the files to see if any are locked (see p.89).

Mac laptop batteries

Mac laptops are powered by Lithium-ion batteries that can keep going much longer than the batteries found in most PC laptops. However, over the years, all Lithium-based batteries gradually lose their ability to hold a decent charge, and in the end they give up the ghost completely. If you run your Mac laptop from the battery every day, you may find that it needs to be replaced after a year or two. This is, unfortunately, quite normal, and is true of PC laptops – and iPods – as well as Macs. New batteries can be purchased from the Apple Store for $129/£99.

To increase the overall life of your battery:

▶ **Stay up to date** Among the various good reasons for accepting all updates to OS X (see p.37) is the fact that they sometimes relate to battery management. Also accept updates for your various applications, when offered.

▶ **Temperature** Your battery will last much longer if you use and store your laptop at room temperature or thereabouts. Avoid any extremes of temperature – hot or cold – especially for extended periods of time.

▶ **Plug it in** Plug in your laptop whenever possible, including when the battery is half charged. However, if you leave it plugged in nearly all the time, let the battery run down completely around once a month.

▶ **Storage** If your laptop is likely to remain unused for six months or more, switch it off when the battery is around 50 percent charged. To view your battery's charge status in the menu bar, check the box within the **Options** pane of the **Energy Saver** > **Battery** panel illustrated below.

To increase the time you get from a single charge:

▶ **Contrast** Turn down your screen contrast to the lowest acceptable level using the **F1** and **F2** keys.

▶ **Quit applications** Quit all programs that you're not using.

▶ **Switch off AirPort** If you're not using it, switch off AirPort via the fan-shaped icon in the menu bar. Also switch off Bluetooth, if you have it on.

▶ **Explore the settings** Open **System Preferences** > **Energy Saver** and select **Battery** from the **Settings For** menu. Then choose **Better Battery Life** from the **Optimization** menu. Your Mac will be slightly slower, but slightly more energy efficient. To tweak the settings further, click **Show Details** and explore the **Sleep** and **Options** tabs.

Tip: If you're worried about the possibility that your hard drive might crash, download SMARTReporter, a free application that will try to warn you in advance – by email or with an on-screen alert – if disaster is about to strike. Grab it from: homepage. mac.com/julianmayer

My Mac won't sleep

First, make sure DVD Player (see p.255) isn't running. Next ensure that Sleep isn't turned off in the **Energy Saver** panel of **System Preferences**. Finally, if you have a Mac laptop, make sure the keyboard hasn't come loose; if it has, push it back into position.

My Mac kicked the bucket

If your Apple's truly crumbled, resist the temptation to throw it in the kitchen bin. Find out how to dispose of it properly here:

Mac Recycling apple.com/environment/recycling

I deleted the wrong file!

If you've accidentally deleted – or overwritten – an important file or folder, and it's no longer in the Trash, you can easily get it back using Time Machine, if you use it (see p.287). If you don't have any form of backup, you can probably still dig the lost data up from the dark depths of your hard drive using data recovery software. Do this ASAP, as the longer you leave it, the smaller your chances of getting your data back. Two of the best Mac data recovery applications are:

Data Rescue II prosofteng.com ($100)
TechTool Pro micromat.com ($98)

You can download a free trial of Data Rescue II and use it to see which files you'll be able to recover (and salvage one file of 500k or less) before having to cough up for the full version.

Macology

Mac websites

There are thousands of sites on the Web that focus on all things Mac, from simple blogs to vast portals with discussion forums, troubleshooting tips, news and reviews. We've gathered together many of the best over the following pages, though you'll find hundreds more links scattered throughout this book. We've dedicated a separate section to online Mac weirdness (see p.307).

Apple

Apple's own site is a very useful resource, though if you can't resist a hard sell, it can be an expensive place to visit. It features stacks of downloads, patches, articles, info and tips.

Apple apple.com
Apple Store apple.com/store

If you're having problems with your hardware or software, drop into the Software Updates and Support sections:

Software Updates apple.com/support/downloads
Service & Support apple.com/support

But don't forget the discussion forums. Post a question or quandary and you may get a reply from a Mac know-it-all within minutes.

Apple Discussions discussions.info.apple.com

> **Tip:** Peeved with your Pod, PowerBook or Power Mac? Send feedback to Apple via:
>
> apple.com/feedback

Supersites, magazines & forums

For news, reviews, opinions and discussions, drop into any of the following:

About This Particular Macintosh atpm.com
EveryMac everymac.com
Mac|Life maclife.com
Macworld macworld.com
Insanely Great insanely-great.com
LowEndMac lowendmac.com
Mac Observer macobserver.com
MacMinute macminute.com
MacNN macnn.com

Rumour sites

Wondering what's in the Mac pipeline? Don't expect to find out from Apple, who usually only make advance announcements about their software. Instead, drop into one of these rumour sites. Expect around half of what you read to be true:

AppleInsider appleinsider.com
Mac Opinion macopinion.com
Think Secret thinksecret.com
Mac Rumors macrumors.com

Mac blogs

There are blogs covering everything these days, and Macs are no exception. A few of the best are:

AppleWatch apple.blognewschannel.com
Daring Fireball daringfireball.net

Mac newsfeeds

The best way to stay up to date with Mac news is to subscribe to some RSS feeds (see p.161 for instructions). Many of the sites and blogs listed here offer feeds.

Mac gaming

Despite what those big bullies with overclocked PCs might tell you, there's plenty of gaming to be done with your Mac. Head to:

macworld.com/games
apple.com/games
macgamesandmore.com
macgamer.com
gamedb.com
insidemacgames.com

And if you like miniaturized, lo-tech games, don't forget the scores of widgets in the "Games" section of:

apple.com/downloads/
dashboard

Tao of Mac the.taoofmac.com
The Unofficial Apple Weblog tuaw.com
The Apple Blog theappleblog.com
The Cult of Mac Blog cultofmac.com

Mac & accessories retailers

Reading the advice offered on p.19 – and scanning the reviews on the supersites listed opposite – should stand you in good stead when buying or selecting a Mac or accessory. Aside from the Apple store, major stockists include:

Amazon amazon.com (US) • amazon.co.uk (UK)
Cancom cancomuk.com (UK)
MacConnection macconnection.com (US)
Mac Zone maczone.com (US)

Mac minis

From the day of its release, the Mac mini has been a source of fascination and wonder to many people. No surprise, then, that there are a number of sites and blogs devoted to using, upgrading, discussing and generally worshipping the crab apple of the Mac family.

123Macmini 123macmini.com
Mac HTPC machtpc.com

iMovie - Render Soft Blur Effect
Time In Seconds – SHORTER bar means FASTER

Mac laptops

WhiteMacBook whitemacbook.com
Phone & Book Zone pbzone.com

Software downloads

Have you ever wished there was a bit of software devoted to carrying out some very specific task? Well, in all probability it already exists and is available for download via one of the following sites, all of which are overflowing with free or inexpensive apps for Macs.

Mac Update macupdate.com
Pure Mac pure-mac.com
Version Tracker versiontracker.com
Download.com download.com
TuCows tucows.com/macintosh

Mac creative

These sites should help you get the best out of the iLife suite and, in the case of design, industry-standard "creative" packages such as Photoshop and Illustrator:

Apple apple.com/ilife
Mac Design macdesignonline.com
MacJams macjams.com
Jim Heid's Macintosh Digital Hub Site macilife.com

Macs & PCs

If you want to make Apple and Wintel work together, see:

Emaculation emaculation.com
MacWindows macwindows.com

And for in-depth facts regarding the Mac vs PC debate, visit:

OS X vs Windows macvswindows.com
PC versus Mac pcversusmac.com

Mac programming & AppleScript

OS X software tends to have a friendly face, but behind the shiny icons lies a sprawling sub-culture of pale-skinned scripters and programmers, beavering away on everything from Actions (see p.123) and AppleScripts (see p.124) to full-on applications. If you fancy joining their ranks, the *de facto* introduction to hacking – which among the computerati simply means programming, and doesn't imply anything illegal – can be found here:

How To Be A Hacker catb.org/~esr/faqs/hacker-howto.html

Once you're prepared, visit the following websites for links and inspiration – or simply to grab a sack-full of readymade scripts to automate your Mac.

AppleScript apple.com/macosx/features/applescript
Apple Developer Connection developer.apple.com
Doug's AppleScripts for iTunes dougscripts.com
MacScripter scriptbuilders.net
MacTech mactech.com

MACTECH.

Linux on a Mac

Want to score maximum geek points? Then why not use your Mac to run the open-source operating system Linux, either instead of, or as well as, OS X. Find out more here:

lowendmac.com/linux
mklinux.org
terrasoftsolutions.com

iPods online

Gone are the days when the iPod was simply a cool Mac accessory. The music player has spawned its own vast online culture of sites…

ilounge.com
everythingipod.com
ipoding.com
ipodhacks.com
ipodstudio.com

…and blogs:

ipod-news.blogspot.com
myipodblog.blogspot.com
theipodblog.com

Help, hints & hacks

Whatever your Mac-related problem or question, the answer is bound to be online. A good place to start looking for help and advice is the Apple Discussions site (see p.301), but there are loads more sites out there. Try one of these:

About macs.about.com
Apple applefritter.com
MacFixit macfixit.com
MacZealots maczealots.com
MacOSX.com macosx.com
Mac OS X Hints macosxhints.com
XLR8yourmac xlr8yourmac.com

Troubleshooting Solutions for the Macintosh

Old Macs

Wondering what to do with, or need a driver for, your old Mac Quadra or Performa? Drop in to:

Classic Mac Addict thor.prohosting.com/classicm
MacDriverMuseum macdrivermuseum.com
LowEndMac lowendmac.com

Apple history

Want to know how it all started? These links offer the story of Apple – the highs, the lows, the beige boxes…

Apple History apple-history.com
Wikipedia en.wikipedia.org/wiki/Apple_Macintosh

Mac madness

Endemic among the Mac-using minority is a condition known as Apple Obsession Syndrome. While some AOS symptoms are serious (casual first-name references to Steve Jobs, for example) others can be entertaining, from gratuitous Mac modifications to ridiculous software. So grab your iHymn sheet and join us to pay homage at the high altar of Macdom.

iBook picture frames

Bored of using your iBook or PowerBook as a laptop computer? Why not turn it into an all-singing, all-dancing wall-mountable digital picture frame? A surprising number of people have done just this, and posted instructions online. Grab your glue gun and screwdriver, and head for:

DuoDigital applefritter.com/hacks/duodigitalframe
PowerBook Picture Frame barr104.spymac.com/index.htm

The HollowScreen project

A "project" in the loosest sense. Take a digital photograph of something and set it as your desktop background on your MacBook, iBook or PowerBook. Then cunningly position your laptop in such a way that the screen appears to be transparent. Disarmingly funny.

HollowScreen hollowscreen.com

SlashNOT

SlashNOT is a pasquinade of the computing supersite Slashdot (which, by the way, bubbles over with Mac news and discussions and is well worth a visit). When you reach the front page, click on the big blue Apple logo to dig your way through to the Mac news section. There you'll get the lowdown on everything from the iToaster (see left) to Apple's attempts to sue Gwyneth Paltrow for naming her daughter Apple Martin, and not forgetting the rumours that Apple is in fact owned by Microsoft.

SlashNOT slashnot.com

◄ *This picture of the mythical iToaster can be found on the All-Electric InterWeb at: worth1000.com*

Hack a Mac

We've already showed you how to mess with the appearance of OS X (see p.115), so now it's time to think about your Mac's delightful outer shell – white and silver is just so Nineties.

If you hark back for the days when Macs came in such delicate hues as "tangerine", consider handing your Mac over to a re-skinning service, such as:

ColorWare colorwarepc.com

Naturally, however, you'll have more fun doing it yourself. Get inspiration from the following sites, and maybe even enter the annual "Great MacMod Challenge":

Hack A Day macs.hackaday.com
MacMod macmod.com
AppleFritter applefritter.com

Got status anxiety about your old Mac G4 Cube? Why not dress it up as a top-end Power Mac:

G5 Cube Case conf.co.jp/new_folder/making/cube_1.html

Or if you really hate the site of your Mac mini, why not wrap a car around it?

Classic Retro classicresto.com/macmini.html

And where would we be without a Lego option:

Apple Juice apple-juice.co.uk/lego

A modified Mac laptop at macmod.com. Some people clearly have far too much time on their hands.

Terminal has a GSOH

```
Lilly:Purity, sweetness.
Magnolia:Dignity, perseverance.
Marigold:Jealousy.
Mint:Virtue.
Orange blossom:Your purity equals your loveliness.
Orchid:Beauty, magnificence.
Pansy:Thoughts.
Peach blossom:I am your captive.
Petunia:Your presence soothes me.
Poppy:Sleep.
Rose, any color:Love.
Rose, deep red:Bashful shame.
Rose, single, pink:Simplicity.
Rose, thornless, any color:Early attachment.
Rose, white:I am worthy of you.
```

So, you thought Terminal utility was strictly for the serious Mac-head looking to squeeze that little bit extra out of his or her (probably his) machine via the use of the command line interface? Well, this techie-looking tool actually has a sensitive side. Open Terminal from **Applications > Utilities** and type:

`cat /usr/share/misc/flowers`

Hit **Enter**, and you'll see a poetic list of flowers, along with each of their meanings.

Not satisfied? How about a lo-fi game of Tetris? Open Terminal again, type emacs and hit **Enter**. Next press **Escape** and type **x**. Finally, type **tetris** and hit **Enter**.

System Prank

System Prank is a free download that simulates the uninstallation of Mac OS X and its replacement with Windows XP – complete with system bugs and viruses. Try it on your friend's new PowerBook (no harm will come of it).

System Prank titanium.free.fr/english.html

Mini vMac

Leopard may be slick and powerful, but can it match the retro charm of the OS featured on the Macintosh Plus, one of the first Mac computers to hit the market? Grab the Mini vMac emulator and decide for yourself.

Mini vMac minivmac.sourceforge.net

The iToilet must have had a real resonance for one Jonathan Ive (see p.6 to find out why).

Apple spoofs

There are loads of spoof Apple products to be found online, and most have the letter "i" plastered at the start of their name, which makes them pretty easy to track down using Google. At times you might have trouble distinguishing the real ones from the pranks. But often it's not too difficult…

iShave application-systems.de/ishave
iBrew dropcap.co.uk/ibrew

Most spoofs are from Apple fans, but occasionally imaginary products are dispatched from across enemy lines. For example:

iToilet electric-chicken.co.uk/itoilet.html

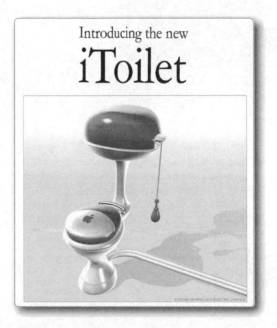

Introducing the new
iToilet

Useless software

P-P-P-PowerBook

This epic tale of scams, pranks, PowerBooks and eBay will have you laughing for days. Download the PDF of the whole story from:

p-p-p-powerbook.com

Our brief survey of Mac madness wouldn't be complete without a warm-hearted endorsement of the software available from:

Useless Macintosh Software Applications jschilling.net/software.php

Among the wonders on offer are The Lonesome Electric Chicken, who spews forth philosophical snippets of wisdom; EarthquakeX, which allows your Mac to experience fully-customizable on-screen earthquakes; Heart Monitor, which places an anatomical heart on your desktop that beats faster or slower depending on the activity of your Mac's processor; and PowerOrgasm X, which, when installed on a Mac laptop, gives your Mac the climax of its life whenever the power cord is plugged into it (remember that scene from *When Harry Met Sally*?).

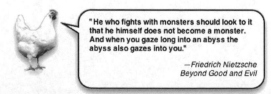

"He who fights with monsters should look to it that he himself does not become a monster. And when you gaze long into an abyss the abyss also gazes into you."

—*Friedrich Nietzsche*
Beyond Good and Evil

Index

Index

index

index

index

index

index

notes

D: Rough Guide
DIRECTIONS for
short breaks

Available from all good bookstores

ROUGH GUIDES

Complete Listing

For more information go to **www.roughguides.com**

ROUGH
GUIDES